Improving Your Speech

JOHN A. GRASHAM
Los Angeles Harbor College

GLENN G. GOODER
Los Angeles City College

HARCOURT, BRACE & WORLD, INC.
New York Chicago San Francisco Atlanta

PART TITLE ILLUSTRATIONS BY *Murray Fleminger*

Library of Congress Catalog Card Number: 60-6845

Printed in the United States of America

To Beth and Virginia

Preface

We believe that students will make an unusual effort to improve their speech if they are shown a straightforward plan for this improvement. As we prepared *Improving Your Speech* we kept in mind five basic needs which we believe a text in voice and diction must meet if it is to be useful to both teacher and student.

First the text must provide a meaningful and consistent organization; second, it must cover the basic elements of voice and articulation in sufficient detail to meet the needs of the student, yet avoid the confusion of too comprehensive a treatment.

Improving Your Speech begins with an evaluation of the individual student's speech, showing him at once his strengths and weaknesses. An introduction to the speech process then gives him a basic understanding of the phonetic, physiological, and psychological factors involved, and the procedures he must follow for speech improvement. The sections on voice and articulation are separated (yet with relationships clearly indicated) to allow student and teacher to select either for first consideration. The chapters on articulation and pronunciation include International Phonetic Alphabet symbols and diacritical marks. The book emphasizes throughout that speech is not merely a mechanical process, that the effective speaker is sensitive to the speaking situation, realizing that his personality contributes to the impression his speech makes upon others. And the final chapters provide text and exercises to help the student integrate all the elements treated.

Third, a satisfactory text must provide for the evaluation of the student's proficiency in as specific terms as possible. In *Improving Your Speech* the general evaluation for diagnosis and motivation is followed by further and more searching evaluations of the individual factors which contribute to each element of speech with which the student will be concerned. A chart to record progress appears in the front of the book;

the tests are keyed to enable the student to refer readily to appropriate explanatory materials and corrective exercises.

Fourth, to be useful, a text must present varied, interesting, and purposeful drill materials. In *Improving Your Speech* the exercises are designed to meet an apparent need; they are based on an understanding of what must be accomplished. They are varied to sustain interest; they are organized consistently from chapter to chapter in sequence from the easiest to the most difficult.

Fifth, a satisfactory book must have eye-appeal. We have tried to make all illustrations clear, accurate, and attractive, consistent in style throughout. All are planned to aid the student to interpret the concepts being discussed. Page make-up, type size, and style have been chosen to make the text easy to read and the exercises easy to follow.

If *Improving Your Speech* does meet these basic needs, the credit must be shared with many persons to whom we extend our thanks.

We are indebted, first of all, to our many students, from whom we have learned much.

We are grateful to our colleagues at Los Angeles City College for many helpful and valuable suggestions.

Special credit should go to those of our colleagues in various parts of the country who have offered critical suggestions during the preparation of the manuscript: Dr. Burton H. Byers, Queens College; Professor Dwight Freshley, Vanderbilt University; Professor Merritt Jones, New York University; Mr. Leslie Mahoney, formerly of University of California, Berkeley; and Dr. W. H. Perkins, University of Southern California. These readers share no responsibility for any weaknesses in the manuscript but deserve much credit for any strengths.

We wish to thank the many authors and publishers who have permitted us to reprint materials.

We are indebted to Miss Marie Sanchez for bringing both accuracy and interest to the illustrations which she prepared for the text.

Finally, to Beth and to Virginia go our deepest thanks. They have graciously contributed countless hours to the tedious tasks of research, typing, and proofreading, leaving us free for the more exciting work in the preparation of the manuscript.

JOHN A. GRASHAM
GLENN G. GOODER

January 1960

Contents

4. Expanding Your Expression

SPEECH EVALUATION

Name ____ *Date* ____________

Work on the elements checked. Exercises are on the pages indicated. Record your proficiency on the profile chart which follows.

Voice

Breathing	
Placement	26
Controlled cxhalation	28
Coordination with phrasing	33
Tone Initiation	
Breathiness	42
Harshness	47
Hoarseness	47
Pitch level	52
Pitch range	54
Tone Resonation	
Nasality	65
De-nasality	67
Open relaxed throat	72
Active tongue, lips, jaw	73
Good tone	74
Vocal Power	
Achieving	84
Using	90

Clarity

Vowels		
Front	[i] (eat)	126
	[ɪ] (it)	128
	[ɛ] (Ed)	130
	[æ] (add)	134
Back	[ɑ] (on)	136
	[ɔ] (awed)	140
	[ʊ] (book)	142
	[u] (boot)	146

Name ______________________________ ***Date*** ____________

Central	[ʌ] (up)	148
	[ə] (arena)	152
	[ɝ] (bird)	154
	[ɚ] (brisker)	156
Diphthongs		
[ɪ]	[eɪ] (aim)	164
	[ɑɪ] (I)	166
	[ɔɪ] (oil)	170
[ʊ]	[ɑʊ] (out)	172
	[oʊ] (oak)	176
Consonants		
Plosives	[p] (peep)	192
	[b] (bib)	192
	[t] (toot)	196
	[d] (dad)	196
	[k] (kick)	202
	[g] (gig)	202
Nasals	[m] (maimed)	206
	[m̩] (chasm)	209
	[n] (noon)	210
	[n̩] (fatten)	212
	[ŋ] (singing)	214
Fricatives	[f] (fife)	216
	[v] (vivid)	216
	[s] (sauce)	220
	[z] (zero)	220
	[θ] (thought)	226
	[ð] (that)	226
	[ʃ] (sheep)	230
	[ʒ] (vision)	230
	[h] (hat)	236
Semivowels	[r] (*ra*rer)	238
	[l] (lily)	240
	[l̩] (litt*le*)	242
Glides	[ʍ] (whale)	244
	[w] (wait)	244
	[j] (yet)	248
	[ju] (use)	250

Name ______________________________ ***Date*** ____________

Expression

SPEECH PROFICIENCY PROFILE

Total the number of check marks for each element on the speech evaluation form. Circle the number on this profile chart which corresponds to the total for each element.

Connect the circled numbers with a solid red line. This will give you a graphic representation of your speech proficiency. The fewer the checks your instructor has made, the more proficient is your speech. You should strive to improve your speech so that all elements will be rated on the far right of the profile chart, thus indicating no deficiencies. Re-evaluate your speech periodically.

Plot your new scores with different colors to show your progress.

VOICE													
Breathing	3				2								0
Tone initiation	5		4			3		2			1		0
Tone resonation	5		4			3		2			1		0
Vocal power	2						1						0
CLARITY													
Vowels	12	11	10	9	8	7	6	5	4	3	2	1	0
Diphthongs	5		4			3		2			1		0
Consonants	29	27	24	21		18	15	12		9	6	3	0
Pronunciation	5		4			3		2			1		0
EXPRESSION													
Vocal variety	4			3			2			1			0
Creative expression	2						1						0

Improving Your Speech

1. Evaluating Your Speech

1. *Improving* SPEECH

Speech improvement is not difficult to achieve, but it does require the same painstaking analysis and care needed to gain competence in any other skill, such as driving, dancing, baseball, or tennis. Even though you are young, your speech patterns have become stubborn habits which will resist change. Only patient adherence to a program of regular drill will enable you to improve your speech.

Your plan for speech improvement must be geared to your individual needs. The first step, therefore, is to evaluate your present speech. Do you have difficulty in producing certain sounds? Is it difficult for people to understand you? Does your voice lack expression? Is it unpleasant to your listeners? Have you been told that your speech is monotonous and uninteresting?

The following voice and speech examinations will give you and your instructor a general picture of your speech capabilities and speech deficiencies. You will want to devote most of your time during this course to those special areas in which you need improvement.

TEST YOUR VOICE Read the following paragraph aloud while your instructor evaluates your speaking voice. His evaluation may be recorded on the voice and speech evaluation chart on pages xi-xvi. If you have voice problems connected with breathing, tone initiation, tone resonation, or vocal power, they should be noted in the appropriate spaces on this chart.

The use of language can become an instrument of health and joy just as its abuse can act as a vehicle of discouragement and misery. We can strike with a word sometimes more effectively than with the fist; by words we can help and hurt, inspire and dishearten, give value to a matter or throw it into oblivion. Words, like deeds, may be constructive or destructive, elements of strength or expressions of decay. Those who learn to speak with charm, precision, vigor, and good diction soon experience the benefits of well-used words.[1]

TEST YOUR CLARITY The clarity of your speech is determined by the accuracy with which you produce the sounds and words of our language. Read the following sentences aloud while your instructor evaluates your clarity. You will want to record your performance in vowel, diphthong, and consonant articulation, together with your proficiency in pronunciation, on the voice and speech examination chart.

[i]	Eat each green pea.
[ɪ]	It is in Italy.
[ɛ]	Ed said "Get ready!"
[æ]	Add and subtract, Dan.
[ɑ]	On top of the rock was Don.
[ɔ]	Awed audiences applauded Claude.
[ʊ]	Books look good.
[u]	Boots and shoes lose newness soon.
[ʌ]	Up the bluff Bud runs.
[ə]	Arenas abound in Australia.
[ɝ]	Birds were heard chirping.
[ɚ]	Brisker than a Saturday in September . . .
[eɪ]	Aim straight at the game.
[ɑɪ]	I tried my kite.
[ɔɪ]	Oil spoils doilies.
[ɑʊ]	Outside the town the crowd howled.
[oʊ]	Oaks grow slowly.
[p]	Peep at the sleeping parrot.
[b]	Bibs belong on babies.
[t]	Toot the trumpet, Tommy.
[d]	Dad didn't drive daringly.
[k]	Kick the pigskin quickly.
[g]	Gig the big frog by the log.
[m]	Maimed animals may become mean.
[m̩]	Chasms may result from cataclysms.
[n]	Noon dances are banned.
[n̩]	Fatten a dozen chickens.
[ŋ]	Singing dispels anger.

[1] William G. Niederland, *Man-Made Plague: A Primer on Neurosis* (New York, Renbayle House, 1948), p. 211. Reprinted by permission of the author.

[f] Fifes and flutes were featured.
[v] Vivid experiences were lived vicariously.
[s] Sauce makes the goose more succulent.
[z] Zeros in zoology caused Buzz to fail.
[θ] Thoughtful thinkers think things through.
[ð] That brother loathes lather.
[ʃ] Sheep shears should be sharp.
[ʒ] Vision, when good, brings pleasure.
[h] Hats hang on cloakroom hooks.
[r] "Rarer, sir," Ruth requested.
[l] Lily, the old lady, seldom is late.
[l̩] Little candles burned on bottles.
[ʍ] Whales, when angry, whip their tails.
[w] Wait, Willie, beware of the wolf.
[j] *Yet* usually is not used to begin a sentence.
[ju] Used uniforms may be useful.
[tʃ] Church benches of birch were chosen.
[dʒ] Judge Jenkins married Judy and James.

TEST YOUR EXPRESSION How expressive is your speech? Read the following paragraphs aloud as your instructor evaluates your vocal variety and your expression. Record the findings in the appropriate spaces on your voice and speech examination chart.

As you improve your speech, you will be studying the most fascinating subject in the world—you! It was Demosthenes who said, "As a vessel is known by the sound whether it be cracked or not, so men are proved by their speeches whether they be wise or foolish."

What do your friends say about your speech? Does one of these classifications apply to you?

Betty sounds like a mouse.
Jean sounds like an angel.
Jim sounds like a hyena.
Bill sounds like a dream.

Your speech is you. An ancient proverb said, "A man's character is revealed by his speech."

ALTERNATIVE SPEECH TESTS Your instructor may prefer to analyze your speech by using one or more of the following tests, or perhaps by using an entirely different speech examination. Results should be recorded on the voice and speech examination chart and graphically represented on the speech improvement profile.

The alternative speech examination forms may also be used to reevaluate your speech at any time during the course.

VOICE AND SPEECH EXAMINATION, I

1. Give your name, your address, and your major in college or your occupation.

My name is . . .
I live at . . .
My major in college is . . . (*or*)
I am employed by . . .

2. Read down the following list of words:

VOWELS

eat, bead, me
it, bid, baby
Ed, get
add, bat
on, cot, spa
awed, bought, saw
book, put
boot, do
up, bud
arena, cinema
birds, word
brisker, sooner

DIPHTHONGS

aim, late, day
I, side, die
oil, coil, boy
out, doubt, now
oak, boat, go

CONSONANTS

peep, pippin
bib, abbey
toot, tighten
dad, eddy
kick, wicket
gig, gagged
maimed, ham
chasm, rhythm
noon, any
fatten, risen
singing, banging
fife, fifty
vivid, save
sauce, sisters
zero, buzzes
thought, ether, bath
that, either, loathe
sheep, usher, dish
vision, barrage
hat, behead
rarer, ear
lily, goal
little, ladle
whale, awhile
wait, aware
yet, onion

use, cute, view
church, butcher
judge, edger

PRONUNCIATION

get, catch, just
because, wash, athlete
film, across, twenty
government, February
picture, asterisk
cavalry, irrelevant
imminent, formidable
hospitable, chastisement
lamentable

3. Read this test passage aloud:

If you could improve your appearance, increase your popu-
larity, and 10
protect your health, you'd be interested, wouldn't you? You
can 20
do all those things with RAINBOW dentifrice. RAINBOW
is the 30
latest in scientific health care for the teeth and gums. 40
If you use RAINBOW—you'll always know—that your smile 50
is fresh. RAINBOW is scientifically prepared to do a superior 60
job of cleaning teeth. And here's something you'll really appreciate. 70
RAINBOW is now available in your favorite flavor. In addition 80
to peppermint and strawberry, you have a choice of grape 90
or cherry flavors. Eminent medical men agree, RAINBOW
contains agents 100
which do the all-important job of cleaning the teeth 110
and at the same time do not mar or scratch 120
precious enamel. Yes, RAINBOW protects your smile of
health and 130
beauty. A large size tube of RAINBOW toothpaste or a 140
large size can of RAINBOW toothpowder costs only twenty-
five 150
cents. And for as little as eighty-five cents you 160
can get a special variety set of four large tubes 170
or cans of delightfully fresh flavors. Now that new RAIN-
BOW 180
is available in all parts of the country, we are 190
sure that you people of the South, the West, and 200
the Middle West will agree with the folks from the East 210
that RAINBOW toothpowder and RAINBOW toothpaste

are the finest you 220
have ever tried. Remember RAINBOW. 225

(*Compare your reading time in seconds with the number listed above it to determine your reading rate in words per minute.*)

Rate	*Too slow*											*Too fast*	
WORDS PER MINUTE	113	117	123	129	135	142	150	159	169	180	193	208	225
READING TIME IN SECONDS	120	115	110	105	100	95	90	85	80	75	70	65	60

4. Tell what you like about your home town:

I like my home town because . . .

VOICE AND SPEECH EXAMINATION, II

1. Give your name, your address, and your major in college or your occupation.

My name is . . .
I live at . . .
My major in college is . . . (*or*)
I am employed by . . .

2. Read the following series of sentences. The words in capital letters contain all of the sounds commonly used in General American speech.

SUTTON, in a SEAT, did SIT near where the hen had SET and where the dog SAT near the SOT, who SOUGHT something to clean the SOOT from his SUIT.

It was necessary for DALE to DIAL DOYLE before the unemployed DOWEL worker could receive his DOLE.

The girl's BEAU was the BOY BY the BAY beneath the BOUGH.

PAULA stopped to JUMP rope with BETTY, whose BABY sister was in the CRIB TEETHING on a METAL BOAT.

DAVID is ADDLED by POPCORN and POP.

COME to the BAKERY QUICK, GARY, and don't ARGUE or LAG.

MARY, it's ALMOST TIME for the NEW, FUNNY CLOWN to lead the SINGERS in SINGING.

FIFTY VIVACIOUS, and yet SOOTHING MOTHERS simulated FOURTH-rate THESPIANS and PLEASED the DESERVING SISTERS.

I RUSHED for the SHIP, but it was a BEIGE MIRAGE.

HOW UNHAPPY I was, WISHING I knew WHAT it was and WHERE it was.

RESCUE ROVER, RUTH, the ORANGE PARROT CRIED.

He's THERE, NEAR the CHAIR.

The GIRL HEARD that the MURDERER had no MOTHER.

The LAD mowed LESTER'S LAWN.

He WHISTLED SOFTLY in the SILENT FALL afternoon.

The soft SOIL was FULL of moisture.

A LITTLE boy on a BICYCLE popped his BUBBLE gum.

A CAMEL carried a CANDLE in a BOTTLE.

It's JUST CABBAGE, YOUR honor, not ONIONS, said the CHASTIZED BACHELOR.

VOICE AND SPEECH EXAMINATION, III

1. Give your name, your address, and your major in college or your occupation.

My name is . . .
I live at . . .
My major in college is . . . (*or*)
I am employed by . . .

2. Read the following excerpts from the Preface to *Pygmalion*.[2]

George Bernard Shaw's successful play, *Pygmalion*, has
been produced in 10
legitimate theater and motion pictures, and as *My Fair Lady* 20
in musical comedy. In his preface, Shaw said: "The English 30
have no respect for their language, and will not teach 40
their children to speak it. They spell it so abominably 50
that no man can teach himself what it sounds like. 60
It is impossible for an Englishman to open his mouth 70
without making some other Englishman hate or despise him.

[2] George Bernard Shaw, *Selected Plays of Bernard Shaw* (New York, Dodd, Mead and Co., 1948), p. 193. Reprinted by permission of the Public Trustee of the Shaw Estate and the Society of Authors, London agents for the Shaw estate for the use of an excerpt from the Preface to *Pygmalion*.

German 80
and Spanish are accessible to foreigners: English is not accessible 90
even to Englishmen. The reformer England needs today is an 100
energetic phonetic enthusiast: that is why I have made such 110
a one the hero of a popular play. There have 120
been heroes of that kind crying in the wilderness for 130
many years past. . . . Finally, and for the encouragement of
people 140
troubled with accents that cut them off from all high 150
employment, I may add that the change wrought by Professor 160
Higgins in the flower-girl is neither impossible nor uncommon. 170
The modern concierge's daughter who fulfills her ambition
by playing 180
the Queen of Spain in *Ruy Blas* at the Théâtre 190
Français is only one of the many thousands of men and 200
women who have sloughed off their native dialects and acquired 210
a new tongue. But the thing has to be done 220
scientifically, or the last state of the aspirant may be 230
worse than the first. An honest and natural slum dialect 240
is more tolerable than the attempt of a phonetically untaught 250
person to imitate the vulgar dialect of the golf club; 260
and I am sorry to say that in spite of 270
the efforts of our Royal Academy of Dramatic Art, there 280
is still too much sham golfing English on our stage 290
and too little of the noble English of Forbes Robertson." 300

(*Compare your reading time in seconds with the number listed above it to determine your reading rate in words per minute.*)

Rate	*Too slow*								*Too fast*			
WORDS PER MINUTE	100	106	113	120	129	138	150	164	180	200	225	259
READING TIME IN SECONDS	180	170	160	150	140	130	120	110	100	90	80	70

VOICE AND SPEECH EXAMINATION, IV

1. Give your name, your address, and your major in college or your occupation.

My name is . . .
I live at . . .
My major in college is . . . (*or*)
I am employed by . . .

2. Answer one or more of the following questions aloud. Talk in a conversational manner and use your normal speaking voice.

a. What is the scholastic training necessary to prepare you for your proposed future occupation?
b. What is the main reason you feel you will enjoy working at your proposed future occupation?
c. How does your proposed future occupation benefit society?
d. What is the value of pleasant and effective speech in your proposed future occupation?
e. Describe the speech of someone you know who speaks very well.
f. In what ways do you feel that your speech should be improved?
g. What one thing would you change about your school if you had the authority to do so?
h. What one thing would you change about your job if you had the authority to do so?
i. What one thing would you change about your community if you had the authority to do so?
j. What one subject do you know more about than any other person in this group?

The Four Steps to Speech Improvement

You have already begun to analyze your speech with the short tests at the beginning of this chapter. Your instructor may wish to evaluate your speech further, and he may ask you to make a voice recording. After he has made his analysis you will want to listen critically in order to detect your own speech deficiencies. This general evaluation will enable you and your instructor to identify the areas which should be of greatest and most immediate concern to you. Be sure that your instructor's evaluation is recorded on the speech evaluation chart and that your proficiency is plotted on the profile chart.

Once you have taken the first step to speech improvement, "Evaluating Your Speech," you are in a position to move toward improvement in the area you and your instructor consider most critical. A great many students devote early attention to developing a normal and natural tone production and to improving the quality of their voices. Part II of this book is planned to help you take the second step to speech improvement, "Enriching Your Voice." You will begin with materials to help you understand the kind of breath control which supports good tone, and then will consider the manner in which tone is initiated and resonated so that it may be pleasant. Finally, you will investigate methods of developing vocal power so that you may be heard in a variety of speaking situations without vocal strain.

When you are satisfied with your progress in voice training, you will be ready for step three to speech improvement, "Increasing Your Clarity." (If you are seriously concerned with your ability to be understood, you may wish to study this section before the chapters on voice.) You will begin your work in this area by examining the nature of spoken American English. Next you will consider the sounds of our language in detail (vowels, diphthongs, and consonants). You will then understand how words are pronounced and will be able to improve your own pronunciation.

After you have developed a pleasant voice and clear articulation, you may turn to the fourth step to speech improvement, "Expanding Your Expression." In this section you will practice blending all the elements into more expressive speech—first, by working with the more mechanical factors in expanding vocal variety and then by integrating all these elements with a pleasant speaking personality and a creative approach to vocal expression.

As you prepare to take these four steps to speech improvement, keep in mind that the responsibility for improvement must lie with the individual student. The instructor or the book can only create a situation within which you may discover and overcome your speech deficiencies and develop more effective speech. You must follow a definite plan. First, you must evaluate your speech to find out where you stand. Second, you need to understand why you speak as you do. Third, you must establish correct speech habits and then practice to make them habitual. Fourth, you must make periodic re-evaluations of your speech to persist in correct speech habits.

This book is planned to help you follow this kind of program. Each of the following chapters except Chapter 2 deals with an individual element of speech. Each begins with a test to assess your strengths and weaknesses in the various factors contributing to this element. On this test are references to the pages on which the individual factors are explained and to those on which exercises begin. After you take the test and determine which factor needs improvement, you may turn to the explanation and then to the exercises for improvement. You can check your progress periodically by taking the test again at the beginning of the chapter.

You need not fear that enriching your voice, increasing your clarity, and expanding your expression will make your speech artificial. Effective speech is not affected speech. Effective speech does not call attention to itself by displaying techniques such as artificial inflections, overly precise articulation, or theatrical voice projection. Instead, if you develop effective speech, your listener will be aware of your ideas and not of your voice or of the manner in which you communicate your ideas.

It will be necessary for you to consider the elements of speech in isolation as you work through your speech improvement program. You should never lose sight of the fact, however, that speech is an integrated activity. It will be helpful for you to understand the over-all process as you work to improve each element. A very brief overview of the speech process is presented in the next chapter to give you this basic background.

2. *Understanding* THE SPEECH PROCESS

The human voice is produced in much the same way that sound is produced by a wind instrument. The reed in the wind instrument must vibrate, as must the vocal folds in the larynx when air is expelled from the lungs, if sound is to be heard. This process of producing vocal sounds and, ultimately, human speech can be broken down into four parts for the purpose of analysis.

The first step is respiration, a process which furnishes air to set the vocal folds in vibration. We breathe to live, to supply the blood stream with oxygen, and to remove the carbon dioxide (the chief waste product of oxidation) from the blood stream. Oxygen is absorbed by minute blood vessels in the lungs in exchange for carbon dioxide.

Air is able to move into the lungs because the lungs can expand in size. As they expand, air rushes into them to maintain equal air pressure inside and outside of the lungs.

The body is so constructed that the volume of the lungs can be increased in several ways to make breathing possible. The lungs are encased in the rib cage. The ribs can be raised by muscles running between them in such a way as to increase the size of the rib cage. The lungs are elastic and fill the rib cage at all times. Consequently, when the dimensions of the cage are increased, the lungs expand.

Attached to the lowest ribs and forming a floor for the lungs is a membrane made up of muscle and sinew called the *diaphragm*. The diaphragm separates the *thorax* (the area bounded by the rib cage, the breastbone, and the backbone) from the *abdomen* (the area which includes the stomach, intestines, liver, and other vital organs) and is attached to the lower ribs, the breastbone, and the backbone. When the rib cage is in its lowered position and air has been expelled from the lungs, the diaphragm is dome-shaped, protruding upward into the thorax. Since it is partly muscle, it can contract, and it does this by flat-

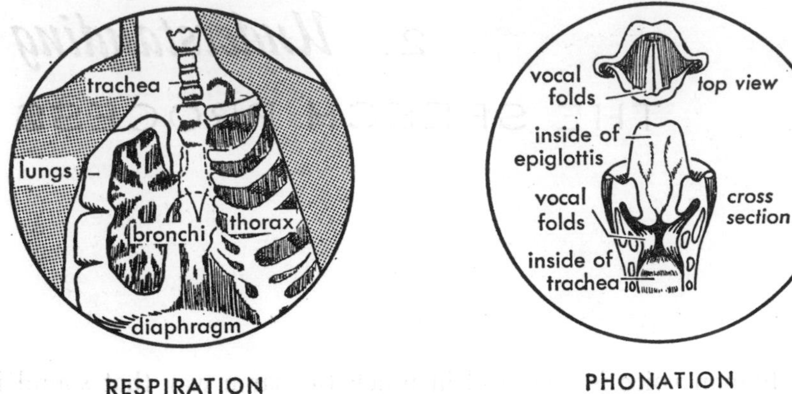

Figure 1. Steps in the speech process

---

tening out, pushing against the abdomen, and increasing the area at the base of the thorax.

As the diaphragm contracts and as the ribs are raised, the lungs fill the enlarged space, and air simultaneously flows into the lungs. This air not only brings oxygen to the blood but provides the power for vibrating the vocal folds when the air is later exhaled between them.

To expel this air, the ribs return to their lowered position partly because of their own weight. The diaphragm, being muscle, can pull only in one direction. It can, however, be pushed back into its domed position by the abdominal muscles and by the elastic recoil of the internal organs that were displaced downward by the contracting diaphragm. With such movements as these, air is forced out of the lungs and the cycle of respiration is completed.

Phonation is the second stage in producing speech. As the air is expelled, it must pass through the bronchi, then through the trachea to the larynx, where the vocal folds are located, then through the pharynx and out of the body through the mouth or nose.

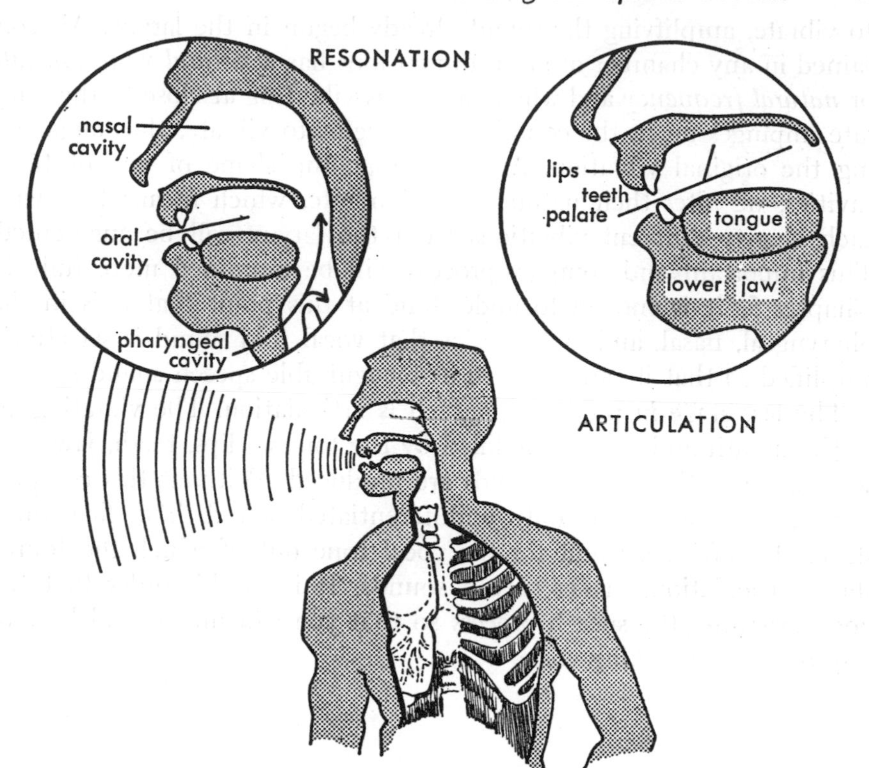

The *larynx*, which forms the upper part of the trachea, consists of muscles and cartilage which allow the larynx to adjust itself so that air can pass through it when we breathe, so that food can be kept from going down into the lungs, and so that the vocal folds can be adjusted to restrict the passage of air between them. The vocal folds, which lie within the larynx, are of elastic tissue. When we breathe silently, the folds are open. When we wish to speak, they become taut and come together or approximate so that they form a slit through which the air must pass. This opening is called the *glottis*. The air escapes through the narrowed glottis in puffs, since the elastic folds snap back together after a small amount of air has passed between them. This fluttering of the folds produces vibration which is the source of the sound we hear.

Some of these sounds would be scarcely audible if it were not for the third part of the speech process, resonation. As the folds vibrate, they in turn vibrate the molecules of air surrounding them, and these disturb other molecules farther away. In turn the air in the back of the nose and throat (*pharynx*), the mouth, and sometimes the nose begins to vibrate, amplifying the sound already begun in the larynx. Air contained in any chamber of given dimensions has a *natural vibration rate* or *natural frequency* and when air that is vibrating at close to the same rate impinges on it, the contained air begins to vibrate, thus augmenting the original vibration. As we change the shape of any of these cavities, we alter their natural vibration rate, which means that with each change different vibrations from the larynx will be augmented. This important and complex process will be examined more fully in Chapter 5. It is enough to understand at this point that it is in the pharyngeal, nasal, and oral cavities that vocal fold sound is selectively amplified so that it can be heard as recognizable speech sounds.

The last stage in producing speech is articulation. The vibrating air in the mouth and nose is modified by the tongue, lips, teeth, jaw, and soft palate so that speech sounds are produced. Without this complex action, we would hear only undifferentiated sound. The first three stages, therefore, account for the vocal tone out of which the fourth stage, articulation, makes speech sounds. It is in this order that the book examines the speech process so that you can understand how to improve your speaking voice.

2. Enriching Your Voice

3. *Controlling* BREATHING

test your breathing

BREATHING PLACEMENT

(EXPLANATION, P. 23; EXERCISES, P. 26.)

1. Use good standing posture. Place the tips of the fingers together at the waistline and press the hands firmly against the body. Inhale and exhale normally for 20 seconds. Read the following aloud, keeping your hands on your waistline:

> How wonderful is the human voice! It is indeed the organ of the soul. The intellect of man sits enthroned, visibly, on his forehead and in his eye, and the heart of man is written on his countenance, but the soul reveals itself in the voice only.
>
> —Henry Wadsworth Longfellow

2. Use good standing or sitting posture. Place your thumbs on your shoulders and extend the fingers so they meet at the junction of the collarbones and breastbone. Inhale and exhale normally for 20 seconds. Read the following aloud, keeping your fingers on your shoulders and collarbones:

> To live is not merely to breathe, it is to act; it is to make use of our organs, senses, faculties, of all those parts of ourselves which give us the feeling of existence.
>
> —Jean Jacques Rousseau

3. Use good standing or sitting posture. Inhale and exhale normally for 20 seconds. Read the following aloud:

> We live in deeds, not years; in thoughts, not breaths; in feelings, not in figures on the dial; we should count time by heart-throbs. He most lives who thinks most, feels the noblest, acts the best.
>
> —Gamaliel Bailey

POSTURE AND BREATHING PLACEMENT

(EXPLANATION, P. 25; EXERCISES, P. 26.)

4. Breathe deeply and slowly for 20 seconds. Next, allow only one-half of your breath supply to be exhaled before inhaling again. Breathe this way for 20 seconds. Maintain good posture throughout.

PRODUCING FORCEFUL TONES

(EXPLANATION, P. 27; EXERCISES, PP. 28-31.)

5. Read this sentence, using strong tones throughout:

> Strong tones are produced by controlled contraction of the abdominal muscles.

AN ADEQUATE SUPPLY OF AIR FOR SPEECH

(EXPLANATION, P. 27; EXERCISES, PP. 28-31.)

6. Read the following aloud, inhaling as frequently as necessary:

> In order to have breathing habits which are conducive to good speech, the speaker must have good posture, must have the correct relationship between muscular relaxation and tension, and must keep an adequate reserve of air in his lungs.

THE USE OF EXHALED AIR IN SPEECH

(EXPLANATION, P. 27; EXERCISES, PP. 28-31.)

7. Read the following sentence on one breath:

> He showed Hester his sealskin slippers which Herman had shipped him from Seattle, Washington.

BREATHING AND PHRASING

(EXPLANATION, P. 31; EXERCISES, PP. 33-34.)

8. Read the following aloud. Phrase it so that the meaning and dramatic effect are heightened:

> This living hand, now warm and capable
> Of earnest grasping, would, if it were cold
> And in the icy silence of the tomb,
> So haunt thy days and chill thy dreaming nights
> That thou wouldst wish thine own heart dry of blood
> So in my veins red life might stream again,
> And thou be conscience-calmed—see here it is—
> I hold it towards you.
>
> —John Keats, "This Living Hand"

*Name*______________________________	*Rating*
1. Student achieves expansion in the abdominal region.	____
2. Student's upper chest and shoulders are quiet during breathing.	____
3. Student avoids tense, constricted throat, weak and breathy tones of clavicular breathing.	____
4. Student's posture facilitates abdominal breathing.	____
5. Student produces strong tones by controlled contraction of the abdominal muscles.	____
6. Student avoids speaking on residual air by taking inhalations frequently enough to maintain an adequate reserve of air.	____
7. Student avoids wasting breath before the *h, s,* and *sh* and before he begins to speak.	____
8. Student coordinates his phrasing and breathing so that the reading is meaningful and dramatic.	____
Total	____

Rating: It is suggested that the student be scored on a 5 to 1 point scale, 5 being used to indicate an excellent and 1 a poor rating.

Introduction Perhaps your score indicates that your breathing habits are adequate for your speech needs, even though you have not studied breath control for speech. But if you scored low on a few items, it is important that you should learn exactly how your breathing mechanism functions so that you will understand why there is a better and a worse way of breathing for speech.

Did your instructor say that you spoke with a tense throat, or that your voice was constricted? Is your voice weak, lacking in vitality? Do you tire quickly when you speak? Do you sound breathless, and have you insufficient air to complete a phrase or a sentence? This chapter should enable you to understand and overcome these problems by (1) achieving correct breathing placement, (2) controlling and making the best use of your exhalations during speech, and (3) inhaling at the proper intervals during speech.

Inhalation

BREATHING PLACEMENT Sit comfortably relaxed and breathe in and out several times without speaking. If your breathing mechanism is operating at maximum efficiency, you will note the rhythmic outward and inward movement of the abdomen. If your collarbones, upper chest, or shoulders rise and fall with each cycle of respiration, you are not breathing properly for the most efficient voice production.

The reason for this becomes clear as we review how air moves through one respiratory cycle, noting the actions involved. (See Chapter 2, p. 13.)

The dome-shaped diaphragm (the principal muscle of inhalation) forms the floor of the chest cavity or thorax. The fibers of the diaphragm are attached to the fifth through the tenth ribs on the sides and to the vertebral column in the rear. The enlargement of the chest cavity, which permits inhalation, is partly accomplished by the lowering of the diaphragm. To permit inhalation, the fibers of the diaphragm contract or shorten and the domes of the diaphragm are pulled down and flattened out. This movement displaces the contents of the abdomen (the abdominal viscera) downward and outward if the abdominal walls are relaxed. Thus, in proper breathing, the abdomen moves out with each inhalation. (See Fig. 2 on page 25.)

At the same time, muscles (external intercostals) which run upward and outward between the ribs contract and pull the ribs upward, allowing for an even further expansion of the chest cavity. The ribs are attached to the vertebral column in back, and all but the floating ribs are joined to the breastbone in front by means of elastic cartilages. Attachment of the ribs to the spinal column is such that in an adult they form an angle of 64° [1] As they are pulled upward and their angle of attachment to the spinal column more nearly approaches 90°, there is an increase in the size of the chest cavity from side to side. (See Fig. 2.)

The increase in the size of the chest cavity, caused by the movement of the diaphragm and by the movement of the ribs, permits air to rush into the lungs to fill the cavity and keep the air pressure equalized outside and inside the chest.

The bony and cartilaginous nature of the rib cage, with its narrow dimensions and firm attachments at the top, makes expansion in the upper chest difficult and inefficient, whereas the lower ribs are freer to expand in a bucket-handle movement. (See Fig. 2.) The most efficient breathing makes full use of this freedom of movement in the lower ribs. Whenever the "wasp waist look" becomes fashionable, the movement of the abdomen and the lower ribs is restricted, resulting in clavicular or upper-chest breathing. It was once thought that it was natural for women to breathe in this inefficient fashion, but when tightly laced corsets went out of style, so did clavicular breathing. In natural breathing, the abdomen will protrude slightly on inhalation just below the lower ribs so that the diaphragm can move freely; and the chest bones and lower ribs are raised to enlarge the thorax further.

Try breathing incorrectly. Breathe deeply a few times while trying to force yourself to expand only in the region of the upper chest. Hold your abdomen in as you inhale. Probably you will find that this inefficient breathing is unnatural for you. You will notice excessive throat tension as you exhale. Try to speak while breathing in this manner. Is your voice breathy and weak? Speak forcefully. Do you detect a harsh quality in your voice? Over a period of time you would find it tiring to speak while breathing in this manner.

Clavicular breathing has another drawback. People who breathe this way frequently run out of breath when they speak. Breathing properly allows the speaker enough air for phonation so that his tones will be strong and so that he can inhale again when a phrase requires it, not just when he must because of shortness of breath. You should avoid upper-chest, clavicular breathing with its accompanying rising and falling of the breastbone, collarbones, and perhaps even the shoulders.

[1] Lyman Spicer Judson and Andrew Thomas Weaver, *Voice Science* (New York, F. S. Crofts and Co., 1942), p. 4.

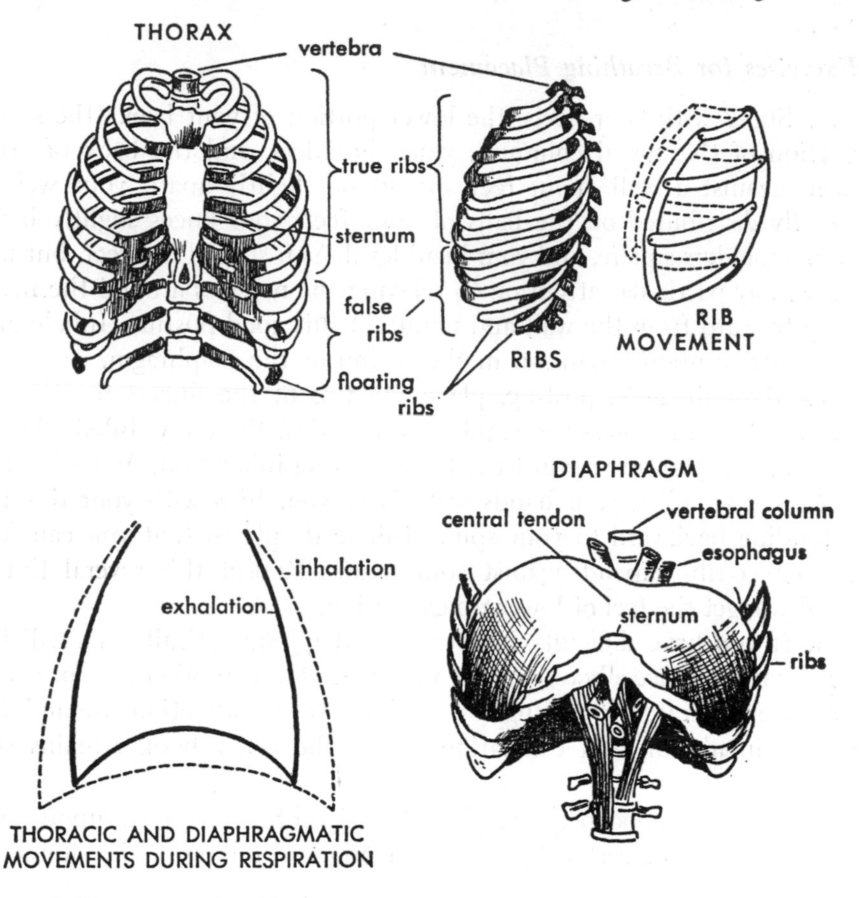

Figure 2. The process of respiration

It does not follow, however, that because you breathe abdominally (or medially) you must always take long, deep breaths. Not only is this unnecessary, but such deep breathing can cause undue tension in your throat so that you are unable to produce pleasant tones. Take short and frequent inhalations to maintain the reserve of air you need for phonation. But in making these short inhalations, make sure that you breathe medially, in the middle region of your body, so that the breathing movement is always free and relaxed.

POSTURE AND BREATHING PLACEMENT To make the best use of your breathing mechanism, try to maintain good posture. Keep your head held high, your shoulders held back, though not tensed, and your body erect, allowing the rib cage to expand in a natural manner.

Exercises for Breathing Placement

1. Stand with your heels, the lower portion of your back (the sacral portion of the spinal column), your shoulders, and the back of your head against a wall. Your feet should be slightly apart, your weight equally distributed on the balls of your feet, your knees slightly bent, your shoulders square, and your head level. You should be erect, but not tense. Pay particular attention to relaxing the muscles around the neck. Step forward from the wall and maintain this good posture. Inhale and concentrate upon expansion in the region of the diaphragm.

2. Maintain good posture, place the tips of the fingers together at the waistline and press the hands firmly against the body. Inhale deeply and feel the pressure against the hands during inhalation. Assuming the same stance, place your hands just above your hips with your thumbs extending backward to your spine. Inhale deeply so that you can feel the lower ribs expand against your hands. Repeat this several times, until you get the feel of lower rib expansion.

3. If you have difficulty in breathing diaphragmatically or medially, lie down and place a book on your upper chest and another at your waistline. Concentrate on making the book on your midsection rise and fall during inhalation and exhalation, while the other book remains stationary.

4. Maintain good posture, place the tips of your fingers upon your shoulders, and be certain there is no rising and falling of the shoulders as you breathe.

5. Maintain good posture. Place your thumbs on your shoulders and extend the fingers so they meet at the junction of the collarbones and breastbone. Be certain there is no rising and falling of the collarbones during respiration.

Exhalation

PASSIVE AND ACTIVE EXHALATION Keep your hands against the abdomen as you inhale. Now exhale. You should be able to feel the action of the abdominal muscles that govern exhalation. It is partly these muscles which enable you to control the breathing process during speech.

Exhalation is the second half of the respiratory cycle. At this point, the diaphragm relaxes, and as a result of their elasticity, the lungs, costal cartilages (connecting the ribs to the sternum or breastbone) and the abdominal viscera return to their original position. This action, aided by the contraction of the abdominal muscles and muscles which run upward and inward between the ribs (internal intercostals) reduces the size of the chest cavity. In exhalation, air is expelled from the lungs to maintain an equal pressure of air inside and outside the chest.

In breathing for life, air is exhaled passively, because of the elastic recoil of the rib cage and the recoil of the muscles, viscera, and cartilages, and the pull of gravity on the ribs. In breathing for speech, however, active control of the exhaled breath stream is necessary. The abdominal muscles, in contracting, force the viscera against the diaphragm which returns to the domed position. By means of these muscles you can control the uninterrupted flow of speech for an extended period of time. It is this control, also, which makes it possible to achieve the pressure necessary to produce variations in the strength of tones.

PRODUCING A FORCEFUL TONE To produce forceful tones, tense the muscles of the abdomen while closing the glottis so that no air escapes. Build up pressure in the lungs and then phonate *ah.* Use the exhaled breath stream to sustain the sound. Continue to tighten the abdominal muscles as you exhale, meanwhile continuing the production of a forceful tone. It is this action which you should practice, not only in the production of a single sound such as *ah,* but also when producing connected forceful speech. At no time must you tense the throat muscles. Depend, rather, on abdominal control for a forceful tone.

AN ADEQUATE SUPPLY OF AIR FOR SPEECH Exhale all the air you can. No matter how hard you try, you cannot expel it all since the rib cage does not collapse. That amount of air which remains in your lungs after exhalation is your *residual air,* which is there to sustain life. That maximum amount of air which you can exhale is your *vital capacity.*

Exhale and then try to speak on the residual air as some speakers do when they get to the end of a long phrase. It is likely that your voice will be weak and unpleasant. To avoid this effect, you should always inhale well before you have emptied the lungs of all of the air which you are capable of expelling. Take quick, short inhalations after the first breath that starts you off on your spoken thought. Try to keep your lungs fairly full so that there will always be a reserve of air for the long phrase that cannot be broken.

THE USE OF EXHALED AIR IN SPEECH Many speakers fail to use all of the exhaled air in producing speech. To avoid wasting air during speech it is imperative that you delay exhalation until the vocal folds

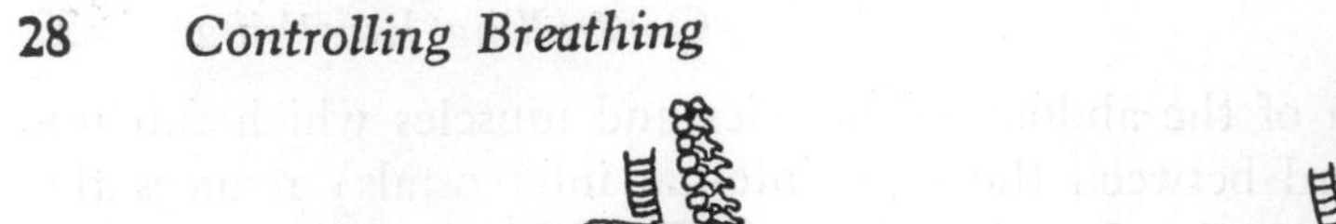

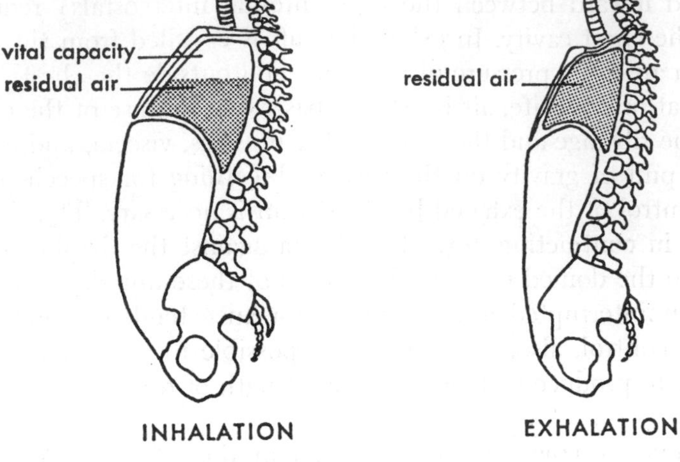

Figure 3. Vital capacity and residual air

have been brought together, otherwise you will expel a great gust of air before it has been used to vibrate the vocal folds. Also avoid wasting air between phonations and wasting air during the production of the *h* sound and sibilant sounds such as *s* and *sh*. Repeat the following words aloud and force yourself to waste air on the initial *h* sound: *heat, hit, hat, hot, hoot, hut*. Now repeat the same words while concentrating on the efficient use of all the exhaled air. If you did this properly, you should find that you can take more words on one breath. The tone should also be pleasanter and more easily produced when air is used efficiently.

Exercises for Controlled Exhalation

1. While maintaining good posture and firm muscular action during exhalation, sustain a strong, phonated *ah* for 20 seconds. Avoid a tense throat. Try to increase the duration to 30 seconds; 40 seconds, keeping the tone strong.

2. Maintain firm action of the abdominal muscles and pant in staccato exhalations, simulating a dog. Repeat, phonating *ah*. Place your hands on your abdomen so you can feel the sharp abdominal contractions as you make each sound.

3. Read the following in strong tones. Place your hands on your abdomen to make sure that you produce these tones by firm muscular action. Avoid a tense throat.

But when the blast of war blows in our ears,
Then imitate the action of the tiger,
Stiffen the sinews, summon up the blood,
Disguise fair nature with hard-favored rage.
—William Shakespeare, *Henry V*

4. Avoiding a tense throat, read each sentence aloud on only one breath, making each succeeding word louder than the one before it. Strive for an efficient, forceful, and sustained tone.

It is important to learn to breathe correctly.
Some people have acquired incorrect breathing habits.
Through proper training, one can learn good breathing for speech.

5. Read each sentence aloud on only one breath, making each succeeding word softer than the one before it. Strive for an efficient, forceful, and sustained tone.

Don't leave, Agatha; Agatha, please don't leave; Aggie.
Don't go near that hill, Billy.
If the plural of "goose" is "geese," shouldn't the plural of "moose" be "meese"?

6. Read the following, taking short breaths to maintain a full reserve of air throughout the speech. Make the end of each phrase as powerful as the beginning:

The light has gone out, I said, and yet I was wrong. For the light that shone in this country was no ordinary light. The light that has illumined this country for these many years will illumine this country for many more years, and a thousand years later that light will still be seen in this country and the world will see it and it will give solace to innumerable hearts. For that light represented the living truth . . . the eternal truths, reminding us of the right path, drawing us from error, taking this ancient country to freedom.[2]

—Jawaharlal Nehru

7. Inhale silently and deeply before you read each of the following sentences. Strive to produce audible, well-sustained phonations throughout. Relax the muscles of the neck and avoid vocal strain. Read each sentence on a single exhalation.

[2] Jawaharlal Nehru, "Nehru Speaks to Mourning Millions a Few Hours After the Murder of Gandhi" (January 30, 1948), in *Jawaharlal Nehru*, by Frank Moraes (New York, The Macmillan Co., 1956), pp. 349-350. Reprinted by permission of the publisher.

Breathing is necessary to sustain life.

One's breath stream is also necessary for speech.

A speaker should avoid raising and lowering his shoulders during inhalation and exhalation.

A good speaker, who has learned how to control his breathing mechanism during speaking, has sufficient reserve power to meet the requirements of almost any speaking situation.

8. This exercise and the next are meant to develop your capacity to handle the unusual speaking situation when you must speak a long phrase on one breath. Repeat the following nonsense saying a number of times on a single breath.

Spring would be a dreary season, were there nothing else but
spring would be a dreary season, were there nothing else but
spring would be a dreary season, were there. . . .etc.

9. Read this sentence aloud on one breath:

A speaker who uses his exhaled breath stream in such a manner that air is not wasted during the process of phonation finds, provided he is using the proper region of expansion during inhalation, that he has sufficient initiating force to enable him to cope with the most unusual demands of a speaking situation.

10. Assume that you are leading a group of 100 people in an open field in calisthenics. Tense the muscles of the abdomen while maintaining closure of the vocal folds. Avoid a tense throat. Build up pressure in the lungs and prohibit the escape of excessive gusts of air as you count:

1, 2, 3, 4; 1, 2, 3, 4; 1, 2, 3, 4; 1, 2, 3, 4.

11. Read the following selection aloud. Use all the exhaled air efficiently, not wasting air between phonations and concentrating on conserving air during production of the *h* sound.

What's Hecuba to him, or he to Hecuba,
That he should weep for her? What would he do,
Had he the motive and the cue for passion
That I have? He would drown the stage with tears
And cleave the general ear with horrid speech.

—William Shakespeare, *Hamlet*

12. Read the following selection aloud. Use all the exhaled air efficiently, not wasting air between phonations and concentrating on conserving air during production of sibilant sounds such as *s* and *sh*.

When to the sessions of sweet silent thought
I summon up remembrance of things past,
I sigh the lack of many a thing I sought
And with old woes new wail my dear time's waste.
Then can I drown an eye, unused to flow,
For precious friends hid in death's dateless night,
And weep afresh love's long since canceled woe,
And moan the expense of many a vanished sight.
Then can I grieve at grievances foregone,
And heavily from woe to woe tell o'er
The sad account of forebemoanèd moan,
Which I new-pay as if not paid before.
But if the while I think on thee, dear friend,
All losses are restored and sorrows end.

—William Shakespeare, Sonnet XXX

Breathing and Phrasing

Breath control for speech means coordinating breathing with what we are saying, and our breathing is properly coordinated when it permits us to phrase our speech so that it is meaningful. Control of breathing must allow for any required adjustments in phrasing. (By phrasing is meant the setting apart of a word or a group of words from adjoining words by means of pauses.)

Two extreme examples will help to indicate the wide range of phrasing possibilities. First, read the following sentence on one breath without pausing. "If there's one thing I dislike, it's the speaker who runs all his words together without trying to set them apart from one another in groups or phrases so that I can follow his meaning." Now, read the next sentence, inserting pauses of equal length between each word as indicated by the slant marks: "I / am / just / as / discouraged / by / the / speaker / who / is / so / inflexible / that / he / methodically / sets / each / word / apart / from / adjacent / words / without / regard / to / the / meaning / he / intends / to / convey."

Neither of these examples is acceptable, since neither contributes to effective communication. Our use of exhaled air must be regulated so that we can group words into phrases (long, short, medium, or varied) to suit our speaking needs and purposes.

First, phrases must be set apart clearly. This is done with pauses—

the punctuation marks of spoken language. The foregoing sentences might be unscrambled by grouping the words into meaningful units and separating the groups by pauses. The same sentences you have read might have been phrased as below. Read them, pausing at each slant mark. This will require that you breathe deeply enough to insure a sufficient breath supply for each phrase, or for as many phrases as you will sustain on a given breath. No more phrases should be taken on a single breath than can be spoken on a firm and steady exhalation. Don't attempt to speak on residual air.

> If there's one thing I dislike, / it's the speaker / who runs all his words together / without trying to set them apart from one another / in groups or phrases / so that I can follow his meaning.
>
> I am just as discouraged by the speaker / who is so inflexible / that he / methodically / sets each word apart from adjacent words / without regard to the meaning he intends to convey.

If you were being introduced as a speaker, which of the following introductions would you prefer?

> Today, / our topic is liars, / and our speaker is one of the best known after-dinner speakers in America.
>
> Today, / our topic is liars, / and our speaker is one / of the best known / after-dinner speakers in America.

Or consider the plight of the woman who asked that her pastor make the following announcement from the pulpit:

> John Smith, / having gone to sea, / his wife asks that you pray for his safety.

Unfortunately, however, the pastor phrased the announcement in the following manner:

> John Smith, / having gone to see his wife, / asks that you pray for his safety.

Sometimes we wish to use breathing for dramatic effects in our speech (as in acting or in the expression of some emotion). This may require a very precise muscular control of breathing. Read the following aloud and try to create the illusion that you are running and are afraid:

> Hurry up, Henry—We've got to get away from here—Hurry up—that —that mad bull—is getting closer—and closer—Hey, Henry—Wait for me!

You probably noticed that you inhaled deeply, and rapidly, with violent movement of your chest and abdomen. Air was probably exhaled in short irregular gasps. Your voice was probably breathy or perhaps even harsh, reflecting correctly the feeling of fear you wanted to communicate.

Exercises for Breathing-Phrasing Coordination

1. Read the following numbers aloud, pausing at each dash. Inhale as often as it is necessary to sustain a firm tone.

1 – 2 – 3 – 4 – 5 – 6 – 7 – 8 – 9 – 10.
1 2 – 3 4 – 5 6 – 7 8 – 9 10.
1 2 3 4 5 – 6 7 8 9 10.
1 2 3 4 – 5 6 – 7 8 9 10.
1 2 3 4 5 6 7 – 8 9 10.

2. Read the following sentences aloud and pause when you reach each slant mark. Inhale at these pauses when necessary to maintain an adequate reserve of air.

A speaker / when he begins to talk / is never sure at the outset exactly how long he will speak before it appears appropriate for him to pause. / It is necessary, therefore, / for him to be in such complete command of his breathing / that he has a reserve of air in his lungs / to meet whatever demands the process of communication places upon it.

3. Read the following selections aloud and pause when you reach each slant mark. Inhale at these pauses when necessary.

Freedom means / the supremacy of human rights / everywhere. / Our support / goes to those / who struggle to gain those rights / or keep them. / Our strength / is our unity of purpose. /
To that high concept / there can be no end / save victory.

—Franklin Delano Roosevelt, Message to Congress, January 6, 1941

Like an armed warrior, / like a plumed knight, / James G. Blaine / marched down the halls of the American Congress / and threw his shining lance / full and fair / against the brazen foreheads / of the defamers of his country / and the maligners of his honor.

—Robert G. Ingersoll, "Plumed Knight" speech nominating James G. Blaine for President, June 15, 1876

For now / we see through a glass, / darkly; /
but then / face to face: /
now I know / in part; /
but then shall I know / even as also I am known. /
And now abideth / faith, / hope, / charity, / these three; /
but the greatest of these is charity.

—St. Paul, *I Cor. 13*

4. Read the following selection aloud. Concentrate on coordinating breathing with the communication of meaning. It may help to put a slant mark in the copy wherever you plan to inhale.

Never is the deep, strong voice of man, or the low, sweet voice of woman, finer than in the earnest but mellow tones of familiar speech, richer than the richest music, which are a delight while they are heard, which linger still upon the ear in softened echoes, and which, when they have ceased, come, long after, back to memory, like the murmurs of a distant hymn.

—Henry Giles

5. Read the following selection aloud. Concentrate on coordinating breathing with the communication of feeling. It may help to put slant marks in the copy where you plan to inhale.

Black Hawk is a true Indian, and disdains to cry like a woman. He feels for his wife, his children, and his friends. But he does not care for himself. He cares for the Nation and the Indians. They will suffer. He laments their fate. Farewell, my Nation. Black Hawk tried to save you, and avenge your wrongs. He drank the blood of some of the whites. He has been taken prisoner, and his plans are crushed. He can do no more. Farewell to Black Hawk!

—Black Hawk to General Street

6. Read the following selection aloud, using quick inhalations for dramatic effect:

(As if running) I've just got—to get to that corner—before the bus does—If—I miss that bus again—the boss will fire me—If the boss—fires me—I'll be broke in a week—If I'm broke—I'll have to get a new job—If I get a new job—I may really have to work—my life will be ruined—I've got to catch that bus.

4. *Initiating* VOCAL TONE

test your vocal tone initiation

BREATHINESS

(EXPLANATION, P. 39; EXERCISES, PP. 42-44.)

1. Read the following aloud:

Which of us has known his brother? Which of us has looked into his father's heart? Which of us has not remained forever prison-pent? Which of us is not forever a stranger and alone? [1]

—Thomas Wolfe, *Look Homeward, Angel!*

2. Read the following sentences aloud:

The vocal folds should function with a minimum of fatigue, whether you are singing or speaking.

Unhappy is he who has a voice hampered and hindered by harshness or hoarseness.

HARSHNESS AND HOARSENESS

(EXPLANATION, P. 45; EXERCISES, PP. 47-50.)

3. Read the following aloud:

Alone, alone, all, all alone;
Alone on a wide, wide sea.

—Samuel Taylor Coleridge,
"The Rime of the Ancient Mariner"

4. Read the following sentences aloud:

Each listener appreciates the essential importance of a voice which is initiated efficiently and resonated effectively.

Every exercise included in this book is here to enable each student to overcome speech deficiencies in accordance with his individual needs.

5. Read the following sentences aloud:

Use of an improper pitch level may aggravate harsh voice quality.
Continued vocal misuse may induce hoarseness.

PITCH (EXPLANATION, P. 50; EXERCISES, PP. 52-57.)

6. Read the following excerpts aloud. Each sentence should be read so that the increasing depth of feeling is reflected by your voice.

Mr. President: No man thinks more highly than I do of the patriotism, as well as abilities, of the very worthy gentlemen who have just addressed the House. . . .

They tell us, sir, that we are weak; unable to cope with so formidable an adversary.

But when shall we be stronger? . . .

I know not what course others may take; but as for me, give me liberty, or give me death!

—Patrick Henry

7. Beginning at the lowest pitch level you can produce, sing up the musical scale as many octaves as possible, through falsetto. Although some tenseness may result at the limits of your range, avoid excessive tension.

do	re	mi	fa	so	la	ti	do	re	mi	fa	so	la	ti	do	re	mi	fa	so	la	ti	do
1	2	3	4	5	6	7	8	9	10	11	12	13	14	15	16	17	18	19	20	21	22

←——one octave——→←——two octaves——→←——three octaves——→

Instructor's Test Sheet for Chapter 4

*Name*____	*Rating*
1. Student achieves proper balance of relaxation and tension to avoid breathiness.	____
2. Student avoids wasting air on initial unvoiced consonants.	____
3. Student achieves proper balance of relaxation and tension to avoid harshness and hoarseness.	____
4. Student's vowel sound initiation is free from glottal attack.	____
5. Student's pitch level docs not contribute to guttural or strident quality.	____
6. Student's pitch level is appropriate.	____
7. Student's pitch range (singing) is sufficiently great (approximately 3 octaves) to indicate likelihood of potentially adequate pitch range for speaking.	____
Total	____

Rating: It is suggested that the student be scored on a 5 to 1 point scale, 5 being used to indicate an excellent and 1 a poor rating.

Introduction The test you have just taken should reveal whether or not the vocal tone produced in your larynx is adequate for your speech needs and whether your voice is pitched properly and has sufficient range. Note that we are not for the moment interested in the way your words sound, but rather the way your voice sounds apart from the words. The kind of sound produced in your larynx contributes at least as much to the effectiveness of your speech as your breathing habits. If the tone you initiate in the larynx is of poor quality or if it lacks range, your words will not hold your listener's attention. A breathy voice may be too weak to hear, and even if it is heard it will irritate listeners, just as a harsh or hoarse voice will annoy them. If you have any of these disorders or if you spcak in a monotone, it is almost certain that you have needlessly limited the effectiveness of your spoken thoughts. The vocal power and beauty that you need for effective communication originate with well-produced laryngeal sounds. For this reason a study of phonation logically precedes the study of resonance and articulation.

Breathiness

Inhale deeply. Open your mouth wide and make a silent and prolonged exhalation. There is an absence of sound because the air is not blocked as it passes from the chest cavity through the open glottis to the outer air.

Inhale deeply once again. Produce a prolonged whispered *ah.* Listen to the aspirate quality which is characteristic of whispered sounds. This sound occurs as the glottis is narrowed by the partial approximation, or drawing together, of the vocal folds. (See Fig. 4.) The somewhat tensed folds are set into vibration by the exhaled air. Separate two leaves of this book about one-half an inch and blow sharply between them. Their vibration produces a sound in the same way as do the vibrating, partially approximated vocal folds.

Inhale deeply once again. Produce a prolonged vocalized *ah.* This sound should be very unlike the whispered *ah,* because the vocal folds are brought together even more closely and are then forced apart by the pressure of air from below. After each outward vibration of the vocal folds, the action of the laryngeal muscles causes the folds to close. Air forces them apart again and the cycle is repeated. Phonate the sound of middle C and your vocal folds will complete 256 cycles of opening

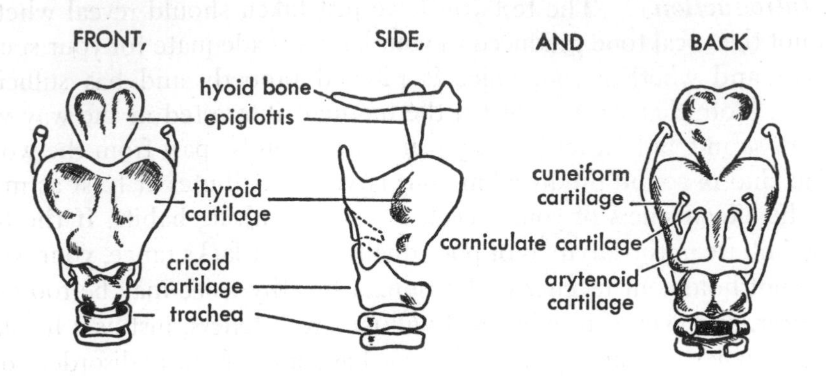

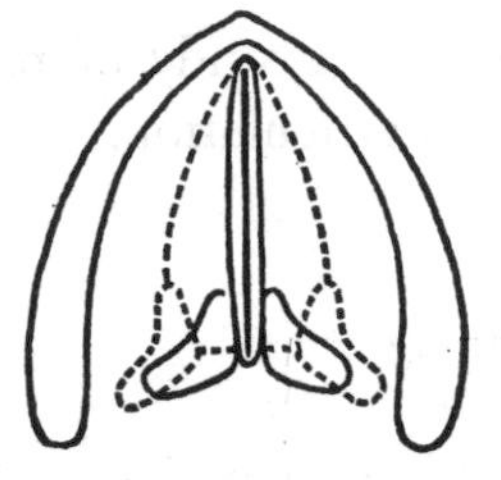

SCHEMATIC DIAGRAM
SHOWING OPENING AND
CLOSING OF VOCAL FOLDS

Figure 4. The larynx

and closing every second; which is the same thing as saying that their vibration rate is 256 cps.

Sound occurs whenever some force sets a vibrating body in motion. In a violin, the bow on the strings is the force, and the strings are the vibrating agent. In the human voice, the column of air lying below the larynx is the potential force, and the vocal folds are the vibrating agent. Place your fingers against your Adam's apple, the protrusion formed by your larynx. Say *ah* and you will feel the vibration of the folds in the larynx.

Some speakers make a sound during phonation which has superimposed on it the aspirate quality you observed when you produced the whispered *ah.* Whisper this paragraph. Now read it again, adding a slight phonation to your whispered speech. This is *breathy speech.* Although your vocal folds are vibrating, an excessive amount of air is rushing past the vocal folds because they are too far apart or not taut enough. Such breathy speech is wasteful of exhaled air; it tires the speaker, as you probably observed; its quality is unpleasant, and the effect is weak.

Breathy speech can often be traced to the speaker's childhood or adolescence. If you have a breathy voice, perhaps you were an impressionable teenager who imitated an older sister or a reigning movie siren whose breathy speech may have seemed alluring to you. If so, you must first re-examine your values to determine which is more important to you—a good voice or an artificial allure. Then listen carefully to your own voice and compare it with properly phonated speech until you can hear the difference. You must train your voice by first training your ear. Once you have become conscious of the aspirate quality of your voice, you are ready to correct it by drilling on the exercises provided later in this chapter, particularly the exercises on relaxation.

Since breathiness is due to insufficient tension in the vocal folds, it may seem paradoxical to counsel the breathy speaker to practice relaxing his throat and body. However, if the throat muscles are tense, the muscles of the larynx will be unable to function properly and may be incapable of drawing the vocal folds as taut as they should be for phonation. If your instructor diagnoses your speech as breathy because you are too tense, pay particular attention to the exercises on relaxation so that your laryngeal muscles will be able to give sufficient tautness to your vocal folds.

Sometimes breathiness is the result of an over-all lack of muscular *tonus.* If the body is run down, the laryngeal muscles are likely to be as flaccid and unresponsive as those in the rest of the body. If breathiness is traced to such a condition, improvement can only be expected when health is restored.

Breathiness may be the result of a condition quite different from the lack of proper muscular control. Speakers sometimes waste an excessive amount of air pronouncing certain words, and the flow of unphonated air adds a breathy quality to the voice. In Chapter 3 we found that more exhaled breath is needed for certain sounds than for others. But the expenditure of air can be greatly overdone. When the voiceless *h* occurs before a vowel, as in the word *heat,* too much air may escape before the vowel is sounded. The same is true in pronouncing any word with certain unvoiced consonants (the sound of which is not made by the vibration of the vocal folds): *wh* in *where, th* in *thing, s* in *set, f* in *far, sh* in *shoe*. By practicing how to move quickly from the voiceless sound to the voiced, this kind of breathiness can be eliminated.

Exercises for Avoiding Breathiness

RELAXATION

1. Stand at exaggerated military attention. All muscles should be excessively tense. Hold the head high. The chin should be pulled back, the chest thrust forward, and the abdomen sucked in. The purpose of this is to give you the feeling of extreme tension which comes from holding such an uncomfortable position. Concentrate on the physical tension in all parts of the body. Now, slowly relax all of these tense muscles. Let the arms and hands hang limp, the shoulders droop, the knees sag, the head fall forward. Instead of the extreme tension you had at first, you should have the feeling of contrasting relaxation.
2. Sit down and assume rigid muscular tension in all parts of the body. Slowly release this tension until you are wholly relaxed.
3. Now alternately tense and relax various parts of the body. Tense one foot. Make the muscles as rigid as possible. Now relax them slowly. Note the difference in muscle tension in other sections of the body. Now tense and relax the other foot. Now tense each leg, then relax it. Repeat with the hands and arms.
4. Contrast the condition of tension and lack of tension in the trunk, first by tensing and then relaxing the muscles of the abdomen. Next, tense the shoulder mucles, then let them sag.
5. Apply excessive tension to the muscles of the neck and throat so that the cords stand out, then relax them. Open your mouth and yawn. If you find this difficult, continue to practice simulating a yawn until you can yawn at will. Let your head fall forward and turn it from side to side gently until you achieve relaxation of the neck and shoulders. Retain the open feeling inside your throat that accompanies a yawn.

EAR TRAINING

1. Inhale deeply. Count *one* using the entire breath supply. Inhale deeply. Count *two* using the entire breath supply. Continue this process through the count of ten. Speak as if you had been running hard for some time and were gasping for air. Note and try to avoid the breathy

tone quality which results from inadequate breath control. Now count from one to ten, taking care to use the breath supply as efficiently as possible. Note the quality of the sound produced and try to develop it.

2. Listen to recordings of the voices of persons who have breathy voice quality and also to recordings of voices of persons with normal voice quality. Notice how excessive amounts of air escape during breathiness.

3. Make recordings of your own voice, alternately recording what you consider to be breathy and nonbreathy samples of speech. Ask your instructor to check you on this. If necessary, ask your instructor to record samples of breathy and nonbreathy speech. This should help you to become aware of the acoustical qualities of these two types of speech. After practice, you should be able to tell even without recordings whether your own voice has normal or breathy voice quality.

4. Read the following paragraphs aloud, simulating the voice quality suggested by the content of each paragraph.

> I am now speaking with breathy voice quality. This condition occurs when excessive air is expelled between only partially approximated vocal folds.
>
> Now I am attempting to eliminate the loss of excessive amounts of air. As long as I maintain proper muscular control and expel a sufficient quantity of air with neither too much nor too little tension, I should be able to produce normal voice quality. It is important that I hear the difference between breathy and nonbreathy voice quality and strive to eliminate the condition of breathiness.

CONSERVING BREATH

1. Keep your body relaxed as suggested in the exercises above. Draw air deeply and easily into the lungs. Relax completely as you release the air in a sigh. Breathe deeply and easily once again and sigh audibly, just vocalizing a single sound *ah*. Repeat with the sounds *aw* and *oh*.

2. Produce a series of slow, silent *h* sounds. These should be made with little effort. Then add voiced sounds to the *h* sound. Do not prolong the unvoiced *h*. Move quickly to the next sounds: *hah, hah, hah, hah, hah, hah, hah; haw, haw, haw, haw, haw, haw, haw; ho, ho, ho, ho, ho, ho, ho*. Maintain the open feeling that accompanies a yawn. Repeat with the sounds *wh, th, s, f,* and *sh*.

3. Read the following words aloud. Be sure that air is not wasted on the unvoiced consonants and that the body remains relaxed.

hat, hail, hair, hall, anyhow, ahead, mohair, uphold, what, when, where, why, anywhere, awhile, horsewhip, nowhere, thick, thimble, thin, three, anything, authentic, author, authority, sat, saw, sew, sun, essay, fast, guest, mister, few, for, furnace, further, afar, differ, offer, refuse, shall, sharp, shop, show, ashamed, dishes, pushing, washing.

4. Follow the instructions given in Exercise 3, above, as you read the following sentences aloud.

Helen had breathy voice quality.
She had not heard of proper vocal fold approximation.
She hurried to a speech correctionist, who told her that hours of practice were ahead.
Helen is now happy that she has eliminated her defect.

5. Follow the instructions given in Exercise 3, above, as you read the following selections aloud:

He who knows, and knows that he knows,
  He is wise—follow him.
He who knows, and knows not he knows,
  He is asleep—awake him.
He who knows not, and knows not he knows not,
  He is a fool—shun him.
He who knows not, and knows he knows not,
  He is a child—teach him.

—Arabian Proverb

The skies they were ashen and sober;
  The leaves they were crispéd and sere,
  The leaves they were withering and sere;
It was night in the lonesome October
  Of my most immemorial year;
It was hard by the dim lake of Auber,
  In the misty mid region of Weir;
It was down by the dank tarn of Auber,
  In the ghoul-haunted woodland of Weir.

—Edgar Allan Poe, "Ulalume"

Harshness and Hoarseness

A tense throat may not only contribute to breathiness but may also cause its opposite, harshness and hoarseness. When the vocal folds are too tightly and inflexibly approximated, harsh tones are produced. If the tension continues, the voice will become hoarse and laryngitis or permanent damage to the vocal folds may result.

Try to apply extra tension to the neck and larynx as you say, "My neck is so stiff, I can hardly turn my head." Now, apply this tension to the upper throat as you say, "I have a sore throat." Probably you noted an unpleasantly harsh quality. You could hear the same results if you spoke with a tense jaw, or if your body were tense. For this reason an angry person may have a harsh voice, and anyone who is emotionally disturbed is likely to have an unpleasant vocal quality.

The elimination of harshness or hoarseness is also often found in exercises for relaxation. If your tests indicate that your voice has these qualities, practice the exercises in this chapter for relaxed phonation, continuing the practice throughout your entire voice improvement program.

As you practice relaxed phonations, concentrate on breathing from the center of your body. Sound is produced in the throat, but the breathing that sets the vocal folds vibrating should be supported abdominally so that there is no unwanted tension in the throat and no harshness in the voice. (See Chapter 3, page 23, on breathing placement.)

GLOTTAL ATTACK Some speakers accompany harsh voice quality with a click or glottal shock, especially on the initiation of vowel sounds, at the beginning of syllables. This unwanted and unpleasant sound (like the sound of a cough) occurs when pressure builds up below the overtensed folds, forcing them apart abruptly with a glottal click.

Hypertension in the throat and larynx must be avoided if this explosive-like vowel initiation is to be avoided. The speaker who initiates vowels with such a glottal attack habitually should first learn to recognize these sounds. Then he should learn to relax the laryngeal muscles until he can initiate vowel sounds easily and naturally. It sometimes helps to overcompensate the fault by producing breathy initial vowel sounds at first. Pronounce *eat* as *heat, it* as *hit,* and *at* as *hat.* Muscles of the larynx should be relaxed and air should not be allowed to build up beneath tightly closed vocal folds. Eventually, as vocal control is achieved, the excessive amount of air escaping between the vocal folds can be reduced. Thus both breathiness and its opposite, glottal attack, can be eliminated.

Failure to correct this fault may cause damage to the vocal folds. If the tension is excessive and the misuse is prolonged, permanent hoarseness may result.

Closely akin to glottal attack in the initiation of vowels is the glottal stop. This sound is used in some dialect regions in substitution for the sound *t*. Thus, *bottle* may be pronounced as *boʔl*, *rattle* as *raʔl*, and *cattle* as *caʔl*. In such instances the glottal stop is likely to be an articulatory problem and is discussed in Chapter 10, on page 196. Here, we are concerned with the glottal attack as a voice quality problem.

THE RELATION OF PITCH TO HARSHNESS AND HOARSENESS A voice is sometimes harsh because it has been pitched too high or too low. Pitch will be discussed in more detail in the next section, but its relation to harshness needs to be stressed here. To get the feeling of a low-pitched (guttural), harsh tone, read the next sentence at the lowest pitch level you can possibly manage while trying to imitate a person expressing a feeling of extreme disgust. "If I talked like this very long, I would soon have a sore throat." This unpleasant voice quality is the result of forcing the vocal folds to vibrate under abnormal muscular conditions. The vocal folds are of a given length, thickness, and elasticity for each individual. A wide range of normal variations in these properties is possible through the action of the muscles controlling the cartilages of the larynx and thus the action of the vocal folds. However, when you force these muscles to adjust the vocal folds to produce an abnormally low tone, you are seeking a response outside their normal limits. It is as unnatural to produce bass vocal tones on tenor vocal folds as it is to play bass viol tones on a violin.

This problem is magnified by the fact that a low tone has very little intensity and does not carry. In an attempt to compensate for this lack of carrying power, speakers often force additional muscular effort, thus compounding an already unfortunate situation.

High-pitched harshness (stridency) results from attempting to produce tones which are beyond the normal limits of the mechanism in the opposite direction. To get the feeling of stridency, read the following sentence at the highest pitch level you can possibly manage, while imitating a very angry speaker. "This kind of speech is not only unpleasant to listen to, but may also damage the vocal folds."

You will find that either of these extremes (too low a pitch or too high a pitch) causes undue muscular strain which is evident in an unpleasant vocal tone.

Exercises for Avoiding Harshness and Hoarseness

RELAXATION

1. Sit or lie down in a comfortable position. (You should be in a quiet place, by yourself.) Imagine that you are in a secluded retreat. Try to recall some lake or landscape that seemed particularly peaceful to you at the time, and remember the feelings which accompanied that experience. Do not allow yourself to be interrupted by other sounds or thoughts. Now clench the left hand and then let it relax as completely as possible. Follow this by concentrating on relaxation of the lower arm, then the upper arm, then the shoulder. Repeat this with the right hand and arm, and then with both feet and both legs. Now concentrate, in turn, upon relaxing the muscles of the entire body; the abdomen, chest, throat, neck, face, and head. Repeat this several times until you have a feeling of well-being with an absence of muscular tension.

2. Sit in a comfortable position, with good posture. Let the head fall forward of its own weight and let the jaw drop, and the mouth fall open. (Do not force the head down, just let it fall.) Gently rotate the head several times to the right, back, left, and forward, maintaining a sense of relaxation in the neck muscles. Reverse the rotation, going several times to the left. Now let the jaw fall open even farther and yawn. Keep this feeling of the relaxed open throat as you repeat *ah* several times; *aw* several times; *oh* several times. Count to ten, maintaining this open feeling. Now read the following selection aloud.

Blest, who can unconcern'dly find
Hours, days, and years, slide soft away
In health of body, peace of mind,
    Quiet by day:
Sound sleep by night; study and ease
Together mixt, sweet recreation,
And innocence, which most does please
    With meditation.

—Alexander Pope, "Solitude"

EAR TRAINING

1. Put your hands on your neck and add muscular tension to the throat so that you can feel the tension of the muscles with your fingers. Count from one to ten and note the quality of the tone which results from tension in the neck and throat. This harsh voice quality should be avoided. Now yawn once again, open the mouth wide, and avoid tension both in the jaw and in the neck and throat as you count from one to ten. Note the nature of the quality produced, and try to develop it.

2. Listen to the voices of your friends and of speakers on radio and television who have a harsh or hoarse voice quality, as well as to the voices of persons with normal voice quality. Learn to recognize these qualities. If you are unable to identify the quality of your own voice as you speak, record it and compare your voice quality with that of other speakers.

CORRECTING GLOTTAL ATTACK

1. Say the word *hod* aloud several times. Concentrate on beginning the word with an open throat on the *h* sound and a smooth initiation of the vowel *ah* without glottal attack. Once you are positive that you are moving from the *h* sound to the vowel sound without an abrupt glottal initiation, repeat the word *hod* aloud several times to reinforce the habit of producing sound initiation correctly without glottal attack. Repeat with the words *hold, heat,* and *hit*.

2. Repeat the following pairs of words aloud several times, being certain that the absence of glottal attack which you have achieved in the production of the first word is carried over to the second word of the pair. *hod-odd, hold-old, heat-eat, hit-it, head-Ed, hat-at, haul-all, hurl-Earl.*

3. Strive to avoid glottal attack as you read the following paragraphs aloud:

> It is on the initiation of words with vowel sounds in the initial position that glottal attack is most likely to occur. Excessive air pressure in the trachea should be avoided. Unless unusual muscular tension in the larynx is eliminated, it is almost impossible to initiate the sound easily without the occurrence of the glottal click.
>
> Notice that there is less likelihood of glottal attack at the beginning of words in this paragraph than in the preceding one, since fewer of the words in this paragraph begin with vowel sounds.

Here we have held to initial *h*'s to hammer home the handy habit of initiating vowels easily, hence hampering harshness and hoarseness.

4. Strive to avoid glottal attack as you read the following selections loud:

> Out—out are the lights—out all!
> And over each quivering form,
> The curtain, a funeral pall,
> Comes down with the rush of a storm—
> While the angels, all pallid and wan,
> Uprising, unveiling, affirm
> That the play is the tragedy, "man,"
> And its hero the Conqueror Worm.
>
> —Edgar Allan Poe, "Ligeia"

> All the world's a stage,
> And all the men and women merely players.
> They have their exits and their entrances,
> And one man in his time plays many parts,
> His acts being seven ages.
>
> —William Shakespeare, *As You Like It*

CORRECTING PITCH

Consult the exercises on pitch range, page 54.

VOICE PRODUCTION WITHOUT HARSHNESS OR HOARSENESS

1. Make sure your body is relaxed. Draw the air easily and deeply into the lungs. Maintain the feeling of an open throat and avoid laryngeal tension. Read the following words aloud, watching for any trace of harshness as you begin each word:

> eat, ever, all, over, up, aid, ire, oil
> out, ode, omen, oust, ear, ant, on, am

2. Follow the instructions given in Exercise 1, above, as you read the following sentences aloud.

Arthur's harsh voice annoyed everyone.

He was often obstinate about his faults and avoided self-improvement.

Unfortunately, his tension increased, and the harsh quality became even more unbearable.

Eventually, Arthur's annoying harshness evolved into permanent hoarseness.

Eliot's vocal habits encouraged the growth of nodules on his vocal folds.

Excessive strain increased his vocal abnormalities.

Eventually, his voice became unbearably hoarse.

Relaxation of body and serenity of mind were prerequisites to his vocal rehabilitation.

3. Follow the instructions given in 1, above, as you read the following selections aloud:

> A man said to the universe:
> "Sir, I exist!"
> "However," replied the universe,
> "The fact has not created in me
> A sense of obligation."
>
> —Stephen Crane, "A Man Said to the Universe"

> Death be not proud, though some have called thee
> Mighty and dreadful, for, thou are not so,
> For, those, whom thou think'st thou dost overthrow,
> Die not, poor death, nor yet canst thou kill me.
>
> —John Donne, Sonnet V from *Holy Sonnets*

Pitch

We have already indicated that a voice may become guttural if it is pitched too low, and strident if pitched too high. What, then, is the right pitch? The answer is to be found by examining why voices vary in pitch.

The pitch of a human sound is determined by the rapidity with which the vocal folds vibrate; this frequency of vibration is determined partly by the length, thickness, and tension of the vocal folds. The pitch level varies directly with the length and thickness of the vibrating agent and indirectly with its tension. Other things being equal, the longer or thicker the vibrating body, the lower the pitch; the more tension it is under, the higher the pitch. The bass notes on a piano have long, thick strings, whereas its top notes have shorter and slender strings. Similarly, men's vocal folds tend to be longer and thicker than women's, consequently they tend to vibrate more slowly and thus have a lower pitch.

PITCH LEVEL For every pair of vocal folds there is what is referred to as an *optimum pitch level* (sometimes called natural or structural pitch level). Since vocal folds vary in their dimensions from one person to another, so will the optimum pitch level vary from person to person. For each person, the vocal mechanism operates most efficiently when optimum pitch is used.

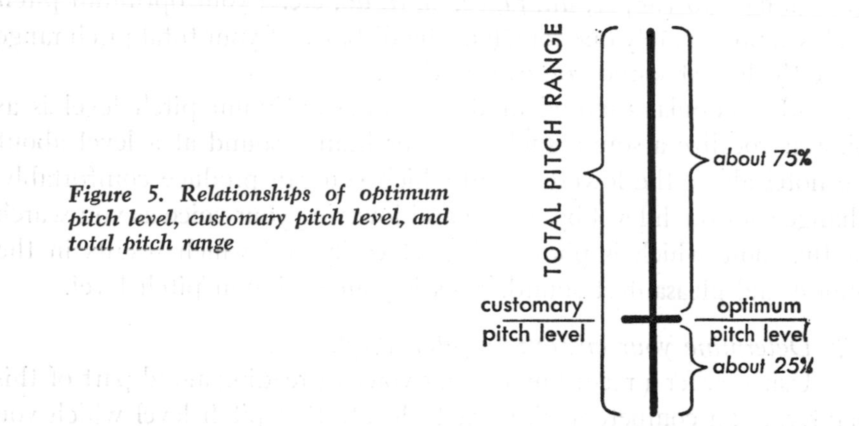

Figure 5. Relationships of optimum pitch level, customary pitch level, and total pitch range

When a speaker's voice tends to center on this level, rising above and falling below it so that the voice is not monotonous but uses this pitch more than others, his pitch is optimum. But if the pitch he generally uses, his customary pitch level, lies above or below his optimum pitch, he will not be making the most effective use of his voice. Let us suppose your *customary pitch level* is too high. If you raise your voice at times to avoid monotony, the laryngeal muscles will be placed under strain and the quality of your voice will suffer. Furthermore, you will have limited severely the possibilities of pitch flexibility in an upward direction, since you will already be speaking close to the top of your range.

If, on the other hand, your customary pitch level is below your optimum pitch, it will be difficult to vary your pitch downward to deliver a command or to emphasize a declarative statement. You will probably speak in a monotone with a dull and expressionless voice. It is also difficult to be heard when you speak at the floor of your pitch. It is entirely possible, if you attempt to use loud tones at this low pitch level, that you may damage the vocal folds and develop a permanently unpleasant voice quality.

Exercises for Pitch Level

1. *Determine your optimum pitch level.*

One of the standard methods of determining the pitch level at which your voice functions most efficiently is as follows: sing down the scale to the lowest note your voice can produce (*do, ti, la, so, fa, mi, re, do*, etc.); sing up the scale from your lowest note to your highest note through falsetto (*do, re, mi, fa, so, la, ti, do*, etc.); your optimum pitch level is approximately one-fourth of the distance of your total pitch range above the lowest sound you can produce.[2]

Another popular method of determining optimum pitch level is as follows: vocalize a sound such as *ah* or hum a sound at a level about five notes above the lowest sound which you can produce comfortably. Change your pitch level by raising and lowering your voice as you search for that note which is phonated most easily and which results in the loudest and pleasantest sound. This is your optimum pitch level.

2. *Determine your customary pitch level.*

Using either a recording of your voice or reading aloud part of this chapter, ask a competent observer to locate that pitch level which you use most often. He should listen carefully while you speak and compare your pitch level with hummed tones or with notes struck on a piano until he finds that pitch level which appears to be the base from which your voice varies upward and downward. This is your customary pitch level.

3. *Compare your optimum pitch level with your customary pitch level.*

If your customary pitch level deviates more than two or three notes from your optimum pitch level, it *may* be desirable to change your customary pitch level so that it coincides more nearly with your optimum pitch level. However, before you decide to make any drastic changes in the customary pitch level of your voice, consult a competent speech authority to be sure that the level which you believe to be your optimum pitch level has been determined correctly and that a false level has not

[2] Grant Fairbanks, *Voice and Articulation Drillbook* (New York, Harper and Brothers, 1940), pp. 168-70.

been chosen when your vocal mechanism was under unnatural tension or strain.

PITCH RANGE Unless you vary your pitch when speaking, so that the highest pitch you use is between one and one and one-half octaves above your lowest, the chances are that your voice will be monotonous. In fact, expression of certain emotions may demand that you use a pitch range varying as much as two octaves.

As you set about to increase your pitch range, it is important to note that it is much easier to increase range upward than downward. Since your optimum pitch is close to one-quarter of the way up from the lowest pitch you can produce, you can see that it might be as much as three times as easy to expand pitch range upward from your optimum pitch as to expand the range downward from the optimum pitch level. This may be bad news for those who want to speak in a deeper rather than a higher voice. More encouraging is the fact that there is no necessary correlation between high pitch and unpleasant voice quality. Harshness, hoarseness, or breathiness (types of unpleasant voice quality) are the result of improper voice production. A soprano or tenor voice, properly produced, is considerably more pleasant to the ears of a listener than is a baritone or alto voice produced through unnatural and forced tension in the throat.

People who are unable to distinguish between higher and lower tones frequently have such a limited speaking range that their voices are uninteresting. Test your ability to distinguish pitch levels by having someone strike notes on a piano while you tell him which tones are high and which are low. If no piano is available, you may perform the same test by having someone with good tone perception produce vocal tones at varying pitch levels while you identify the level. People with good hearing can generally distinguish differences in pitch ranging from a frequency of 50 vibrations per second to 20,000 vibrations per second, although there are wide variations in these limits from individual to individual. If you cannot distinguish pitch levels easily, you probably should have your hearing tested further.

Speaking range and singing range are not to be confused. The normal effective singing range is about two octaves, although it may be extended considerably with proper training. Peruvian Yma Sumac is well known for her singing range, which covers four octaves. Alfred Wolfson, in support of his theory that the human voice has an inherently wide singing range, points to his star pupil Jennifer Johnson.[3] Miss Johnson, according to her teacher, has a useful singing range of four and a half octaves—everything from bass to soprano—and can cover almost two additional octaves, although the latter have little musical value.

Unless you intend to use the voice for singing or perhaps for professional acting, you need not concern yourself with the extreme pitch range development which is possible for the human voice. However, it is not unreasonable to assume that almost any student can train his voice so that he can use it for expressive speaking over a range of one or two octaves.

In developing an expanded pitch range, you need have no fear that your speech will call attention to itself or be affected because of the use of varying pitch levels. There is nothing affected about an expressive voice. It is the insincere speaker who sounds affected, not the expressive one. In fact, you will fail to present your total personality in the most favorable light if, through embarrassment about using your voice, you limit your range to a few notes.

Exercises for Pitch Range

1. Starting at a comfortably low pitch, count from 1 to 5 making each number higher in pitch than the one before. Maintain the feeling of the "open throat" and avoid the use of excessive force as you produce the sounds.

2. Repeat the following words aloud slowly and easily, starting with a comfortably low pitch and raising the pitch of each repetition. Go to as high a pitch as is comfortable. Avoid the feeling of tension in the tongue, lips, palate, and lower jaw while maintaining an open throat:

see, Sue, tea, too, me, moo, key, coo

3. Beginning at a point near your optimum pitch level, sing down the musical scale until you reach the floor of your pitch. Maintain a well-supported tone and attempt to increase your range gradually as you practice this exercise a number of times. If possible, use a piano to assist you. Repeat, singing upward from your optimum pitch level instead of downward.

4. Beginning at the lowest tone which you can produce, sing upward

[3] "The Omnitone," *Time Magazine*, Vol. LXVII, No. 12 (March 19, 1956), p. 56.

through the highest tone you can produce. Attempt to increase this range gradually and without undue muscular tension. Return to this exercise and to other exercises in this section regularly, until you have achieved a total singing range of about three octaves.

5. Say *ah* at a low, medium, or high pitch level, as indicated:

(low) *ah* (medium) *ah* (high) *ah* (low) *ah*
(high) *ah* (low) *ah* (medium) *ah* (high) *ah*

6. Read the following words and phrases aloud at a pitch level appropriate to the meaning expressed by each.

Begin low—then talk high—a little higher still—now low again—now very low—speak at a medium pitch—now very high—now higher still —can you make it higher?—now very low.

7. Read the following military commands aloud, making the first half low in pitch and the second half (the execution) higher in pitch. Avoid vocal strain.

Atten	-	shun
Right	-	Dress
Ready	-	Front
Right shoulder	-	Arms
Left	-	Face
Forward	-	March
Company	-	Halt
Dis	-	missed

8. Read the following military commands aloud, making the first half high in pitch and the second half (the execution) lower in pitch. Avoid vocal strain.

Atten	-	shun
Forward	-	March
Column right	-	March
Column left	-	March
By the right flank	-	March
By the left flank	-	March
Company	-	Halt
Dis	-	missed

9. Read the following selection aloud as though you were:

a. Speaking of the heart of someone very close to you;
b. Speaking of your watch;
c. Speaking of the engine of an airplane in which you are a passenger.

Pay particular attention to exaggerating the different pitch levels of each situation.

At first it never occurred to me that it might become serious. And then the rhythm became more irregular and erratic. I began to get really worried. I wondered if it would come to a complete stop. I listened, and wondered, and hoped. The rhythm steadied down finally and I thought everything would be all right until five minutes ago. Now the rhythm is all out of phase, and it's getting weaker and weaker. . . . Now it's slowing down . . . way down. . . . Now it's stopped!

10. Read the following selections aloud. Pay particular attention to using a wide pitch range without vocal strain.

O sinner! Consider the fearful danger you are in: 'Tis a great furnace of wrath, a wide and bottomless pit, full of the fire of wrath, that you are held over in the hand of that God, whose wrath is provoked and incensed as much against you, as against many of the damned in hell. You hang by a slender thread, with the flames of divine wrath flashing about it, and ready every moment to singe it, and burn it asunder; and you have no interest in any Mediator, and nothing to lay hold of to save yourself, nothing to keep off the flames of wrath, nothing of your own, nothing that you ever have done, nothing that you can do, to induce God to spare you one moment.

—Jonathan Edwards, "Sinners in the Hands of an Angry God"

I hear America singing, the varied carols I hear,
Those of mechanics, each one singing his as it should be blithe and strong,
The carpenter singing his as he measures his plank or beam,
The mason singing his as he makes ready for work, or leaves off work,
The boatman singing what belongs to him in his boat, the deckhand singing on the steamboat deck,
The shoemaker singing as he sits on his bench, the hatter singing as he stands,

The wood-cutter's song, the plowboy's on his way in the morning,
  or at noon intermission or at sundown,
The delicious singing of the mother, or of the young wife at work, or
  of the girl sewing or washing,
Each singing what belongs to him or her and to none else,
The day what belongs to the day—at night the party of young fellows,
  robust, friendly,
Singing with open mouths their strong melodious songs.

—Walt Whitman, "I Hear America Singing"

5. *Resonating* VOCAL TONE

test your resonance

NASALITY AND DE-NASALITY

(EXPLANATION, P. 63; EXERCISES, PP. 65-68.)

1. Read the following aloud:

deem, dim, dumb, doom, dame, dime, dome
ring, rang, rung, sin, send, sand, sun, soon
wrongdoing, sandstone, ringworm, wineskin, winsome
Sing and hum and run home soon.

2. Read the following aloud:

knee, knit, net, gnat, knot, nut, nigh, neigh
meet, mit, met, mat, might, mate, mote
nevermore, amenable, management, nonentity, moment
Mike and his mate moved next to my neighbor.

3. Read the following aloud:

deed, did, dead, dad, dude, tat, tot
taught, toot, tight, pad, tad, bat, bad, gag
statistics, electric, capable, capital, tactics
Successful speakers give others pleasure.

4. Read the following aloud:

Some are born great; some achieve greatness; and some have greatness thrust upon them.

—William Shakespeare, *Twelfth Night*

Know then thyself, presume not God to scan;
The proper study of Mankind is Man.

—Alexander Pope

RESONANCE

(EXPLANATION, P. 68; EXERCISES, PP. 72-75.)

5. Read the following aloud:

Every duty which we omit, obscures some truth which we should have known.

—John Ruskin

6. Read the following aloud:

The Curfew tolls the knell of parting day,
The lowing herd wind slowly o'er the lea,
The plowman homeward plods his weary way,
And leaves the world to darkness and to me.

—Thomas Gray,
"Elegy Written in a Country Churchyard"

7. Read the following aloud:

The influence of temper upon tone deserves much consideration. In the voice there is no deception; it is, to many, the index of the mind, denoting moral qualities; and it may be remarked that the low, soft tones of gentle and amiable beings, whatever their musical endowments may be, seldom fail to please; besides which the singing of ladies indicates the cultivation of their taste.

—Charles Mordaunt

8. Read the following aloud:

How often the spell of beauty is rudely broken by coarse, loud talking! How often you are irresistibly drawn to a plain, unassuming woman, whose soft, silvery tones render her positively attractive. In the social circle how pleasant it is to hear a woman talk in that low key which always characterizes the true lady. In the sanctuary of home how such a voice soothes the fretful child and cheers the weary husband!

—Charles Lamb

9. Read the following aloud:

This is pre-eminently the time to speak the truth, the whole truth, frankly and boldly. Nor need we shrink from honestly facing conditions in our country today. This great nation will endure as it has endured, will revive and will prosper. So first of all let me assert my firm belief that the only thing we have to fear is fear itself—nameless, unreasoning, unjustified terror which paralyzes needed efforts to convert retreat into advance.

—Franklin Delano Roosevelt, "First Inaugural Address"

10. Read the following aloud:

Then darkness enveloped the whole American armada. Not a pinpoint of light showed from those hundreds of ships as they surged on through the night toward their destiny, carrying across the ageless and indifferent sea tens of thousands of young men, fighting for . . . for . . . well, at least for each other.[1]

—Ernie Pyle, *Brave Men*

[1] Ernie Pyle, *Brave Men* (New York, Henry Holt and Company, 1944), p. 18. Reprinted by permission of the publisher.

Instructor's Test Sheet for Chapter 5

*Name*____	*Rating*
1. Student avoids nasalizing vowel sounds before nasal consonants.	____
2. Student avoids nasalizing vowel sounds after nasal consonants.	____
3. Student avoids nasalizing vowel sounds when they are not adjacent to nasal consonants.	____
4. Student achieves adequate resonance of nasal consonants.	____
5. Student amplifies tone with open throat, avoiding pharyngeal constriction.	____
6. Student's resonance is enhanced through proper tongue movement.	____
7. Student's resonance is enhanced through proper lip movement.	____
8. Student's resonance is enhanced through proper jaw movement.	____
9. Excessive sound reflection of tensed walls of resonators is avoided.	____
10. Excessive sound absorption of relaxed walls of resonators is avoided.	____
Total	____

Rating: It is suggested that the student be scored on a 5 to 1 point scale, 5 being used to indicate an excellent and 1 a poor rating.

Introduction If your instructor has found that your voice lacks resonance or is improperly resonated, you may be inclined to think that the fault is a minor one, especially if you are convinced that people hear what you say. It is also quite likely that you will not be able to detect the vocal fault even after your instructor calls your attention to it. One purpose of the exercises in this chapter is to make you aware of how unpleasant a poorly resonated voice really is. For once your ear has been trained to *hear* any resonating faults you may have, it should be obvious why poor resonance should be corrected. The man who whines may be understood, but his point of view is seldom appreciated. The strident voice, the thin voice, the muffled voice are not likely to win a sympathetic hearing for the speaker. You, like others, undoubtedly are attracted to those who have full, harmonious, mellow voices. They succeed in communicating with you whereas you may be reluctant even to listen to a person with a pinched or nasal voice. Therefore, if your speech is poorly resonated, it is important that you should remedy this fault if you wish others to listen to you with interest and pleasure.

Nasality and De-nasality

Close your mouth and hum the sound of *m*. Pinch your nose slightly and you will feel the vibration. Produce the sounds of *n* and *ng* in the same way. These three sounds (*m*, *n*, and *ng*) are the nasal sounds of American speech and are distinguished from other sounds in that air escapes through the nose as they are made.

Stand in front of a mirror and shine a flashlight in your mouth. You will see at the back of the mouth the velum, or soft palate, ending in the uvula, which hangs down toward the throat. Inhale through your nose with your mouth open, and you will see the velum lower. Prepare to say *ah* and the velum will lift. As you can see in the diagram, when the velum is raised, it prevents air from passing through the nose to the outer air. When it is lowered, air can be exhaled through the nose. In the latter position, the nasal sounds can be made properly.

In the next section, the nature of resonance will be explored in detail. But to anticipate that discussion slightly, the nasal sounds *m*, *n*, and *ng*, since they are emitted through the nose, should be resonated and thus amplified in the nasal passages as well as in the mouth and the back of the throat. When the nasal resonating chamber is closed off by raising the velum, the air cannot escape through the nose, and the quality of these nasal sounds becomes unpleasant. A voice that produces them is called de-nasal.

Say "Mel and Minnie were singing in the rain." Did it sound as though you were saying, "Bel and Biddie were sigig id the raid"? If you had a severe head cold, it might be de-nasalized this way because your blocked nasal passages would prevent the proper resonating of the *m*'s, *n*'s, and *ng*'s. A broken nose, adenoids, sinus, hay fever, or anything else that tends to close off the nasal passages will produce de-nasalized speech.

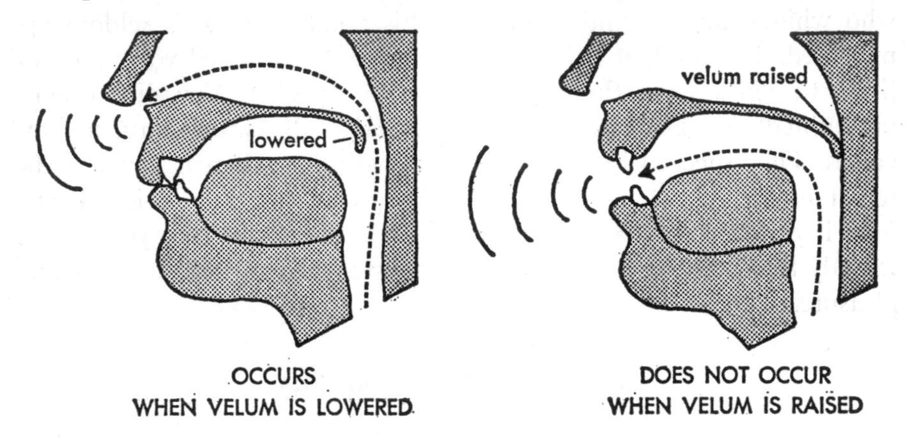

Figure 6. Nasal resonance

Nasal speech, however, is more common than de-nasal speech. Some forms of it are even acceptable in certain parts of the country. Try to count from one to ten with the soft palate lowered, so that air can pass through the nose, and with the mouth almost closed. Many sounds besides the three nasal ones will be nasalized. The effect is unpleasant to most people. Your speech has a twang when you speak this way, or it may sound as if you are whining. We say that a person talking this way is "speaking through his nose" and this is quite literally true. People with cleft palates speak this way because there is a hole in the roof of the mouth through which air escapes into the nasal cavity whether the velum is lowered or raised. But many people whose resonators are perfectly formed speak nasally. If you are one of these, the exercises given below will help you to shut off your nasal passage completely except when you are making one of the three nasal sounds.

Exercises for Eliminating Nasality and De-nasality

NASALITY

1. Hold a hand mirror and look at the soft palate in the back of the roof of the mouth. Inhale through the nostrils and note that the velum is lowered. Now say *ah.* You will see the velum raise. Alternately inhale and say *ah* until you are aware of the feeling accompanying the raising and lowering of the soft palate. Practice raising and lowering it without inhaling and without sounding *ah.*

2. Repeat the vowel sounds *ee* and *a* as in *bat* with the velum lowered so that air escapes through the nose. Check to make sure that you are phonating with a lowered velum by alternately pinching and releasing the nostrils. If your velum is lowered, there will be a distinct difference in the quality of the sound produced; if it is raised, there should be no audible difference. Repeat with *ah* and *oo.* Note the unwanted nasal resonance which results from this distortion in the production of vowel sounds and try to avoid it. Now, repeat the same vowel sounds, taking care to keep the velum raised so that no air escapes through the nose. Note the nature of the quality produced and try to develop this kind of production of nonnasal sounds.

3. Place a small hand mirror under your nostrils and read the following words aloud:

read rid red rod rude road

There should be no moisture on the mirror. Now place the mirror under your nostrils again and read the following words aloud:

mean men mine man moon moan

There should be moisture on the mirror as a result of correct production of the nasal sounds in these words. If moisture appeared after you read the first group of words (*read, rid,* etc.), practice reading words without nasal sounds until there is no escape of air during their production.

4. Practice feeling velar action by repeating the vowel sound *a* (as in *man*) several times, alternately lowering and raising the velum.

a	a	a	a	a	a
(normal)	(nasal)	(normal)	(nasal)	(normal)	(nasal)

5. Practice avoiding the nasalization of vowel sounds before nasal consonants by reading the following words aloud. First, separate the

word into its individual sounds and produce each sound in isolation. Then, pronounce the word aloud, concentrating upon keeping the velum lowered for nasal sounds and raised for nonnasal sounds.

s—ee—n	seen	s—ee—m	seem	s—i—ng	sing
i—n	in	h—i—m	him	r—a—ng	rang
h—e—n	hen	h—e—m	hem	s—a—ng	sang
a—n	an	a—m	am	s—o—ng	song
r—u—n	run	h—u—m	hum	s—u—ng	sung

6. Practice avoiding the nasalization of vowel sounds after nasal consonants by reading the following words aloud. Follow the instructions given in Exercise 5, above.

n—ea—t	neat	m—ea—t	meat
n—e—t	net	m—i—tt	mitt
N—a—t	Nat	m—e—t	met
n—o—t	not	m—a—t	mat
n—u—t	nut	m—oo—t	moot

7. Practice avoiding the nasalization of vowel sounds before and after nasal consonants by reading the following words aloud. Follow the instructions given in Exercise 5, above.

m—ea—n	mean	N—a—n	Nan
m—e—n	men	n—a—me	name
m—a—n	man	a—n—o—n	anon
m—oo—n	moon	n—oo—n	noon
m—oa—n	moan	n—u—n	nun

s—i—ng—i—ng	singing
h—e—mm—i—ng	hemming
h—a—ng—i—ng	hanging
i—nn—i—ng	inning
h—u—mm—i—ng	humming

8. Read the following sentences aloud. Pay particular attention to the avoidance of nasality in nonnasal sounds.

Mary's nasal resonance produced a disturbing twang.
Her soft palate did not close off the nasal passage completely on nonnasal sounds.

Her twang detracted from her otherwise pleasant tone.
Mary needs to hear her voice as others hear it before she can eliminate the twang.

9. Read the following selection aloud. Avoid nasalizing nonnasal sounds.

> Jenny kissed me when we met,
> Jumping from the chair she sat in;
> Time, you thief, who love to get
> Sweets into your list, put *that* in . . .
> —Leigh Hunt, "Jenny Kissed Me"

DE-NASALITY

1. Repeat the sentence "I cannot sing because I have a cold in my nose" with the velum raised so that no air escapes through the nasal cavity. It will sound as though you are saying "I caddot sig because I have a cold id by dose." Note the voice quality which results from this omission of nasal resonance; this kind of de-nasal quality should be avoided. Now repeat the sentence, taking care that the nasal resonance cavity is used correctly. Note the nature of the quality produced and try to develop it.
2. Place the forefinger against the nostril lightly. Close the mouth and hum a tone at your optimum pitch level. Sustain the tone and concentrate on gaining maximum nasal resonance. Place the tips of the fingers on the bridge of the nose as you say *hum, sing, run, none, home.* Lower the velum for the nasal sounds. Prolong the production of the nasal sounds and exaggerate the resonance until you can feel the vibration of the nose with the fingers.
3. Repeat the following words aloud. Sustain the final sounds. Amplify them with full nasal resonance.

> beam, bam, bomb, boom, bum
> bean, bin, Ben, ban, boon
> bing, bang, bong, ding, dong
> mean, men, man, moan, moon

4. Read the following pairs of words. Take care to avoid nasality in the first word and to produce nasal resonance on the nasal sounds in the second word.

bit—mitt	deed—need	rig—ring
bet—met	dead—Ned	rug—rung
bat—mat	dote—note	sag—sang
lid—limb	lead—lean	tag—tang
lad—lamb	Tad—tan	tug—tongue
load—loam	load—loan	lug—lung

5. Read the following sentences aloud. Pay particular attention to the avoidance of de-nasality in nasal sounds.

Ned's nasal passages are partly blocked because his nose has been broken.

Nasal sounds are hampered by this abnormal physical condition.

It frequently sounds as if Ned is suffering from a constant head cold.

Ned's physician may try to eliminate this defect by recommending an operation to reopen the nasal passages.

6. Read the following selection aloud. Avoid de-nasalizing nasal sounds.

A noiseless patient spider,
I mark'd where on a little promontory it stood isolated,
Mark'd how to explore the vacant vast surrounding,
It launch'd forth filament, filament, filament, out of itself,
Ever unreeling them, ever tirelessly speeding them.

And you O my soul where you stand,
Surrounded, detached, in measureless oceans of space,
Ceaselessly musing, venturing, throwing, seeking the spheres to connect them,
Till the bridge you will need be form'd, till the ductile anchor hold,
Till the gossamer thread you fling catch somewhere O my soul.

—Walt Whitman, "A Noiseless Patient Spider"

Improving Resonance

Resonance is not an easy process to understand, nor is it necessary to understand all the physics and physiology involved in order to improve one's speech. But there are aspects of the resonating process which it is important to know if you wish to increase the richness and over-all quality of your voice.

No vocal sound is ever made up of one pitch only. Each sound has its fundamental pitch and its overtones which are higher than the fundamental pitch. Strike middle C on the piano. The full length of the C string vibrates at 256 cycles per second. But it also vibrates in sections. Since the sections are shorter than the whole, the vibration of each section produces a higher pitch than the vibration of the full length.

The higher pitches are the overtones. The pitch you are particularly conscious of is the fundamental pitch, the middle C in this case. But you also hear the higher pitches, the overtones, even though they are so blended with the fundamental that you probably cannot distinguish them as separate notes. It is these overtones that make up the richness of the middle C to your ear.

No two people produce middle C in exactly the same way because differences in their vocal mechanisms will provide different overtones, and they will resonate these sounds somewhat differently. You hear a friend whom you cannot see speaking, and yet you can tell who it is because your ear is familiar with the kind of overtones his voice produces and resonates; that is to say, you recognize the resonant quality of his voice.

The differences between the sounds of speech are also partly due to the differences in the overtones that you hear. If you sing *ah* at middle C, then *ee* at middle C, the fundamental pitch for both is the same. But the overtones of the fundamental pitch which your vocal mechanism is amplifying when you say *ah* are different from the ones being amplified when you say *ee*. It is the different patterns of overtones that account for our hearing it as *ah* or *ee*.

When you say *ah*, the vibrations of the fundamental pitch and its overtones enter the pharynx and the mouth (the nasal passage is closed off by the raised velum). The air in these chambers begins to vibrate at the same rates as the fundamental and some of the overtones. The result is a greatly enlarged sound.

Why does the enclosed air vibrate at these same rates? As you adjust your lips, tongue, mouth, velum, and throat to make the sound *ah*, you are forming your resonators into a chamber with a certain shape and volume, and with an aperture into the outer air of certain dimensions. Even the texture of the walls of this chamber is changed as you prepare to say *ah*. The air in the chamber you have formed has a natural frequency, and when it is affected by air vibrating at the same frequency it too will begin to vibrate. You unconsciously formed your mouth and throat in just this way because the natural frequency of the resonators shaped thus are the same as the frequencies that make up the sound *ah*. You might say that the resonator is shaped so that it will select just those overtones for amplification that belong to the sound *ah*.

Shape your mouth differently and the chamber will have different dimensions and therefore a different natural frequency. Thus it will amplify different frequencies of the phonated sound. You will no longer produce *ah* but a different vowel that has a frequency rate similar to the natural frequency of your reshaped resonators. For one sound we amplify certain of the overtones coming from the larynx; at other times we unconsciously amplify different overtones by altering the resonating chamber. If it were not for this ability to modify the shape of the resonators, we should be unable to make the different vowel sounds.

Resonating chambers will have different natural frequencies depending on their volume, their shape, and the size of their aperture, as well as the material of the chamber itself. Of two chambers with the same sized opening, the one with the greater spatial volume will generally have a lower natural frequency. The larger organ pipes produce the low tones, the small ones the high tones. On the other hand, two chambers of the same volume but with different sized openings will have different natural frequencies. The small, apertured one will have a lower natural frequency than the one with the larger aperture.

Let us examine briefly some of the ways in which the human resonators can be altered so that we can understand how they amplify different kinds of fundamentals and overtones to produce different vowel sounds and the sounds of some consonants.

The lips form one exit for the exhaled air, the other being the nostrils. Purse your lips and phonate a sound. You will probably produce the *oo* as in *food*. The sound *oo* has a low natural frequency and the small aperture amplifies these low frequencies. The air in the mouth vibrates in response, then, to the low frequencies rather than the high frequencies of the sound coming from your larynx: the low frequency sound of *oo* results. Now open your mouth wide and phonate a sound again. *Ah*, with its higher frequencies, is probably the vowel sound you will make because the wider aperture permits the amplification of the higher frequencies in the phonated sound. Therefore, for properly resonated tone you must avoid being lip lazy. By actively shaping the oral aperture as you speak, your voice will be stronger, your vowels clearer.

We alter the shape of the oral cavity chiefly by the tongue, a complex muscle structure which can change its dimensions in a great variety of ways. If you make the vowel sound *ee* as in *feet*, your tongue will shape the resonators as shown on page 126. The high frequencies of this sound are amplified by the small chamber in the front of the mouth. The chamber being small, its natural frequency is high and so will amplify the high frequencies of the laryngeal sound. Move the tongue back to say *aw* as in *awful.* The front chamber is enlarged (see page 140) and can resonate the lower frequencies of that sound. To make these adjustments properly and easily so that good resonance is achieved, neither the tongue nor the jaw must be tense. Nor can they be so relaxed that they are not brought into correct position to resonate each sound. The muscles involved should have the same kind of tonicity and freedom from tension that all muscles need in order to govern the movements of the body properly.

The shape of the vocal resonators can also be changed in the pharynx. The action of the velum as it affects the nasal resonator has already been described. The volume of the pharynx can be decreased by raising the larynx, as when we swallow. The pharyngeal cavity can be reduced in size by raising the back of the tongue. Its upper dimension can be decreased by the lowering of the velum. Its width can be reduced by the contraction of the muscles at the back of the throat. The pharynx forms an elongated chamber which, like the long pipes on the pipe organ, has a low natural frequency. It can, therefore, resonate the low fundamentals and overtones issuing from the larynx. Furthermore, the soft walls of a relaxed throat have much the same kind of damping effect on the higher overtones as heavy wall hangings have in the concert hall. Speaking with a relaxed open throat gives the voice desirable mellowness, whereas a tense throat not only prevents the initiation of good tone in the larynx, but resonates the higher overtones at the expense of the lower ones.

Chapter 4 was devoted to the initiation of good vocal tones. Good resonance cannot improve faulty tone. It can only amplify the particular vibrations that come from the larynx. But if these tones are good, then it is possible to reinforce the overtones and fundamentals so that a strong, rich, and clear voice results. In the process of studying the physics and physiology of resonance, the importance of the following factors in improving the voice has become apparent: the throat must be open and relaxed; the jaw must move freely and easily; the tongue and lips must be active, their movements quick and sure so that the resonators are always adjusted to select and amplify the frequencies that combine to produce a voice of good quality.

Exercises for Improving the Use of the Resonators

OPEN, RELAXED THROAT

1. Open the mouth wide. Let the tongue lie relaxed at the bottom of the mouth. Inhale so that the stream of air is felt against the back of the throat, inducing a yawn. Maintain this open feeling in the throat as you produce the vowels *ah* and *oo* alternately.

2. Count from one to ten with the tongue pulled back in the mouth and the throat tensed. Note the voice quality which results from this constriction of the pharyngeal resonance cavity. Try to avoid this distortion of resonance. Now yawn, keep the tongue low in the mouth, open the mouth and throat, avoid tension, and count from one to ten. Note the nature of the quality produced, and try to develop this kind of sound amplification by keeping an open throat.

3. Differentiate between tones which are too metallic and those which are too much absorbed. First, pretend to be angry. Tense the muscles of your throat, mouth, and jaw as you say, "I can't stand this kind of voice because it is so unpleasantly brittle." Second, pretend to be very lazy. Try to over-relax the muscles of the throat, mouth, and jaw as you say, "This kind of speech is unpleasant because the structures damp out the overtones and rob the voice quality of brilliance."

4. Maintain relaxed, open resonators as you read the following selections aloud:

> Laws are like cobwebs, which may catch small flies, but let wasps and hornets break through.
>
> —Jonathan Swift, "A Critical Essay upon the Faculties of the Mind"

> Were I so tall to reach the pole,
> Or grasp the ocean with my span,
> I must be measured by my soul:
> The mind's the standard of the man.
>
> —Isaac Watts, "False Greatness"

5. Read the following selections aloud and strive to achieve a proper balance between tension and lack of tension as you speak.

> Farewell! a long farewell, to all my greatness!
> This is the state of man: Today he puts forth
> The tender leaves of hopes; tomorrow blossoms
> And bears his blushing honors thick upon him;

The third day comes a frost, a killing frost,
And when he thinks, good easy man, full surely
His greatness is aripening, nips his root,
And then he falls, as I do. I have ventured,
Like little wanton boys that swim on bladders,
This many summers in a sea of glory;
But far beyond my depth. My high-blown pride
At length broke under me, and now has left me,
Weary and old with service, to the mercy
Of a rude stream that must for ever hide me.
Vain pomp and glory of this world, I hate ye!
I feel my heart new opened. O, how wretchèd
Is that poor man that hangs on princes' favors!
There is betwixt that smile we would aspire to,
That sweet aspéct of princes, and their ruin,
More pangs and fears than wars or women have.
And when he falls, he falls like Lucifer,
Never to hope again.

—William Shakespeare, *King Henry the Eighth*

Forenoon and afternoon and night—
  Forenoon,
And afternoon, and night—Forenoon, and
  —what!
The empty song repeats itself. No more?
Yea, that is Life: make this forenoon sublime,
This afternoon a psalm, this night a prayer,
And Time is conquered, and thy crown is won.

—Edward Rowland Sill, "Life"

ACTIVE TONGUE, LIPS AND JAW

1. Alternately repeat the sounds *oo* and *ee* in rapid succession, exaggerating lip movements. Alternately repeat the sounds *oo* and *ah* in rapid succession, exaggerating lip movements. Alternately produce the sequence of sounds *oo, ee, oo, ah, oo, ee, oo, ah* several times in rapid succession, exaggerating lip movements.

2. Count from one to ten with the tongue lifted up and held across the middle of the hard palate. Note the unpleasant voice quality which results from this distortion of the oral resonance cavity by the tongue. Now repeat the numbers one through ten, taking care to place the

tongue in the proper position for each sound with which it is involved and making the tongue inactive in the floor of the mouth for each sound with which it is not involved. Note the nature of the quality produced, and develop this kind of sound amplification by using the tongue actively to maintain open oral resonators.

3. Count from one to ten with the teeth clenched tightly together. Note the muffled quality of the tone which results from this distortion of natural resonance, and try to avoid it. Now yawn, open the mouth wide, and avoid excessive tension in the jaw as you count to ten. Note the nature of the quality produced, and develop this kind of sound amplification through active movement of the jaw to maintain open resonators.

4. Count from one to ten with the lips remaining passive. Note the muffled quality of the tone which results from this unwanted distortion of natural resonance. Now yawn, open the mouth, avoid tension in the jaw, flare the lips away from the teeth, and use them actively in articulation. Count from one to ten with the lips being used to exaggerate the sharpness of the articulation of the sounds. Note the nature of the quality produced, and develop this kind of amplification through the active participation of the lips.

GOOD TONE

1. Read the following words aloud. Pay particular attention to maintaining open pharyngeal and oral resonators, using the tongue, jaw, and lips actively:

arena, Ethiopia, ideally, inspirational, authority, essential, elegantly, oratorical, alternately, ultimately, unilateral, argumentatively, uniformity, ambiguity, effectively, enormously

2. Read the following sentences aloud. Pay particular attention to maintaining open pharyngeal and oral resonators, using the tongue, jaw, and lips actively.

Alan always wanted to be an orator.
He hoped that ultimately he could speak inspirationally.
An authority, whom he admired enormously, revealed that, to speak effectively, he must avoid ambiguity.
He thought clearly and communicated ably, his effectiveness being enhanced by strong oral and pharyngeal resonance and all-around excellent speech delivery.

3. Read the following selections aloud. Pay particular attention to maintaining open pharyngeal and oral resonators, using the tongue, jaw, and lips actively.

There was a young lady of Niger
Who smiled as she rode on a tiger.
They returned from the ride
With the lady inside
And the smile on the face of the tiger.

—Anonymous

There once was a man so benighted
He never knew when he was slighted;
He'd go to a party
And eat just as hearty
As though he'd been really invited.

—Anonymous

The night has a thousand eyes,
And the day but one,
Yet the light of the whole world dies
With the dying sun.

The mind has a thousand eyes
And the heart but one,
Yet the light of the whole world dies
When love is done.

—Francis Bourdillon,
"The Night Has a Thousand Eyes"

6. *Increasing* VOCAL POWER

test your vocal power

ACHIEVING VOCAL POWER THROUGH BREATHING, PHONATION, AND RESONANCE (EXPLANATION, P. 81; EXERCISES, PP. 84-89.)

1. Read the following phrases sharply and loudly:

Watch out! Don't move! It's on fire! Jump!

2. King Lear addresses a raging storm. The stage sound effects are deafening, yet Lear's voice must rise above them. Speak these lines so that everyone could hear you in a theater. Say them slowly and inhale wherever you think the meaning of the line permits.

> Blow, winds, and crack your cheeks! Rage! Blow!
> You cataracts and hurricanoes, spout
> Till you have drench'd our steeples, drown'd the cocks!
> You sulph'rous and thought-executing fires,
> Vaunt-couriers to oak-cleaving thunderbolts,
> Singe my white head! And thou, all-shaking thunder,
> Strike flat the thick rotundity o' th' world,
> Crack Nature's moulds, all germains spill at once,
> That make ingrateful man!
>
> —William Shakespeare, *King Lear*

3. Repeat these famous words with which William Jennings Bryan concluded the "Cross of Gold" speech. Speak as though you were addressing a great crowd outdoors, without a microphone to aid you.

. . . we will answer their demand for a gold standard by saying to them: You shall not press down upon the brow of labor this crown of thorns, you shall not crucify mankind upon a cross of gold.

—William Jennings Bryan, speech at the National Democratic Convention, 1896

4. Read the following sentence as though you were addressing a class of 35 students:

When seeking information, have you considered how helpful are "who, what, when, where, how, and why?"

5. Read the following excerpt aloud:

Was it possible they heard not? Almighty God!—no, no! They heard!—they suspected—they *knew!* they were making *mockery* of my horror! this I thought, and this I think. But anything was better than this agony! Anything was more tolerable than this derision! I could bear those hypocritical smiles no longer! I felt that I must scream or die!—and now—again!—hark! louder! *louder!*—

"Villains!" I shrieked, "dissemble no more! I admit the deed!—tear up the planks! here, here!—it is the beating of his hideous heart!"

—Edgar Allan Poe, "The Tell-Tale Heart"

6. Read the following excerpt aloud:

God of our fathers, known of old,
Lord of our far-flung battle-line,
Beneath whose awful Hand we hold
Dominion over palm and pine—
Lord God of Hosts, be with us yet,
Lest we forget—lest we forget!

—Rudyard Kipling, "Recessional"

7. Read the following excerpt aloud:

Alone, alone, all, all alone,
Alone on a wide, wide sea!
And never a saint took pity on
My soul in agony.

—Samuel Taylor Coleridge, "The Rime of the Ancient Mariner"

USING VOCAL POWER

(EXPLANATION, P. 89; EXERCISES, PP. 90-93.)

8. Read the following sentences aloud as though you were in a small group at a quiet reception:

Mr. Smith, I would like you to meet Bill Jones.
I'm having a wonderful time.
My mother told me there would be days like this.

9. Read the sentences above as though you were speaking across the room at a banquet.

10. Read the sentences above as though you were in Times Square at 12:01 A.M., January 1.

11. Read the following excerpts aloud, adjust the loudness of your voice to suit the meaning of the poem, and heighten the feeling of the lines:

The chief's eye flashed; but presently
Softened itself, as sheathes
A film the mother-eagle's eye
When her bruised eaglet breathes;
"You're wounded!" "Nay," his soldier's pride
Touched to the quick, he said:
"I'm killed, Sire!" And his chief beside,
Smiling the boy fell dead.

—Robert Browning,
"An Incident of the French Camp"

JULIET. Good night, good night! Parting is such sweet sorrow,
That I shall say good night till it be morrow.
ROMEO. Sleep dwell upon thine eyes, peace in thy breast!
Would I were sleep and peace, so sweet to rest!

—William Shakespeare, *Romeo and Juliet*

Instructor's Test Sheet for Chapter 6

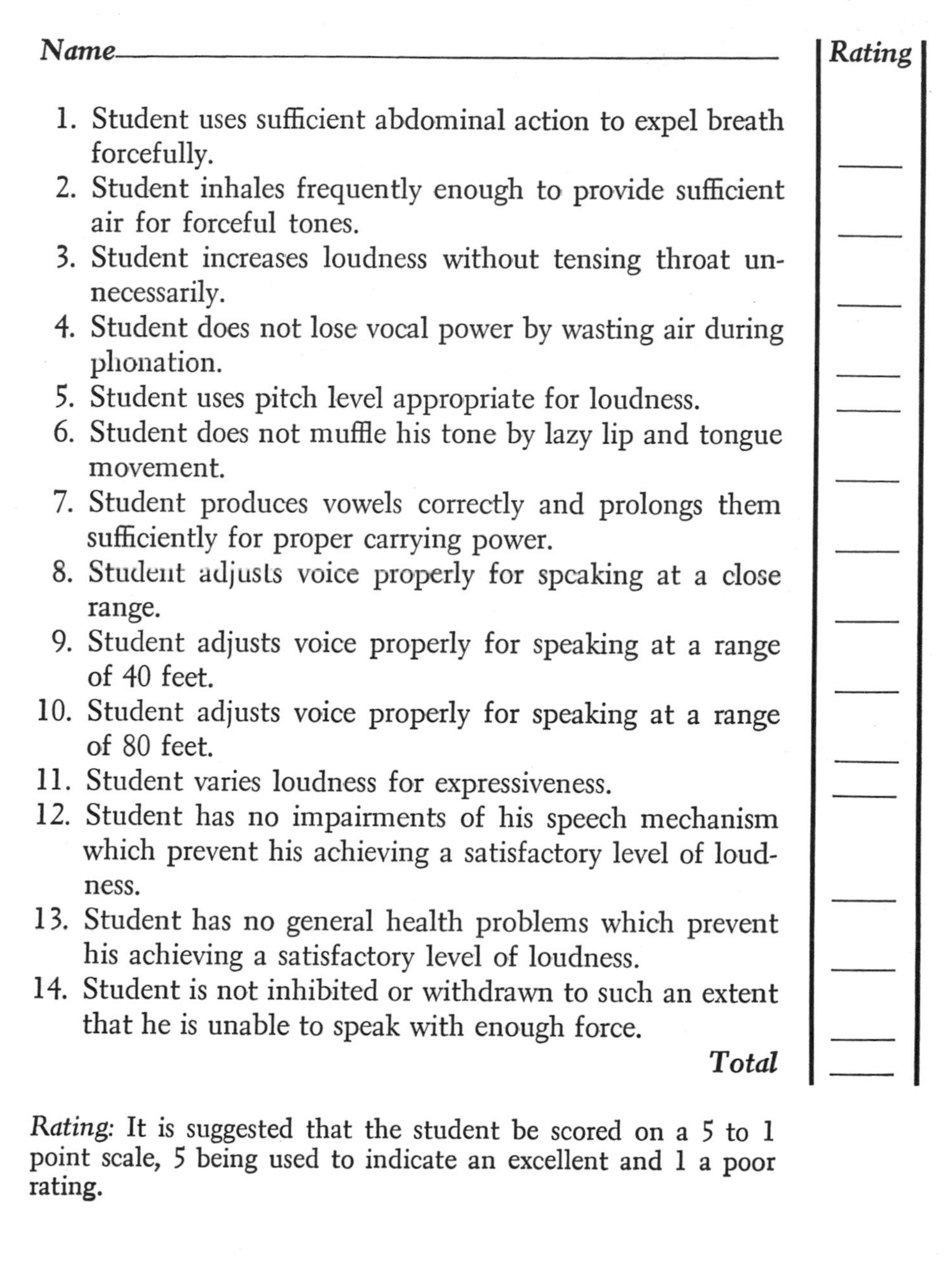

*Name*____	*Rating*
1. Student uses sufficient abdominal action to expel breath forcefully.	____
2. Student inhales frequently enough to provide sufficient air for forceful tones.	____
3. Student increases loudness without tensing throat unnecessarily.	____
4. Student does not lose vocal power by wasting air during phonation.	____
5. Student uses pitch level appropriate for loudness.	____
6. Student does not muffle his tone by lazy lip and tongue movement.	____
7. Student produces vowels correctly and prolongs them sufficiently for proper carrying power.	____
8. Student adjusts voice properly for speaking at a close range.	____
9. Student adjusts voice properly for speaking at a range of 40 feet.	____
10. Student adjusts voice properly for speaking at a range of 80 feet.	____
11. Student varies loudness for expressiveness.	____
12. Student has no impairments of his speech mechanism which prevent his achieving a satisfactory level of loudness.	____
13. Student has no general health problems which prevent his achieving a satisfactory level of loudness.	____
14. Student is not inhibited or withdrawn to such an extent that he is unable to speak with enough force.	____
Total	____

Rating: It is suggested that the student be scored on a 5 to 1 point scale, 5 being used to indicate an excellent and 1 a poor rating.

Introduction A strong voice is dependent on abdominal breathing, on a relaxed throat, and on open resonators. If you had tried to gain more power before establishing good speech habits in these three areas which we have just discussed, you might have done serious damage to your larynx, and it is more than likely that the tone you produced would have been extremely unpleasant.

You may never have addressed a large group without the aid of a microphone or you may never have acted in a theater. Possibly you never will. But many people cannot give their voices the power needed to communicate effectively in conversational tones. In fact, inadequately projected voices are almost as common as voices of poor quality. It is difficult to hear what a person who mumbles is saying. But even when articulation is clear, unless the voice carries well, what is being said might as well not be said at all.

Furthermore, in case you are called on occasionally to address large groups, you should know how to produce a voice that carries well without straining. The voice must be produced properly when speaking loudly or the speaker tircs his voicc and himself. He also tires his listeners, for a strained tone is never pleasant. The first part of this chapter is concerned with those speech habits which need to be improved by anyone interested in increasing the power of his voice, whether he wants to reach a small or large group. The second part discusses the problem of finding the right level of loudness for various public-speaking situations, and the varying levels of loudness needed for expressiveness. Integrating loudness with the other vocal elements in order to convey meaning and feeling is discussed in Chapter 13, "Increasing Creative Expression."

Achieving Vocal Power

INADEQUATE VOCAL PROJECTION You undoubtedly notice that whenever you are ill your voice sounds "tired." Loudness, or rather, lack of loudness, is the principal reason for this impression. The debilitated person lacks the muscular energy to produce the air pressure needed for louder tones. If you were not feeling well when you took the test, you may simply have lacked the energy to speak with much strength.

Poor hearing as well as poor health is often a cause of inadequate volume. The speaker who is unable to hear himself properly may select too loud or too soft a lcvel for his listener's comfort. The hard of hearing often need special help to adjust their voices to the proper level of loudness.

The speech diagnostician sometimes finds that a person whose voice is too weak has been brought up in surroundings where unusually subdued tones have been required, as in a home where someone was ill for a long time. Some people are trained at home to keep their voices down to such a degree that it is difficult for them to speak out with a full voice when the situation requires that they do so. The kind of exercises provided in this chapter should help to correct this vocal inadequacy.

A more difficult problem is faced by the person who lacks confidence and speaks softly so that he will not draw attention to himself. Exercises to increase vocal power seldom solve his difficulty completely, since they do not get to the root of the problem. Yet they are not without effect, for by making himself speak up, an insecure or timorous person may gain confidence. Shakespeare wrote, "Assume a virtue, if you have it not." There is a good chance that the sound of his well-projected voice will instill in a speaker the confidence he lacks initially.

A far more common cause of the poorly projected voice is the actual misuse of the speech mechanism through ignorance of its structure. Let us review this structure, then, as it affects vocal power.

BREATHING AND VOCAL POWER Abdominal breathing has been recommended as the most efficient way of breathing for speech. It is also the best way to produce strong tones, as a review of certain characteristics of sound and the vocal folds will reveal. As you know, sound is the product of vibration. Slightly pluck a resilient string which is fixed at both ends, and it will vibrate only a little. Pluck it hard and the center of the string moves much farther from its position of rest. (See Fig. 7.) The extent or *amplitude* of the swing determines the intensity of the vibration, which in turn determines the loudness of the sound. Therefore, the greater the pressure on the vibrating medium, the wider the swing of vibration and the louder the resultant sounds tend to be.

The equivalent of the resilient string in the vocal mechanism is, of course, the vocal folds, and the source of vibration is the column of air lying below the larynx. If the folds are to vibrate to their fullest extent to produce a powerful sound, the air must rush between them with the kind of force that can be supplied only by a strong contraction (pulling in) of the abdominal muscles.

As you work on this phase of increasing your loudness level, determine how much strength your abdominal muscles are providing for the necessary powerful exhalations. By placing your hands just below your lower ribs, you will be able to feel how firmly your muscles contract as they provide pressure for increased tone. The contraction of the muscles should be sustained and firm for the long, loud phrase and sharp for a short command.

A relaxed, open throat is as necessary in powerful speech as it is in pleasant speech. We have said that the intensity of a sound tends to increase with the amount of pressure applied to the vocal folds. However,

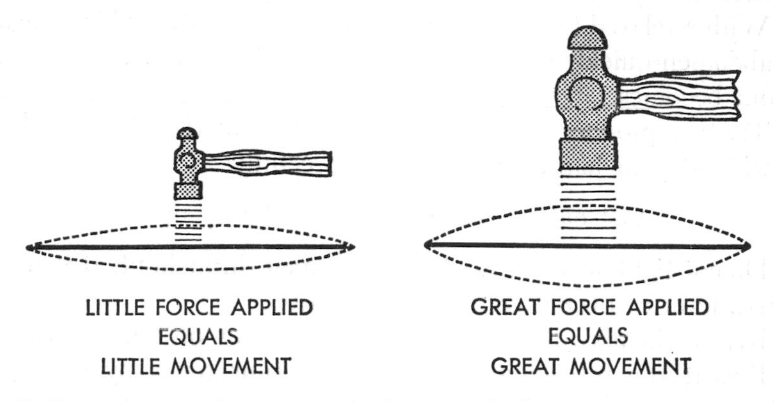
LITTLE FORCE APPLIED
EQUALS
LITTLE MOVEMENT
GREAT FORCE APPLIED
EQUALS
GREAT MOVEMENT

Figure 7. Greater extent of movement equals greater loudness

if the vocal folds are tense, lacking resiliency, they will not vibrate over as wide an arc as they would if the muscles in the throat were relaxed, and the intensity of sound will thus be less than it might be. You cannot control the vocal folds directly, but you can control them indirectly by relaxing the throat and the jaw. Try, therefore, for a relaxed throat as you practice strengthening your voice. In this way you can maximize the tonal effect which the strong pressure from the abdomen is capable of producing. Reduce the resiliency of the vocal folds by tightening the throat, and the strength of the tone is lessened.

Keep these suggestions in mind as you practice the following exercises. Designed to develop the full volume needed for addressing a large group or speaking in an auditorium, they are equally useful for anyone whose voice is weak in conversation. Once the power of your voice has been built up by better breathing habits, your voice may be adjusted more easily to your everyday speaking needs.

Exercises for Breathing and Vocal Power

1. Relax. Let your head fall forward of its own weight, then let it roll loosely from side to side until your neck and shoulders are relaxed. Raise your head, now yawn to gain an "open" feeling in your throat.

2. Repeat Exercise 1, and when you have inhaled on the yawn, exhale on the sound *ah*. Make the tone as loud as you can without tightening your neck muscles. If they tighten, reduce the force of the tone.

3. With a relaxed throat, phonate a loud *ah*. Push your hands against your abdomen quickly during this phonation. Note how much stronger the tone becomes.

4. Try to reproduce this sudden contraction of the abdominal muscles, without your hands, while saying forcefully:

Get out! March! Hurry up!

Do not tighten your throat. Keep it open throughout. If you begin to tense, return to the exercises for relaxation.

5. Repeat the above three commands forcefully on one breath.

6. Repeat the following lines, building your tones by strong and steady abdominal contractions. Take no more words on one breath than can be phonated by an abdominal contraction which you can feel with your hands.

> I have seen tempests when the scolding winds
> Have riv'd the knotty oak, and I have seen
> Th' ambitious ocean swell and rage and foam
> To be exalted with the threat'ning clouds.
>
> —William Shakespeare, *Julius Caesar*

7. Read the following selections aloud with great vigor. Now mark the passage with slant marks (/) where you think it would be proper to breathe. Read the passages forcefully again, breathing at the places you have marked. Be sure you sustain strong tones on every phrase.

> The longer I live, the more deeply I am convinced that that which makes the difference between one man and another—between the weak and powerful, the great and insignificant, is energy—invisible determination—a purpose once formed, and then death or victory.—This quality will do anything that is to be done in the world; and no talents, no circumstances, no opportunities will make one a man without it.
>
> —Charles Buxton

"We're going through!" The Commander's voice was like thin ice breaking. He wore his full-dress uniform, with the heavily braided white cap pulled down rakishly over one cold gray eye. "We can't make it, sir. It's spoiling for a hurricane, if you ask me." "I'm not asking you, Lieutenant Berg," said the Commander. "Throw on the power lights! Rev her up to 8,500! We're going through!" The pounding of the cylinders increased: ta-pocketa-pocketa-pocketa-*pocketa-pocketa*. The Commander stared at the ice forming on the pilot window. He walked over and twisted a row of complicated dials. "Switch on No. 8 auxiliary!" he shouted. "Switch on No. 8 auxiliary!" repeated Lieutenant Berg. "Full strength in No. 3 turret!" shouted the Commander. "Full strength in No. 3 turret!" The Crew, bending to their various tasks in the huge, hurtling eight-engined Navy hydroplane, looked at each other and grinned. "The Old Man'll get us through," they said to one another. "The Old Man ain't afraid of Hell!" . . .

"Not so fast! You're driving too fast!" said Mrs. Mitty. "What are you driving so fast for?" [1]

—James Thurber, "The Secret Life of Walter Mitty"

TONE INITIATION (PHONATION) AND VOCAL POWER Another reason why it is important to maintain relaxation in the throat in order to produce larger vocal sounds was mentioned in Chapter 4. Tension in the throat can prevent the vocal folds from approximating (coming together) properly, so that air is wasted as an excessive amount rushes through the half-open glottis. This outpouring of air makes speech breathy and weak, totally lacking in force. Those whose voices lack power because of breathiness should return to the exercises on page 42 before attempting to build vocal power in other ways.

In the opening tests, the evaluator was asked to determine whether the pitch you employed when you spoke loudly was too far above your optimum or natural pitch as suggested by the range of your voice. (See page 52 in Chapter 4 "Initiating Vocal Tone.") It would not be surprising if, when speaking loudly, you did in fact speak above your natural pitch; but if you use too high a pitch, your voice will become strained in a short time.

When a person increases the loudness of his voice he usually raises not only the loudness level but also the pitch. The higher pitch tends

[1] From "The Secret Life of Walter Mitty" by James Thurber, from *The New Yorker*, March 18, 1939, p. 19. Reprinted by permission, copr. © 1939 The New Yorker Magazine, Inc.

to carry better than the lower, as you have at least unconsciously noticed many times. A whistle, siren, or yodel can be heard at great distances. Even eight men in a marching band blowing sousaphones with great vigor will not drown out the shrill notes of a single flute or piccolo. If a soprano and bass are singing a duet, the soprano must be extremely careful lest her high notes overbalance those of the bass.

But the lesson to learn here is not that you should try to raise a bass voice to a tenor or an alto to a soprano whenever you speak loudly. You may raise the pitch to achieve certain effects of loudness, but you should not raise the average pitch much above your optimum level, since to do this the vocal folds must be tensed. If you keep them tensed for long, you may do them damage and suffer from the same hoarseness you feel after yelling at a football game. Moreover, the quality of the tone will suffer, and the louder voice you achieve by raising the pitch will be less pleasing to hear.

Exercises for Tone Initiation (Phonation) and Vocal Power

1. Increase loudness without increasing tension unnecessarily. Say *ah* at a soft, medium, or loud level, as indicated. Keep the pitch close to your optimum level.

(soft) *ah* (medium) *ah* (loud) *ah* (soft) *ah*
(loud) *ah* (soft) *ah* (medium) *ah* (loud) *ah*

2. Read the following selection, increasing the loudness of each succeeding descriptive adjective. Avoid undue tension. Keep the pitch close to your optimum level.

> Required in every good lover . . . the whole alphabet . . . Agreeable, Bountiful, Constant, Dutiful, Easy, Faithful, Gallant, Honorable, Ingenious, Kind, Loyal, Mild, Noble, Officious, Prudent, Quiet, Rich, Secret, True, Valiant, Wise . . . Young, and Zealous.
>
> —Miguel de Cervantes, *Don Quixote*

3. Repeat the above selection, decreasing the loudness of each succeeding descriptive adjective.

4. Repeat the above selection, making each succeeding descriptive adjective louder through the word *Mild* and then decreasing the loudness of each succeeding word thereafter.

5. Read the following selections aloud. Achieve the vocal power necessary for proper expression of meaning, while avoiding undue tension.

If ye are men, follow me! Strike down your guard, gain the mountain passes, and then do bloody work, as did your sires at old Thermopylae! Is Sparta dead? Is the old Grecian spirit frozen in your brains, that you do cower like a belabored hound beneath his master's lash? O comrades, warriors, Thracians! If we must fight, let us fight for ourselves. If we must slaughter, let it be under the clear sky, by the bright waters, in noble, honorable battle!

—Elijah Kellogg, "Spartacus to the Gladiators"

I gasped for breath—and yet the officers heard it not. I talked more quickly—more vehemently; but the noise steadily increased. I arose and argued about trifles, in a high key and with violent gesticulations, but the noise steadily increased. Why *would* they not be gone? I paced the floor to and fro with heavy strides, as if excited to fury by the observation of the men—but the noise steadily increased. Oh God! what *could* I do? I foamed—I raved—I swore! I swung the chair upon which I had been sitting, and grated it upon the boards, but noise arose over all and continually increased. It grew louder—louder—louder! And still the men chatted pleasantly, and smiled. . . .

—Edgar Allan Poe, "The Tell-Tale Heart"

RESONANCE, VOWEL STRESS AND VOCAL POWER The relation of precise lip and tongue movement to the resonance of vowels and to that of some consonants was examined in Chapter 5. Adjusting the resonators with care is equally important whether you speak in conversational tones or at the top of your lungs. If you initiate a loud tone properly but restrict the adjustment of the resonators by lazy lip and tongue movement, the vocal sounds will be muffled as well as unpleasant and perhaps unintelligible. Therefore, be sure you allow the resonators to amplify the phonated sound by shaping them so that they form exactly the vocal effect that you want.

The sounds of speech vary not only in pitch but also in carrying power. Any sound which must be made with an open mouth tends to carry well since the mouth acts as a megaphone in amplifying it. Open your mouth to yawn. Your tongue is lowered, your velum is raised and the oral cavity is thereby enlarged. Now exhale on the sound *ah,* making it a strong tone but keeping the open feeling. This sound is one of your biggest tones because it is resonated by the full oral cavity. The vowels made with an open mouth, such as *ah, a* as in *man,* and *aw* as in *fall* are all big sounds. Vowel sounds, particularly the open ones, carry better than do most consonant sounds such as *f* in *fun, g* in *gang,* or *th* in *that.*

Notice how little carrying power such sounds as these have. Since sounds vary in intensity it follows that in order to increase loudness, the speaker should give special stress to the stronger sounds. He should give them fuller value than the weaker ones and should keep each of the open sounds strong through its duration. The drill sergeant does just this when he stresses and prolongs the second syllable of *attention.* So does the newsboy when he stresses the first syllable of *extra* and the open *ow* sound in "Read all ab*ou*t it." In the exercises that follow, pay particular attention, therefore, to the open vowels as you practice increasing your level of loudness.

Exercises for Resonance, Vowel Stress, and Vocal Power

1. Assume that you are the ranger in charge of the world-famous "Fire Fall" at Yosemite National Park. Your voice will be heard thousands of feet above you and by persons all over the floor of the valley if you prolong the vowels and keep them strong throughout their duration.

Hello!	Hello up there!
Are you ready?	Let the fire fall!

2. Read the following selections aloud. Underline the sounds which you will want to prolong slightly to give full volume to the selection. Avoid undue exaggeration.

> I have seen man in the glory of his days, and the pride of his strength. He was built like the tall cedar that lifts its head above the forest trees; like the strong oak that strikes its root deeply into the earth. He feared no danger; he felt no sickness; he wondered that any should groan or sigh at pain. His mind was vigorous, like his body; he was perplexed at no intricacy; he was daunted by no difficulty; into hidden things he searched, and what was crooked he made plain.
>
> —Lydia Huntley Sigourney, "The End of All Perfection"

> Strike—till the last armed foe expires,
> Strike—for your altars and your fires;
> Strike—for the green graves of your sires;
> God—and your native land!
>
> —Fitz-Greene Halleck, "Marco Bozzaris"

> When, O Cataline, do you mean to cease abusing our patience? How long is that madness of yours still to mock us? When is there to be an end of that unbridled audacity of yours, swaggering about as it

does now? Do not the mighty guards placed on the Palatine Hill—do not the watches posted throughout the city—does not the alarm of the people, and the union of all good men—does not the precaution taken of assembling the senate in this most defensible place—do not the looks and countenances of this venerable body here present, have any effect upon you? Do you not feel that your plans are detected? Do you not see that your conspiracy is already arrested and rendered powerless by the knowledge which everyone here possesses of it? What is there that you did last night, what the night before—where is it that you were—who was there that you summoned to meet you—what design was there which was adopted by you, with which you think that any one of us is unacquainted?

—Marcus Tullius Cicero, "First Oration Against Cataline"

Using Vocal Power

ADAPTING LOUDNESS TO THE SPEAKING SITUATION The level of loudness a speaker chooses will depend, first of all, on his desire to be heard. He should speak loudly enough so that his listeners hear what he is saying without strain or undue effort, conscious or unconscious. He should not, however, raise his voice above this, or the effect will be unpleasant for the listeners—no one likes to be shouted at.

Failure to choose the right level of loudness is often due to a lack of awareness of exactly how much sound is needed for easy communication in a given situation. Actors and musicians are keenly aware of this problem when they play in unfamiliar theaters or auditoriums. They may rehearse or practice several hours before a performance to discover how much force they must use to create the desired loud and soft effects; they must get the "feel" of the room. A heavily curtained hall will absorb sound greedily, so the level of loudness must be increased. Another smaller room may perhaps be made more of marble or stone than wood. Here the performer must lower the level to achieve the same effects.

Speech students are often astonished to discover that the classroom in which they are speaking has the same amount of floor space as a conventional two-bedroom house. If they have this image in mind and realize that they must speak loudly enough to be heard from the back door to the front door, they can adjust their voices accordingly.

One of the best ways to check the adaptability of your voice is to tape record your speech, first speaking softly, then in conversational tones, then loudly. The volume control should not be touched during the recording session or during the playback. If a teacher has told you that you have been shouting or not speaking up, the playback will demonstrate what he means, especially when you compare your own taped voice with the voices of others in the class.

Exercises for Adapting Loudness to the Speaking Situation

1. Say *ah.* Begin at a soft level and make it progressively louder. Vary the pitch as required to increase loudness. Pay particular attention to building and maintaining air pressure. Repeat, beginning loud and becoming soft. Repeat, beginning soft, becoming loud, and then becoming soft.

2. Ask someone to stand ten feet away from you. Then read the following lines three times. The first time it should sound soft to the listener; the second time it should sound of conversational strength to him; and the third time your voice should sound loud and pleasant to him. Remember, do not strive for loudness if it leads to vocal strain.

Be quiet.
Forget it.
Look out.
Don't move.

What happened?
Throw it away.
What time is it?
We need gas and oil.

Now ask him to stand twenty feet away and repeat the whole exercise, and again at thirty feet away.

3. Read the following sentences aloud. Imagine that you are seated in a football stadium and speak as you would if your team were four touchdowns ahead. Then read the sentences a second time as if your team were four touchdowns behind. Then read them as if your team were tied with one and a half minutes to play. Do not strain the vocal mechanism.

I wish we had another touchdown.
Come on—let's fight.
Look at the score.
What we need is more points.

What's wrong with the line?
What's wrong with the coach?
Send in the water boy.
Send in the bench.

VARYING LOUDNESS LEVELS FOR EXPRESSIVENESS To borrow a valuable term from music, the expressiveness of our speech will depend in part on our use of dynamics. *Musical dynamics* refers to the variation and contrast in loudness or softness of tones. The effective speaker will use dynamics to convey the meaning and feeling of a phrase. If he has been addressing a large group with a full voice, he may suddenly drop his words to a whisper. The effect is sometimes more dramatic than if he had shouted the phrase. Or he will raise his voice on certain parts of a word or a phrase to provide emphasis that heightens meaning.

But the effective speaker does not only vary the levels of loudness. He combines these changes with variations in pitch, time, and stress to avoid the monotonous effect of varying any of these by itself. Here, loudness is dealt with in isolation, so we will note only that the building of strong tones can ultimately make your voice a much more expressive instrument. Later you will practice varying loudness levels at the same time as you vary other factors to develop a more "interesting" voice.

Exercises for Varying Loudness Levels for Expressiveness

1. Count aloud from one to ten, making each succeeding number louder than the one before. Try to stay on the same pitch. Repeat, making each succeeding number softer than the one before. Repeat, getting louder from one to five, and softer from six to ten.

2. Read each sentence aloud, making each succeeding word louder than the one before it. Maintain the same pitch in this and in the later exercises.

Proper audibility requires muscular control.
Increased loudness results from increased air pressure.
Loudness is a part of the dynamic speech process.
If you speak too softly, concentrate on abdominal breathing.

3. Read each sentence aloud, making each succeeding word softer than the one before it.

An open throat amplifies speech.
Amplification is also enhanced by an open mouth.
Some speakers speak too loudly.
Loudness is a psychological concept, and intensity is a physical one.

4. Read each of the following familiar sayings aloud, making the first half soft and the second half loud.

The bigger they come—the harder they fall.
Two is company—three is a crowd.
Birds of a feather—flock together.

The early bird—catches the worm.
Out of the frying pan—into the fire.
You can lead a horse to water—but you can't make him drink.
A stitch in time—may save nine.
One good turn—deserves another.

5. Read each of the following familiar sayings aloud, making the first half loud and the second half soft.

Figures won't lie—but liars figure.
When the cat is away—the mice will play.
Scratch my back—I'll scratch yours.
Don't look a gift horse—in the mouth.
Here's your hat—where's your hurry?
As large as life—and twice as natural.
Ask me no questions—and I'll tell you no lies.
Tread on a worm—and it will turn.

6. Read the following familiar sayings aloud, making the first one soft and the second one loud.

He who hesitates is lost. Look before you leap.
Make haste slowly. Strike while the iron is hot.
Practice makes perfect. Practice makes permanent.
Too many cooks spoil the broth. Two heads are better than one.

7. Read the following familiar sayings aloud, making the first one loud and the second one soft.

Make hay while the sun shines. Haste makes waste.
Live and let live. Live and help live.
Better late than never. Better never late.
Absence makes the heart grow fonder. Out of sight, out of mind.

8. Read the following selections aloud. Vary the loudness level to suit the meaning and feeling being expressed.

Hear the sledges with the bells—silver bells!
What a world of merriment their melody foretells!
How they tinkle, tinkle, tinkle,
In the icy air of night!
While the stars that oversprinkle
All the heavens, seem to twinkle
With a crystalline delight;

Keeping time, time, time,
In a sort of Runic rhyme,
To the tintinnabulation that so musically wells
From the bells, bells, bells, bells,
Bells, bells, bells—
From the jingling and the tinkling of the bells.

—Edgar Allan Poe, "The Bells"

One afternoon a big wolf waited in a dark forest for a little girl to come along carrying a basket of food to her grandmother. Finally a little girl did come along and she was carrying a basket of food. "Are you carrying that basket to your grandmother?" asked the wolf. The little girl said yes, she was. So the wolf asked her where her grandmother lived and the little girl told him and he disappeared into the wood.

When the little girl opened the door of her grandmother's house she saw that there was somebody in bed with a nightcap and nightgown on. She had approached no nearer than twenty-five feet from the bed when she saw that it was not her grandmother but the wolf, for even in a nightcap a wolf does not look any more like your grandmother than the Metro-Goldwyn lion looks like Calvin Coolidge. So the little girl took an automatic out of her basket and shot the wolf dead.

Moral: It is not so easy to fool little girls nowadays as it used to be.[2]

—James Thurber, "The Little Girl and the Wolf"

[2] "The Little Girl and the Wolf" by James Thurber, from *The New Yorker*, January 21, 1939, p. 19. Reprinted by permission, copr. © 1939 The New Yorker Magazine, Inc.

3. Increasing Your Clarity

7. *Understanding* AMERICAN SPEECH

test your speech standards

PATTERNS OF PHONETIC USAGE

(EXPLANATION, P. 103.)

1. Read the following words aloud:

can't, fast, have, path, wrath
car, ear, for, wear, wire
butter, father, later, rather, water
bird, heard, hurry, learn, word
law, walk, want, wash, watch
bomb, bunch, govern, lunch, psalm
library, necessary, oratory, secretary, stationery

2. Read the following sentences aloud:

The class heard laughter as they passed the library.
Father's secretary was hurt in the crash of the car.
He learned that a hot lunch is necessary.
The governor hurried down the path to hear the oratory.

STANDARDS FOR PRONUNCIATION

(EXPLANATION, P. 104.)

3. Read the following sayings of Benjamin Franklin aloud:

A slip of the foot you may soon recover, but a slip of the tongue you may never get over.

Serving God is doing good to man, but praying is thought an easier service, and therefore more generally chosen.

When prosperity was well mounted, she let go the bridle, and soon came tumbling out of the saddle.

If you would not be forgotten, as soon as you are dead and rotten, either write things worth reading, or do things worth writing.

4. Answer the following questions as frankly and as accurately as possible.

Do you think that your speech is similar to that of most Americans?

Do you regard your speech as regional?

If you believe your speech is regional, what do you think are the boundaries of your region?

Do you think your speech is similar to that of your friends?

Do you think your speech is similar to that of your instructor?

5. Answer the following questions as frankly and as accurately as possible.

Do you think your speech is similar to the best speech in the area in which you live?

Do you think your speech deviates sufficiently from the best speech in the area in which you live so that you are sometimes misunderstood?

Is your pronunciation such that it will help you to achieve whatever personal, social, and vocational goals that you have?

If not, in what way is it inadequate?

6. Answer the following questions as frankly and as accurately as possible.

Name a person in national public life whose speech you admire. Tell why.

Name a person in regional public life whose speech you admire. Tell why.

Do you think it is important to have speech patterns similar to those of the most respected speakers in your area?

What plans do you have for changing or improving your pronunciation?

Instructor's Test Sheet for Chapter 7

*Name*____________________________________	*Rating*
1. In saying isolated words, student uses pronunciation typical of the best speech in the region in which he lives.	____
2. In reading sentences, student uses pronunciation typical of the best speech in the region in which he lives.	____
3. Student speaks with clear articulation and pronounces words in a manner which communicates meaning.	____
4. Student takes an objective view of his own speech patterns.	____
5. Student recognizes his shortcomings in pronunciation.	____
6. Student is motivated to speak more like respected speakers in his general speech area.	____
Total	____

Rating: It is suggested that the student be scored on a 5 to 1 point scale, 5 being used to indicate an excellent and 1 a poor rating.

Introduction Articulation is the process by which voice is transformed into speech sounds. The resonators are primarily involved in the articulation of the vowel sounds, whereas many of the consonants are formed principally by the movement of the lips, tongue, and velum as they check the passage of air flowing out of the mouth and nose. The following chapters not only examine the way sounds are articulated but provide extensive drills in the formation of the sounds common to American speech.

There is one problem, however, that must be solved before you do these drills on articulation. Suppose you are drilling on the vowel sound in the word *yet,* and you are told that the same vowel sound appears in the words *bury, dare, Mary,* and *garish.* You might object that *Mary* and *bury* are not pronounced the same way, that you say *Mary* so that it rhymes with *Larry* and *bury* so that it rhymes with *Murray.* Or that *garish* and *dare* are not at all alike, since the *a* sound in *garish* is pronounced like the *a* sound in *blast,* whereas *dare* and *mare* are similar. In challenging the list, you are implicitly asking, "By what authority do you say the sounds in certain words are produced alike when I think they are not?"

The question is not easy to answer and is seldom resolved to everyone's satisfaction. It is not difficult to discover the ways in which people differ in their pronunciation of words, and to explain these differences in terms of the part of the country from which the speakers come or in terms of the people with whom they grew up or of the speech of their friends today. But difficulties are encountered the moment we ask which of these pronunciations is valid and why your pronunciation should be changed but not mine or his.

We will begin with the easier questions: First, how can you indicate in writing the way a word is or should be pronounced? Second, how do people differ in their pronunciations? Then we will be in a sounder position to answer the question of whether there is a better and a worse way of pronouncing English.

THE TRANSCRIPTION OF SPEECH IN WRITING The English alphabet has twenty-six letters, yet American speech has over forty easily distinguished sounds or *phonemes.* Consequently, some letters in our alphabet must stand for more than one sound, so that the alphabet can be stretched to include all the sounds of American speech. For example, the letter *a* appears in all of the following words, yet many people pronounce the *a* differently in each: *apple, calm, call, umbrella, purchase, was.* When a foreigner tries to pronounce these words, he may pronounce the *a* in each word in the same way, perhaps as it sounds in the word *calm.* The result would not be English. Sometimes you face the same problem when you try to pronounce a word you have not used before. If you came across the word *flaccid* for the first time, you would have no way of knowing whether both *c*'s should have the value of *k,* as in *accomplish,* or have the values of both *k* and *s* in combination, as in *occidental.* Spelling is all too often a poor guide to pronunciation just because many of the letters of the alphabet indicate different sounds at different times.

The International Phonetic Alphabet has been devised to solve this problem. Each symbol of this alphabet indicates one and only one sound or phoneme so that a word written in this alphabet is pronounced the same way by everyone who is familiar with the IPA (International Phonetic Alphabet). A student of speech finds the system invaluable in recording in writing the speech of others. If he reports that a certain speaker says [djuti], all those who can read the alphabet know exactly how the speaker pronounces the word. On the other hand, if he reports that the speaker pronounces the word *duty,* it is not clear whether the speaker says *d-oo-ty* or *d-you-ty.*

If a phonetician asked several people to pronounce the words in the list above that begins with *apple,* his report might read as follows: The *a* in *apple* was pronounced by all of the speakers as [æ]. Two used the vowel [ɑ] in *calm,* and the others used [a]; all gave to the *a* the value of [ɔ] in pronouncing *call,* and [ə] in *umbrella,* whereas three said [ɪ] for the *a* in purchase and the rest said [ə]. The group was evenly divided in saying [ɒ], and [ɑ] for *was.* Anyone trained in phonetics would know exactly how these speakers had pronounced these words.

Other systems have also been developed for equating symbols and sounds on a 1-1 ratio. Dictionaries frequently use what are called diacritical markings. The symbols are the letters of our alphabet instead of the sometimes unfamiliar ones in the IPA, but dots, dashes, and other marks are added to them to indicate which kind of *a* or *i* or *u* is meant. There are several disadvantages to these diacritical systems, the most notable being that few dictionaries use the same one; it is necessary, therefore, to learn a new system each time a different dictionary is consulted. However, if you limit yourself to one dictionary (the diacritical system of the *Webster's New Collegiate Dictionary* is provided in this book as well as the IPA), your instructor may prefer that you use the diacritics rather than the IPA. For a list of the sounds commonly found in American English, with the symbols attached to them of the IPA and *Webster's Dictionary*, see page 111.

PATTERNS OF PHONETIC USAGE A phonetician recording the way *wash* was pronounced by people from different parts of the United States would probably find that some gave the vowel the value of [ɑ], others pronounced it as [ɔ], and still others as [ɒ]. However, the chances are that if he asked several people from the same region to pronounce *wash* they would all give the *a* the same phonetic value. Your own experience tells you that people who learn to speak in the same region of the country tend to pronounce words alike. Students of the speech habits of Americans have found that the country can be divided into several speech areas, in each of which people tend to speak more like the others in the same area than like those in other areas. Perhaps the best-known description of these regions is that which divides the country into three speech areas: Eastern (about one eighth of the population), Southern (about one fifth of the population), and General American (about two thirds of the population).

Generally speaking, Eastern speech is said to include the New England states, New York, the northern half of New Jersey, the northern third of Pennsylvania, and the northeastern tip of Ohio.

Southern speech is said to include the states of the Confederacy as well as southern Delaware, Kentucky, and southeastern Maryland; the southern Appalachian Highlands of Arkansas and Louisiana and all of Texas except the southeastern portion are excluded.

General American speech is the predominant dialect in the rest of the nation.[1] This is obviously a rough classification of speech patterns. Nevertheless, you probably do in fact speak more like the people in your area than like those in the other two areas.

Each of these speech areas indicates a dialect area. The word *dialect* is used here to represent any distinctive speech pattern shared by a group of people.[2] So we have the Eastern dialect, the Southern dialect, and

[1] If you desire to make a detailed study of the dialect regions of American speech, consult Claude Merton Wise, *Applied Phonetics* (Englewood Cliffs, N. J., Prentice-Hall, 1957), pp. 171-238; Giles Wilkeson Gray and Claude Merton Wise, *The Bases of Speech*, 3rd ed. (New York, Harper and Brothers, 1959), p. 258; and Charles Kenneth Thomas, *An Introduction to the Phonetics of American English* (New York, Ronald Press, 1958), pp. 216-41.

[2] W. Nelson Francis defines a dialect as "a variety of a language, regional or social, set off (more or less sharply) from other varieties by (more or less) clear features of pronunciation, grammar, or vocabulary." W. Nelson Francis, *The Structure of American English* (New York, Ronald Press, 1958), p. 480.

the General American dialect. Smaller speech areas within the larger ones, as for example New York City within the Eastern area, or Brooklyn within the New York speech area, are also dialect areas. Note that they are all called dialects. It is not correct to say that you speak American (or English) whereas other people who differ from you speak dialects. The fact is that each person speaks a dialect.

If you reflect for a minute on your own experience, you will also realize that dialect areas or speech families are not only geographically delimited but are also set off by social influences. Within a given geographical area there are dialect subdivisions depending on social groupings. (W. Nelson Francis has suggested that there are three dialect groupings which he refers to as cultivated, common, and uneducated speech.) Not all members of the same class in one area will use the same dialect. But all those who identify themselves with the one group, or aspire to it, will *tend* to speak alike, as will those who identify themselves with another, or aspire to it. Once again, these classifications are extremely rough but have enough descriptive accuracy to be useful in analyzing dialects.

There is still one other way of studying speech patterns: to note the kind of pronunciation people use in formal address, in easy conversation, and in extremely relaxed situations. Any description of a person's speech must take account of such distinctions.

So even within one branch of one tongue—the American branch of English speech—there are innumerable speech families or dialects, and within each of these as many variations of the dialect pattern as there are people. Except for intonation or melody, which is an important contributor to dialect and yet is difficult to represent graphically, a specialist can use the symbolic system of the IPA to record all but the subtlest variations in dialect. The question remains if there is any standard by which we can measure a dialect as more American than another or as better than another. Of the three major American dialects, no single one can be advocated as "correct." Each of the three is correct in the region in which it is used.

STANDARDS FOR PRONUNCIATION In searching for a standard, the first step is to reassert the primary purpose of speech, which is to communicate with others so that the listeners understand the speaker's meaning as fully as possible. So compelling is this purpose that in early childhood we learned to speak as our elders did, partly in imitation and partly to eliminate any chance of misunderstanding. Later, when we went to school, we tended to alter our speech in imitation of our classmates. You probably changed your speech to some degree when you entered college. Next you will move into the environment in which you will earn your living. It is equally important that you adjust your speech once more, if need be, so that those with whom you work will understand you. Moreover, you will usually want to gain a sympathetic hearing, and for this reason you will try to adjust your speech so that it is pleasing as well as intelligible.

By recalling that speech must be effective communication primarily, we begin to see a kind of speech standard. First, if people are to understand your meaning, they must find the words you speak intelligible. You must learn how to speak with greater clarity, forming each word with clear articulation so that there is no chance that those listening to you will miss what you say.

But let us suppose that you speak with the dialect of Tidewater Virginia, and that you are trying to tell someone from Denver about your car. Articulate *car* as carefully as you can. Unless the man from Denver is familiar with your dialect he will have a hard time realizing you are talking about a car when you pronounce it as if it were spelled *kyah.* It will be about as effective to repeat the word carefully as to shout at a foreigner in English when he does not understand English.

Therefore, it is as important to speak in a dialect that is understandable to most people with whom you will come in contact as it is to speak clearly. No matter what dialect you speak, it will never be completely intelligible to everyone. But most of the people with whom you will come in contact will be able to understand without difficulty the three dialects, Eastern, Southern, and General American. If your dialect is close to one of these, others will usually understand you. On the other hand, if your dialect is spoken by only a small segment of the people in one of the three speech areas, you will have more trouble communicating with others outside of your small dialect region.

There is another reason why it is often desirable for a person who speaks a dialect shared by only a small group to modify it in the direction of one of the three more general dialects. Unusual or unfamiliar speech tends to call attention to itself rather than to what is being said. Even if most of those to whom you are speaking understand what you are saying, they may give less attention to your meaning than you would wish just because their attention has been diverted to the unfamiliar in your speech.

By considering the purpose of most speech—effective communication of meaning—it is possible to establish a speech standard for most people who expect to spend their adult years in contact with people not only from their own part of the country, but from other parts as well. The standard requires clear speech that resembles more, rather than less, the speech called Eastern, Southern, or General American.

But an even more specific standard can be found. It certainly seems safe to assume that most college students hope to make their way in a stratum of American life made up mostly of other college graduates, the educated of the country. It follows that the standard proper for most college students is the dialect of the educated of one of the three general speech regions.

Just how exact a guide to pronunciation does this standard provide? It already involves three different dialect possibilities corresponding to the three speech areas. But given these three standards, is there enough uniformity in the speech of the educated in any one region to assure us of an exact guide to pronunciation?

The answer is a qualified affirmative. Although it would be foolish to assume that every educated person has good speech, and with all our regional pride and belief that one man's way is as good as another's, the educated in America are unquestionably influenced by what is held up to them as correct pronunciation. One authority writes that Americans are far more prone than the English to check pronunciations in the dictionary and to accept the dictionary as final arbiter, in spite of the fact that no good dictionary professes to set standards but only reports the way Americans do, in fact, pronounce words. Moreover, educated people in a given speech region tend to agree, rather than disagree, on what pronunciation is better and worse. Though the average college graduate who uses a variant pronunciation may not yield to correction in front of others, he is likely to change his pronunciation of a word if he discovers that respected speakers in the community pronounce it that way. The educated are quick to judge others by their speech—that is to say, by their grammar and their pronunciation. There is a good chance that we will be judged harshly on many scores unrelated to language because of our speech "errors."

To summarize, there is no absolutely correct way to pronounce any word. There is no academy in America as there is in France to settle disputes on pronunciation. An appeal to the dictionary to settle a difference of opinion is not conclusive, because dictionaries purport to do no more than say how Americans do pronounce words; and if they pronounce a word in more than one way, this difference is generally recorded. Although there is no absolute standard of correctness, it is advisable to develop your speech along the lines of one of the three major dialects of the country, if you wish to be easily understood by people from neighborhoods other than your own. Furthermore, if you plan to make your way among other educated people, you will want to listen carefully to their speech in your dialect region so that you can eradicate pronunciations of your own that are not acceptable.

THE PLAN OF THE CHAPTERS ON ARTICULATION The chapters which follow contain drills for each of the sounds commonly found in American English. Each sound is identified by its IPA symbol and the diacritical symbol given in *Webster's New Collegiate Dictionary*. Attached to each sound is a list of words which are frequently pronounced with that sound by educated people in one of the main speech areas in the United States. A note indicates any striking variations in the way a word is pronounced in the three regions. For simplicity's sake, the variations have been kept to a minimum and General American speech has been stressed, since more people speak this dialect.

These drills have two purposes. First, by learning how to make a particular sound and then using that sound in pronouncing the list of words, you will discover which pronunciations differ from your own. When there is a difference between the two, you should establish whether the pronunciation given in the book does represent that of respected speakers in your general speech area. Should you discover that your pronunciation diverges from acceptable pronunciation in your speech area, you should repeat the drill until that pronunciation becomes familiar to you. Second, the drills are constructed so that you will articulate the sounds more accurately and pronounce your words more clearly.

You will recall that people not only differ in their pronunciations from region to region, and from group to group, but also that the same person will pronounce words differently when he is making a formal address, when he is speaking informally to friends, and when he is extremely relaxed. The pronunciation given for the words in the chapters which follow are those that people use when they pronounce them in informal, though not in exceedingly relaxed, speech.

They also represent the way they would be pronounced in isolation from other words, not in connected speech. In connected speech, words are run together and the value of certain sounds is altered by the sounds that precede and follow them. In connected speech, *bread and butter* is likely to become *bread 'n butter,* the reason being that the articulators cannot shift fast enough to give full value to each separate sound. The speech mechanism tends to do that which is most efficient, contributing to the easy flow of sounds within a word (e.g., in the word *lads* the *s* is articulated as a *z*) and of words within a phrase (e.g., in saying *this ship,* the first *s* is usually articulated as *sh* as its sound is assimilated to the beginning of the next word).

Such running together of words is natural and desirable as long as it does not make speech difficult to understand. The speaker who pronounces each word too carefully speaks poorly: his diction is so precise as to be affected. But there is very little danger that drilling on words in isolation will cause such overprecision. Since most of us tend to use our lips, tongue, and jaw too little in speaking, the exercises will help to correct the common speech fault of mumbling. The selection which follows is scarcely a parody of the slovenly speech that so many of us have. By practicing the articulation of words in isolation in the next three chapters, you should be able to eliminate traces of Slurvian in your own speech.

Slurvian Self-taught

Listening to a well-known Hollywood radio commentator some time back, I heard her say that she had just returned from a Yerpeen trip, and had had a lovely time nittly. I at once recognized her as an accomplished Slurvian linguist and, being a student of Slurvian, readily understood that she had just returned from a European trip and while there (in Yerp) had had a lovely time in Italy.

Slurvian is coming into common use in the United States, but I am, so far as I know, the only scholar to have made a start toward recording it. There is no official written Slurvian language, but it is possible, by means of phonetic spelling, for me to offer a brief course of instruction in it. In a short time, the student can learn enough to add immeasurably to his understanding and enjoyment of conversation wherever he travels in the country.

I first heard pure Slurvian fluently spoken by a co-worker of mine who told me that his closest friend was a man named Hard (Howard). Hard was once in an automobile accident, his car, unfortunately, cliding with another, causing Hard's wife Dorthy, who was with him, to claps. Dorthy didn't have much stamina but was a sweet woman—sweet as surp.

I soon discovered I had an ear for Slurvian, and since I began to recognize the language, I have encountered many Slurvians. At ballparks, they keep track of hits, runs, and airs. On farms, they plow furs. In florist shops, they buy flars. When hard up, they bar money from banks, and spend it for everything from fewl for the furnace to grum crackers for the children.

When Slurvians travel abroad, they go to visit farn (or forn) countries to see what the farners do that's different from the way we Murcans do things. While in farn countries, they refer to themselves as Murcan tersts, and usually say they will be mighty glad to get back to Murca. A Slurvian I once met on a train told me he had just returned from a visit to Mexico. He deplored the lack of automobiles down there, and said that the natives ride around on little burrs.

A linguistic authority of my acquaintance, much interested in my work in Slurvian, has suggested to me the possibility that the language may be related to, or a variation of, the one still spoken in England of which such a contraction as "Chumley," for "Cholmondeley," is a familiar example. However, I think the evidence insufficient for drawing such a conclusion. Surnames cannot be considered subject to the ordinary rules of pronunciation. In fact, the only one I have positively identified in Slurvian is Faggot, the name of the American admiral who won the Battle of Mobile Bay.

The name Faggot brings me to a discussion of what I designate as "pure" Slurvian. This includes those Slurvian words that, when spelled exactly as pronounced, also make good English words (such as "Faggot," "burr," and "claps"). The day I can add to the lexicon such a word, hitherto unrecorded, is a happy day for me. Here are some examples of pure Slurvian, alphabetically listed:

bean, *n.* A living creature, as in *human bean.*
cactus, *n. pl.* The people in a play or story.
course, *n.* A group of singers.
fiscal, *adj.* Pertaining to the body, as opposed to the spurt.
form, *n.* Gathering place of the ancient Romans.
gnome, *n.* Contraction for *no, Ma'am. Colloq.*
line, *n.* The king of beasts.
lore, *n.* The more desirable of the two berths in a Pullman section.
myrrh, *n.* A looking glass.
par, *n.* An attribute of strength, as in *the par and the glory.*
plight, *adj.* Courteous.
sears, *adj.* Grave, intent.

sport, *v.t.* To hold up, to bear the weight of.
wreckers, *n. pl.* Discs on which music is recorded for phonographs.

I am presently engaged in compiling a dictionary of Slurvian words, which I hope will prove to be the definitive work on the subject. The help of any interested students is welcomed, but I must caution such students to be certain the words are genuine Slurvian, and not merely regional speech, such as that of Alabama, Texas, or New England.

Let me close with a final example, to make my meaning clear. Wherever you may be in the United States, if you hear the word "tare," the speaker probably is not referring to a Biblical weed growing in the wheat. More likely, he is describing the sensation of extreme fear experienced by a movie fan watching Borse Karloff in a harr picture.[8]

—John Davenport, "Slurvian Self-taught"

The International Phonetic Alphabet

Column 1 of the accompanying table lists those symbols of the International Phonetic Alphabet which represent the sounds generally found in American speech. Note that the symbols of the International Phonetic Alphabet are always enclosed in brackets.

Column 2 lists diacritical markings for the same sounds. These diacritical markings are a simplified version of those used in *Webster's New Collegiate Dictionary*.

Column 3 contains a key word, in the pronunciation of which most Americans use the symbolized sound. The portion of the word in which the sound appears is italicized.

Column 4 includes a representation of each key word in phonetic symbols. The important point to remember is that each phonetic symbol represents only one phoneme, or sound family. Where a multisyllable word appears, the syllable that is accented is preceded by the mark '. (A syllable that receives a secondary accent is preceded by the mark ˌ, appearing below the line.)

Look over this phonetic alphabet several times, first noting which of the IPA symbols are the same as the letters in our alphabet. Then write each one, saying it aloud as you write, until it becomes familiar to you.

In the next few chapters you will study each of these sounds in detail,

[8] "Slurvian Self-taught," by John Davenport, from *The New Yorker*, June 18, 1949, p. 26. Reprinted by permission, copr. © 1949 The New Yorker Magazine, Inc.

and their symbolization should then become more fixed in your mind. However, exercises are provided at the end of this chapter to give you some facility in handling the symbols even before you begin the study of individual sounds.

	2	3	
PHONETIC SYMBOL	DIACRITIC * SYMBOL	KEY WORD	PHONETIC REPRESENTATION
[i]	ē	*eat*	[it]
[ɪ]	ĭ	*it*	[ɪt]
[e]	ā	ch*a*otic	[ke'ɑtɪk]
[ɛ]	ĕ	b*e*t	[bɛt]
[æ]	ă	b*a*t	[bæt]
[a]	ȧ	*a*sk †	[ask]
[ɑ]	ä	c*a*lm	[kɑm]
[ɒ]	ŏ̊	m*o*ck ‡	[mɒk]
[ɔ]	ô	*aw*l	[ɔl]
[o]	ō	*o*bey	[o'beɪ]
[ʊ]	o͝o	f*oo*t	[fʊt]
[u]	o͞o	sh*oe*	[ʃu]
[ʌ]	ŭ	s*u*m	[sʌm]
[ə]	*ŭ*	*a*ren*a* §	[ə'rinə]
[ɝ]	ûr	b*ir*d	[bɝd]
[ɜ]	û	b*ir*d ‖	[bɜd]
[ɚ]	ẽr	brisk*er*	['brɪskɚ]
[eɪ]	ā	*a*te	[eɪt]

* A somewhat simplified version of the system used in *Webster's New Collegiate Dictionary* has been employed. A single diacritic symbol has been selected to represent each individual phonetic symbol from the International Phonetic Alphabet. Thus, for example, the symbol *ŭ*, used in the second syllable of the word *circus*, has been employed in all words in which this sound occurs, rather than the symbols *ă*, *a*, *ĕ*, *ĭ*, *ŏ*, and *ŭ* which are variously employed in the dictionary to represent the single sound *ŭ*.

† Not common in General American speech. This sound is used in words such as *ask* in some Eastern and some Southern areas.

‡ Not common in General American speech. This sound is used in words such as *mock* in some Eastern and some Southern areas.

§ See footnote *, above. This sound is used in place of the sound [ɚ] by speakers who drop their *r*'s in some Eastern and Southern areas.

‖ Not common in General American speech. This sound is used by speakers who drop their *r*'s in some Eastern and some Southern areas.

1 PHONETIC SYMBOL	2 DIACRITIC SYMBOL	3 KEY WORD	4 PHONETIC REPRESENTATION
[ɑɪ]	ī	b*i*de	[bɑɪd]
[ɔɪ]	oi	v*oi*ce	[vɔɪs]
[ɑʊ]	ou	h*ow*	[hɑʊ]
[oʊ]	ō	*oa*t	[oʊt]
[p]	p	*peep*	[pip]
[b]	b	*bib*	[bɪb]
[t]	t	*toot*	[tut]
[d]	d	*dad*	[dæd]
[k]	k	*kick*	[kɪk]
[g]	g	*gig*	[gɪg]
[m]	m	*maim*ed	[meɪmd]
[m̩]	'm	chas*m*	['kæzm̩]
[n]	n	*noon*	[nun]
[n̩]	'n	fatte*n*	['fætn̩]
[ŋ]	ng	si*ng*i*ng*	['sɪŋɪŋ]
[f]	f	*fif*e	[fɑɪf]
[v]	v	*viv*id	['vɪvɪd]
[s]	s	sauce	[sɔs]
[z]	z	*z*ero*s*	['zɪroz]
[θ]	th	*th*ought	[θɔt]
[ð]	t̶h̶	*th*at	[ðæt]
[ʃ]	sh	*sh*eep	[ʃip]
[ʒ]	zh	vi*s*ion	['vɪʒən]
[h]	h	*h*at	[hæt]
[r]	r	*r*a*r*er	['rɛrɚ]
[l]	l	*l*i*l*y	['lɪlɪ]
[l̩]	'l	litt*l*e	['lɪtl̩]
[ʍ]	hw	*wh*ale	[ʍeɪl]
[w]	w	*w*ait	[weɪt]
[j]	y	*y*et	[jɛt]
[ju]	ū	*u*se	[juz]
[tʃ]	ch	*ch*ur*ch*	[tʃɝtʃ]
[dʒ]	j	*j*u*dg*e	[dʒʌdʒ]

Listen to speech in terms of the phonemes that compose it, and try to forget the way it is spelled in English. In the beginning of this chapter, we saw that the *a* that appeared in several words was articulated differently in each word and so had to be recorded by a different phonetic symbol in each case. On the other hand, in a list of words such as the following, though the italicized sounds are all spelled differently in English, they all should be transcribed by the same phonetic symbol since they are all pronounced alike: *ee*l, bel*ie*ve, gl*ea*m, dec*ei*ve, b*e*, f*oe*tal, p*eo*ple, m*ae*nad, mar*i*ne.

Furthermore, a word may be spelled in English with more letters than are needed to transcribe it phonetically. The word *kick* has four letters, but only three sounds are made, so that the word is transcribed as [kɪk]. On the other hand, in a word like *ice*, it takes two different phonetic symbols to indicate the way the single letter *i* is articulated in that word since it is produced as a diphthong, with the sound of [ɑ] closely succeeded by [ɪ].

Make sure, therefore, to listen carefully to the actual sounds as they are spoken, and then record the sound of the word as you hear it, and not the way you think it should sound by referring to the spelling. One of the great advantages in learning to transcribe speech phonetically is that it makes the student aware, sometimes for the first time, of the way other people actually speak and then of the way he speaks. Awareness of your own speech habits must precede any attempt to alter them, consequently training in phonetic writing is invaluable to anyone who wishes to improve his articulation.

Exercises on Sound Symbols

1. Select the symbols (phonetic and/or diacritic) which identify the sounds in the italicized portions of the following words. Transcribe them in the spaces provided.

		PHONETIC	DIACRITIC
sho*e*	______	[i]	ē
m*e*t	______	[ɪ]	ĭ
c*u*t	______	[ɛ]	ĕ
ps*a*lm	______	[æ]	ă
m*ee*t	______	[ɑ]	ä

		PHONETIC	DIACRITIC
h*a*t	______	[ɔ]	ô
dat*a*	______	[ʊ]	o͝o
h*i*t	______	[u]	o͞o
c*a*ll	______	[ʌ]	ŭ
f*oo*t	______	[ə]	*ŭ*

2. Select the symbols (phonetic and/or diacritic) which identify the sounds in the italicized portions of the following words. Transcribe them in the spaces provided.

t*oi*l	______	[eɪ]	ā
g*o*	______	[ɑɪ]	ī
m*i*le	______	[ɔɪ]	oi
m*ai*l	______	[ɑʊ]	ou
n*ow*	______	[oʊ]	ō

3. Select the symbols (phonetic and/or diacritic) which identify the sounds in the italicized portions of the following words. Transcribe them in the spaces provided.

*th*at	______	[m̩]	'm
*y*es	______	[n̩]	'n
*u*se	______	[ŋ]	ng
ra*ng*	______	[θ]	th
*ch*op	______	[ð]	t̶h̶
*sh*ow	______	[ʃ]	sh
*wh*ite	______	[ʒ]	zh
chas*m*	______	[ɝ] or [ɜ]	ûr
channe*l*	______	[ɚ] or [ə]	ẽr
a*z*ure	______	[l̩]	'l
ribbo*n*	______	[ʍ]	hw
bette*r*	______	[j]	y

ba*th*	______	[ju]	ū
thi*r*d	______	[tʃ]	ch
*j*ump	______	[dʒ]	j

4. Supply the missing phonetic symbols and/or diacritic markings in the following words. Note that these symbols are already familiar to you.

WORD	PHONETIC SYMBOLS	DIACRITIC MARKINGS
1. peep	[_i_]	_ē_
2. bib	[_ɪ_]	_ĭ_
3. toot	[_u_]	_o͞o_
4. dud	[_ʌ_]	_ŭ_
5. kick	[_ɪ_]	_ĭ_
6. gag	[_æ_]	_ă_
7. maim	[_eɪ_]	_ā_
8. noon	[_u_]	_o͞o_
9. fife	[_ɑɪ_]	_ī_
10. valve	[_æl_]	_ăl_
11. sauce	[_ɔ_]	_ô_
12. buzzes	['bʌ_ə_]	bŭ_'*ŭ*_
13. haha	['_ɑ_ɑ]	_ä'_ä
14. rare	[_ɛ_]	_ĕ_
15. lull	[_ʌ_]	_ŭ_
16. wood	[_ʊd]	_o͝od

5. Supply the missing phonetic symbols and/or diacritic markings for the vowels and diphthongs in the following words. Note that these symbols may be new to you.

1. east	[___st]	___st
2. tin	[t___n]	t___n
3. rotate	['roʊt___t]	rōt'___t
4. get	[g___t]	g___t
5. tan	[t___n]	t___n
6. palm	[p___m]	p___m
7. call	[k___l]	k___l
8. obese	[___'bis]	___bēs'
9. put	[p___t]	p___t
10. pool	[p___l]	p___l
11. come	[k___m]	k___m
12. comma	['kɑm___]	käm'___
13. aid	[___d]	___d

WORD	PHONETIC SYMBOLS	DIACRITIC MARKINGS
14. site	[s___t]	s___t
15. boy	[b___]	b___
16. out	[___t]	___t
17. boat	[b___t]	b___t

6. Supply the missing phonetic symbols and/or diacritic markings for the consonants and semi-vowels in the following words. Note that these symbols may be new to you.

1. prism	['prɪz___]	prĭz′___
2. prison	['prɪz___]	prĭz′___
3. ringing	['rɪ___ɪ___]	rĭ___′ĭ___
4. thin	[___ɪn]	___ĭn
5. this	[___ɪs]	___ĭs
6. shop	[___ɑp]	___äp
7. beige	[beɪ___]	bā___
8. heard	[h___d]	h___d
9. runner	['rʌn___]	rŭn′___
10. bottle	['bɑt___]	bät′___
11. wheel	[___il]	___ēl
12. yes	[___ɛs]	___ĕs
13. fir	[f___]	f___
14. chin	[___ɪn]	___ĭn
15. just	[___ʌst]	___ŭst

7. Read the following short poem aloud, pronouncing the words as they are written in phonetic symbols. (You will note that there are no capital letters in phonetic transcription. This should not surprise you in view of the fact that the phonetic alphabet is an alphabet of sounds.)

ðɛr wʌns wʌz ʌ 'fɛlo 'neɪmd 'gɛsɚ
huz 'nɑlɪdʒ gɑt 'lɛsɚ n̩d 'lɛsɚ.
ɪt ðɛn gru soʊ smɔl hi nju 'nʌθɪŋ æt ɔl
ænd nɑu hiz ʌ 'kɑlɪdʒ prə'fɛsɚ.

8. Transcribe the following short poem into phonetic symbols and/or diacritic markings:

If you your lips would keep from slips,
Five things observe with care,
Of whom you speak, to whom you speak,
And how and when and where.

—Sir Walter Scott

8. *Improving* VOWEL SOUND ARTICULATION

test your vowel sound articulation

Read the following words and sentences aloud while your instructor evaluates your vowel sound articulation.

FRONT VOWELS

[i] ē (EXPLANATION AND EXERCISES, PP. 126-27.)

1. Seem, feel, be, eat, deem, fee, keel, eave, me, eel
   Every breeze in the trees seems to whisper Louise.

[ɪ] ĭ (EXPLANATION AND EXERCISES, PP. 128-30.)

2. It, in, pig, mitt, ill, pill, dig, hid, if, sing
   When I was single my pockets would jingle; I wish I was single again.

[ɛ] ĕ (EXPLANATION AND EXERCISES, PP. 130-33.)

3. Etch, men, egg, bet, end, edge, dell, elf, elm, met
   We'll build a nest somewhere in the west and let the rest of the world go by.

[æ] ă (EXPLANATION AND EXERCISES, PP. 134-36.)

4. And, bat, at, man, am, has, as, dad, Sam, add
   Sam planned his hand, and he and Stan made a grand slam.

BACK VOWELS

[ɑ] ä (EXPLANATION AND EXERCISES, PP. 136-39.)

5. Alm, bomb, fa, mollusk, column, ah, la, obstinate, comma, obvious
   Don wants to concentrate on honest policies.

[ɔ] ô (EXPLANATION AND EXERCISES, PP. 140-42.)

6. Awed, naught, bought, awful, sawed, awl, draw, gnawed, jaw, flaw
   Paul broke his jaw in the fall from the awning onto the lawn.

[ʊ] o͝o (EXPLANATION AND EXERCISES, PP. 142-45.)

7. Bull, pull, wood, stood, wool, bush, hood, push, should, put
   He put his soot-covered football away and looked for a book.

[u] o͞o (EXPLANATION AND EXERCISES, PP. 146-48.)

8. Boom, shoe, loot, true, school, threw, noon, blew, moo, boot
   Too few of you juveniles follow the rules in using the pool.

CENTRAL VOWELS

[ʌ] ŭ (EXPLANATION AND EXERCISES, PP. 148-51.)

9. Cull, gun, mutt, come, one, gull, gum, putt, skull, spun
   Cut the tree trunk into chunks and dump it some distance from the other lumber.

[ə] *ŭ* (EXPLANATION AND EXERCISES, PP. 152-53.)

10. Arena, abandon, about, across, account, economy, bacteria, cinema, petunia, pizza
    Among the notable attractions of the circus was the enormous elephant which had recently arrived from India.

[ɝ] ûr or [ɜ] û (EXPLANATION AND EXERCISES, PP. 154-55.)

11. Early, earn, earth, burr, fur, her, bird, curve, work, were
    The early bird caught the worm that turned.

[ɚ] ẽr or [ə] *û* (EXPLANATION AND EXERCISES, P. 156.)

12. Better, brother, cover, fatter, lighter, over, shorter, sooner, winter, water
    Father tried a heavier sinker, while I had better luck with a brighter spinner.

*Name*____

Student produces the following vowel sounds accurately.

	Rating
1. [i]	____
2. [ɪ]	____
3. [ɛ]	____
4. [æ]	____
5. [ɑ]	____
6. [ɔ]	____
7. [ʊ]	____
8. [u]	____
9. [ʌ]	____
10. [ə]	____
11. [ɝ] or [ɜ]	____
12. [ɚ] or [ə]	____
Total	____

Rating: It is suggested that the student be scored on a 5 to 1 point scale, 5 being used to indicate an excellent and 1 a poor rating.

Introduction Vowel sounds are formed in the resonators as air flows out of the mouth. As we have seen, the resonators form a megaphone which amplifies the sound produced by the vocal folds; consequently, our voice is most fully amplified when it is producing the vowels, not the consonants. The next time you listen to a singer, notice that it is usually the vowels that are held on the long notes. This enables the singer's voice to carry. If he sings the word *soothe,* he prolongs the vowel and articulates the *th* only at the last instant. The *th* has very little carrying power since to make that sound air must be restricted as it flows out of the mouth. Produce all of the vowel sounds that appear on the chart on page 125 and watch in a mirror how open your mouth is as you form most of them. This openness provides the amplification of tone needed to project your voice.

The vowels also give color to the sounds of our speech. Try to make the vowel sound in *peek* in as many ways as you can. You will find that you can make the sound by altering the shape of your mouth in many ways, but that some ways produce more pleasant versions of the vowel than others. Now try to say a consonant like the one in *go* in different ways. You cannot vary the production of the consonant nearly as much. Vowels are slippery phonemes, or families of sounds, and each one can be produced in a great variety of ways. We say that some ways are better than others because we prefer the quality of the tone, the color of the vowel, that is resonated when these preferred ways are used. If you wish to improve the quality of your voice, practice the vowel sounds with your instructor's help.

VOWEL PRODUCTION Although you know the list of vowels in the English alphabet and you can find the symbols for the vowel sounds on the IPA chart, it is important to know how a vowel differs from a consonant in the way in which the voice mechanism produces it.

1. Except in whispering, all vowel sounds originate with the vibration of the vocal folds. We say they are *voiced.* Some, but not all, consonants are voiced.

2. The different vowel sounds are made by adjusting the size and shape of the resonating chambers and the texture of their walls. See how your mouth is shaped when you say *awe,* and then *noon.* You will recall that each vowel sound is a particular combination of overtones which are amplified by the resonators shaped in a certain way. Change the shape and the vowel changes. (See Chapter 5, "Resonating Vocal Tone.")

3. The air that flows from the vocal folds is relatively unrestricted as it passes out of the mouth in the formation of vowels. Its flow is, of course, channeled by the resonators, but it is not blocked off, as it is in the production of most consonants.

In summary, a vowel may be described as a speech sound, modified in the oral resonators, produced with relatively little blockage, restriction, or audible friction and with vocal fold vibration.

If you refer to the IPA chart, you will find seventeen vowels listed. Each is identified by a key word. However, there may be slight variations in how a key word is produced from region to region, so that there is value in considering how each sound is produced by the speech mechanism. Each symbol can be linked with a description of the way the sound symbolized is produced: whether it is voiced or unvoiced, how the tongue is placed, the shape of the mouth opening, the action of the lips, and the action of the velum.

This system of equating IPA symbols with positions of the articulators and resonators works well with the consonants, since, as you saw when you articulated the consonant in *go*, a particular consonant can be made in only a few, slightly different ways. It works less well with the vowels. The vowel symbols cannot be so accurately described in terms of lip and tongue movement because it is possible to make each vowel by shaping the mouth in many different ways. Say the vowel sound in *peek*, first with your lips and teeth close together. Gradually widen them and see how many different shapes your mouth can take which nevertheless permit you to pronounce the word so that it can still be recognized as *peek*. Ultimately, of course, the sound becomes so distorted that it blends into another phoneme. But the fact remains that you can produce an easily recognized [i] sound in a great variety of ways.

Therefore, saying that each vowel in the IPA is linked with a certain position of the lips and mouth does not mean that this is the only way the sound can be produced, but only that an acceptable version of the sound can be made with the articulators in this position. If you have trouble with any of the sounds that follow, pay particular attention to the indicated positions of the articulators, since by following these positions you should be able to reproduce the sounds more accurately.

The tongue and lower jaw are important in vowel production.

For almost all vowel production the tip of the tongue is placed against the lower teeth. The front of it humps up close to the hard palate for what we call the front vowels, the middle of the tongue humps up for

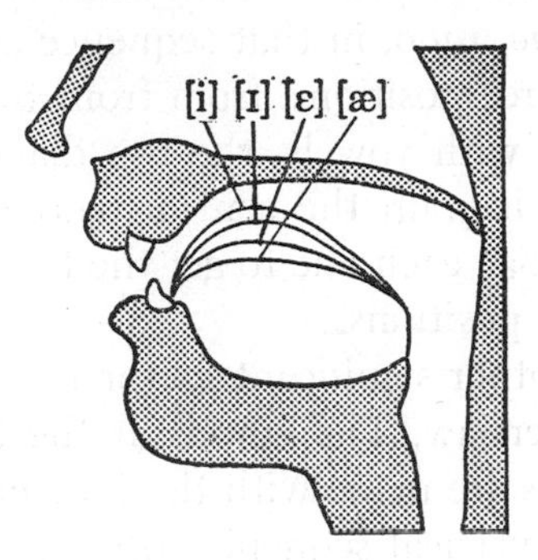

FRONT

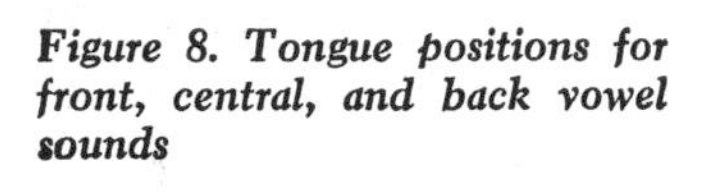

Figure 8. Tongue positions for front, central, and back vowel sounds

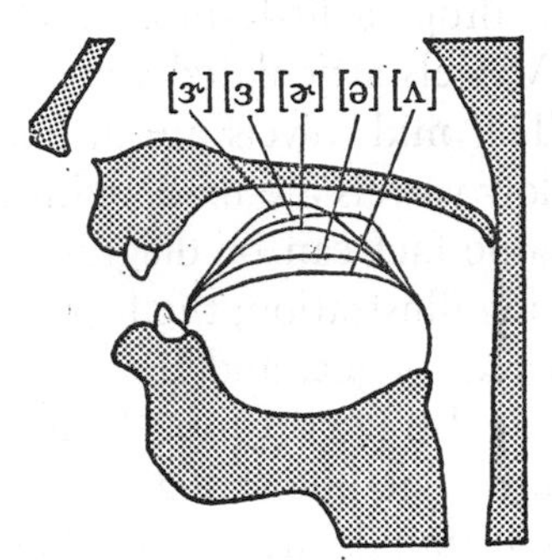

CENTRAL

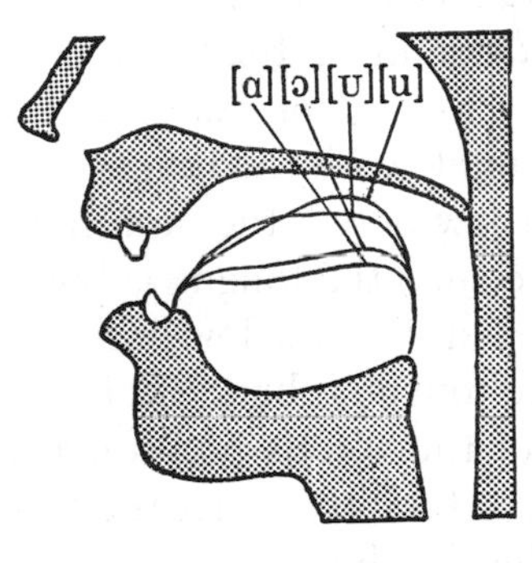

BACK

the central vowels, and the back of the tongue for the back vowels. Say *sea, some, moo,* in that sequence and feel how your tongue bunches in these three positions, from front to back. In the diagrams of the mouth filled in with vowels, the top diagram represents the front vowels, the middle diagram the central vowels, and the bottom diagram the back vowels. Say each one to get the feel of the humping action of the tongue in these positions.

The other significant factor in vowel production is the movement of the lower jaw. The vowels at the top of each vertical sequence in the diagrams are made with the jaws close together; the ones at the bottom of each vertical sequence are made with a more open mouth. Say the sounds in the upper vertical sequence, and you will notice that your lower jaw drops a little more each time you produce the next one on the list. Vowels articulated with the jaws close together are called high vowels. The mid-vowels are articulated with a lower tongue and jaw; and the low vowels are made with the jaw and tongue even lower.

This same fact can be diagramed schematically, as shown on the accompanying illustration; the top line represents the hard palate, the base the flattened tongue, and the vertical line on the left side the closeness of the arched tongue to the front of the mouth. Though the diagrams are obviously no more than rough approximations of what happens when these sounds are made, they are accurate enough to suggest the appropriateness of the terms *front vowels, central vowels,* and *back vowels.* The positions are the same as those shown in Fig. 8, only without the diagram of the mouth surrounding it. By consulting the figures, you can see, for example, that [i] is a high-front vowel, meaning that it is made with the tongue bunched in the front of the mouth and the lower jaw raised, the mouth almost closed. The [ʌ] is a mid-central vowel, meaning the tongue is bunched in the center with the jaw somewhat opened. [ɔ] is a low-back vowel, meaning that in producing this vowel, the tongue is bunched in the back and the jaw is lowered. Define the rest of the vowels positionally, with the help of the diagrams, and at the same time try to get the feel of the position of the articulators as you produce each vowel.

Let us now consider each of these vowels in turn, remembering that (1) the key word indicates the value to be given each vowel only if you pronounce the word as it is generally pronounced by educated people in the General American dialect; (2) the mouth position indicated for the production of the vowel is not the only one that can be used, but it is a good one to use if you have difficulty making the sound.

Figure 9. Vowel diagram

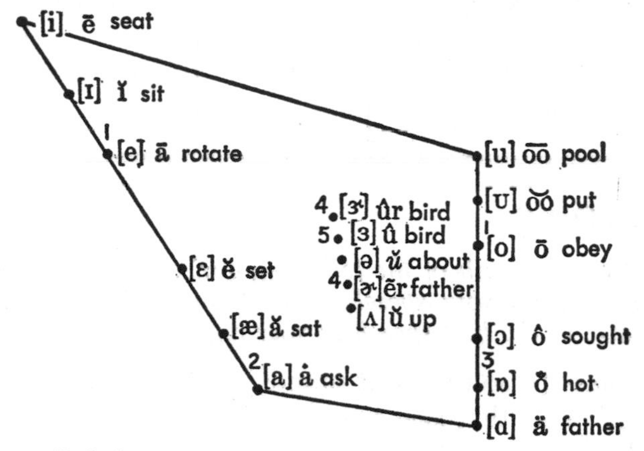

1. Refer to diphthongs.
2. Often used in Eastern speech. (Not common in General American speech.)
3. Often used in Eastern and Southern speech. (Occasionally used in General American speech.)
4. Common in General American speech. (This sound has [r] coloring.)
5. Often used in Eastern and Southern speech. (Not common in General American speech.)

Front Vowels

PHONETIC [i] DIACRITIC ē

KEY WORD	VOCAL FOLDS	VELUM
eat	Vibrating	Raised

DEVIATIONS

Learn to recognize each of the following deviations in the production of [i]. *Eliminate from your speech all of those deviations which are not representative of the best speech in your region.*

1. Substitution of [ɪ] so that *heat* sounds like [hɪt].
2. Addition of [ə] so that *keel* sounds like [kiəl].
3. Nasalized production of [i]—most likely to occur in a word such as *mean*.

EXERCISES

Sound Practice

1. Articulate a series of staccato [i] sounds.
2. Articulate these vowel pairs: *Easy to contrast:* [i-ɛ] [i-ɑ] [i-u]
   Difficult to contrast: [i-ɪ]

Syllable Practice

3. Articulate these syllables: [mi] [li] [bi] [di] [gi]
   [im] [il] [ib] [id] [ig]
   [mim] [lil] [bib] [did] [gig]
4. Articulate these syllable pairs:

   Easy to contrast: [mi-mɛ] [mi-mɑ] [mi-mu]
   [im-ɛm] [im-ɑm] [im-um]
   [mim-mɛm] [mim-mɑm] [mim-mum]
   Difficult to contrast: [mi-mɪ] [im-ɪm] [mim-mɪm]

   Repeat by substituting [l], [b], [d], and [g] for [m].

TECHNICAL DESCRIPTION	MOUTH	LIPS	TONGUE
High front vowel	Nearly closed	Relaxed, slightly spread	Tip behind front teeth, front arched toward hard palate, sides against upper molars

Word Practice

5. Read these words aloud:

Initial: each, eager, ease, east, eastern, eat, eaten, Eden, edict, eek, eel, ego, eagle, easel, easy
Medial: beat, cheat, cheese, deal, feast, feed, feel, least, meal, meat, need, seek, siege, team, yeast, zeal
Final: agree, be, fee, flee, free, he, key, knee, lea, Marie, me, sea, she

6. Read these word pairs aloud:

Easy to contrast:
[i-ɛ] bead-bed, deed-dead, each-etch, feed-fed, lead-led, mean-men, meat-met, read-red, reek-wreck, seat-set
[i-ɑ] beam-bomb, heed-hod, leak-lock, meek-mock, reed-rod, reek-rock, seat-sot, seek-sock, seem-psalm, seep-sop
[i-u] bead-booed, beat-boot, beam-boom, lean-loon, meat-moot, peal-pool, seen-soon, seep-soup, weaned-wound
Difficult to contrast:
[i-ɪ] beat-bit, deal-dill, ease-is, eat-it, feel-fill, feet-fit, keel-kill, peel-pill, seat-sit, seek-sick

Sentence Practice

7. Read these sentences aloud:

Lee sees me greeting people gleefully.
Conceited Pete agrees that eels feed eagerly.
She repeats, "Three mean cheats keep skiing free."
He feels keen as he schemes and dreams.
Marie, Cherrie, and Bea are speaking under a tree.

PHONETIC [ɪ] DIACRITIC ĭ

	KEY WORD	VOCAL FOLDS	VELUM
	it	Vibrating	Raised

DEVIATIONS

Learn to recognize each of the following deviations in the production of [ɪ]. *Eliminate from your speech all of those deviations which are not representative of the best speech in your region.*

1. Substitution of [i] so that *hit* sounds like [hit].
2. Substitution of [eɪ] so that *sing* sounds like [seɪŋ].
3. Substitution of [ɛ] so that *sit* sounds like [sɛt].
4. Substitution of [ʌ] so that *him* sounds like [hʌm].
5. Addition of [ə] so that *big* sounds like [bɪəg].
6. Nasalized production of [ɪ]—most likely to occur in a word such as *him.*

EXERCISES

Sound Practice

1. Articulate a series of staccato [ɪ] sounds.
2. Articulate these vowel pairs:

   Easy to contrast: [ɪ-ɑ] [ɪ-ʊ] [ɪ-u]
   Difficult to contrast: [ɪ-i] [ɪ-eɪ] [ɪ-ɛ] [ɪ-ʌ]

Syllable Practice

3. Articulate these syllables: [mɪ] [lɪ] [bɪ] [dɪ] [gɪ]
   [ɪm] [ɪl] [ɪb] [ɪd] [ɪg]
   [mɪm] [lɪl] [bɪb] [dɪd] [gɪg]

TECHNICAL DESCRIPTION	MOUTH	LIPS	TONGUE
High front vowel	Open slightly more than for [i]	Drawn back, more rounded than for [i]	Tip behind lower front teeth, front arched toward hard palate, lower and more relaxed than for [i]. Sides of tongue against upper molars

4. Articulate these syllable pairs:

Easy to contrast: [mɪ-mɑ] [mɪ-mʊ] [mɪ-mu]
[ɪm-ɑm] [ɪm-ʊm] [ɪm-um]
[mɪm-mɑm] [mɪm-mʊm] [mɪm-mum]

Difficult to contrast:
[mɪ-mi] [mɪ-meɪ] [mɪ-mɛ] [mɪ-mʌ]
[ɪm-im] [ɪm-eɪm] [ɪm-ɛm] [ɪm-ʌm]
[mɪm-mim] [mɪm-meɪm] [mɪm-mɛm] [mɪm-mʌm]

Repeat by substituting [l], [b], [d], and [g] for [m].

Word Practice

5. Read these words aloud:

Initial: if, igloo, ill, illness, imminent, in, infamous, infant, innocent, inside, insist, intake, is, it, Italy, itch

Medial: big, did, dig, dill, dish, ditch, fib, fish, kick, kill, pill, pit, sister, thin, think, this

Final: Because this sound in the final position is articulated as [i] in many areas of the country, no exercises are included.

6. Read these word pairs aloud:

Easy to contrast:

[ɪ-ɑ] hid-hod, kid-cod, kit-cot, lick-lock, rib-rob, rick-rock, rid-rod, sick-sock, tick-tock, win-wan

[ɪ-ʊ] lick-look, bill-bull, fill-full, fit-foot, hid-hood, kid-could, kick-cook, nick-nook, pit-put, sit-soot [ɪ-u] bid-booed, bin-boon, bit-boot, fill-fool, kid-cooed, kit-coot, lit-loot, pill-pool, rid-rude, wind-wound

Difficult to contrast:

[ɪ-i] bit-beat, dill-deal, fill-feel, fit-feet, is-ease, it-eat, kill-keel, pill-peal, sick-seek, sit-seat

[ɪ-eɪ] bit-bait, dill-dale, fill-fail, fit-fate, it-ate, kit-Kate, mill-mail, mitt-mate, pill-pail, rid-raid

[ɪ-ɛ] bid-bed, bit-bet, dill-dell, fill-fell, hid-head, itch-etch, lid-led, mitt-met, rid-red, sit-set

[ɪ-ʌ] bid-bud, gill-gull, hill-hull, kill-cull, kit-cut, knit-nut, mill-mull, pit-putt, rig-rug, sing-sung

Sentence Practice

7. Read these sentences aloud:

Silly Billy insists the intuition of women is a myth.
Nick said to Rick, "I'll lick you with a stick."
Chris thinks Jim fished this thin dish from the ditch.
This innocent infant built the igloo.
The fierce pig bit many thin strips of fish.

PHONETIC [ɛ] DIACRITIC ĕ

KEY WORD	VOCAL FOLDS	VELUM
 *bet*	Vibrating	Raised

DEVIATIONS

Learn to recognize each of the following deviations in the production of [ɛ]. *Eliminate from your speech all of those deviations which are not representative of the best speech in your region.*

1. Substitution of [ɪ] so that *met* sounds like [mɪt].

PHONETIC [e] DIACRITIC ā

The pure vowel [e] seldom occurs in stressed syllables in American speech. Except in a few parts of the country, the vowel sound in words such as *game* is not a pure [e] but the diphthong [eɪ]. The tendency is for the sound to include the [ɪ] element and to become the diphthong when it appears in a stressed position. In an unstressed position the [ɪ] element usually is eliminated. The word *vacation* illustrates the sound in both positions. The first *a* in *vacation* is unstressed and therefore is a pure [e]. The second *a* is stressed and therefore forms the diphthong [eɪ].

Spanish-speaking people characteristically use the pure vowel [e] in their native speech and use it, similarly, when they speak English, rather than using the diphthong [eɪ] as do most Americans. Because these sounds may be interchanged without confusion of meaning the sound often referred to as long *a* is dealt with in the next chapter under the diphthong [eɪ].

TECHNICAL DESCRIPTION	MOUTH	LIPS	TONGUE
Mid front vowel	Open slightly more than for [ɪ]	Unrounded	Tip behind lower front teeth, front arched toward hard palate, less convex and less tense and lower than for [ɪ]. Sides against upper molars

2. Substitution of [eɪ] so that *let* sounds like [leɪt].
3. Substitution of [æ] so that *met* sounds like [mæt].
4. Substitution of [ʌ] so that *bed* sounds like [bʌd].
5. Addition of [ə] so that *head* sounds like [hɛəd].
6. Nasalized production of [ɛ]—most likely to occur in a word such as *men.*

EXERCISES

Sound Practice

1. Articulate a series of staccato [ɛ] sounds.
2. Articulate these vowel pairs:

   Easy to contrast: [ɛ-i] [ɛ-ɑ] [ɛ-u]
   Difficult to contrast: [ɛ-ɪ] [ɛ-eɪ] [ɛ-æ] [ɛ-ʌ]

Syllable Practice

3. Articulate these syllables: [mɛ] [lɛ] [bɛ] [dɛ] [gɛ]
   [ɛm] [ɛl] [ɛb] [ɛd] [ɛg]
   [mɛm] [lɛl] [bɛb] [dɛd] [gɛg]
4. Articulate these syllable pairs:

   Easy to contrast: [mɛ-mi] [mɛ-mɑ] [mɛ-mu]
   [ɛm-im] [ɛm-ɑm] [ɛm-um]
   [mɛm-mim] [mɛm-mɑm] [mɛm-mum]
   Difficult to contrast:
   [mɛ-mɪ] [mɛ-meɪ] [mɛ-mæ] [mɛ-mʌ]
   [ɛm-ɪm] [ɛm-eɪm] [ɛm-æm] [ɛm-ʌm]
   [mɛm-mɪm] [mɛm-meɪm] [mɛm-mæm] [mɛm-mʌm]

   Repeat by substituting [l], [b], [d], and [g] for [m].

Word Practice

5. Read these words aloud:

   Initial: ebb, ebony, echo, Edward, edge, edible, edifice, edit, effigy, egg, elbow, elephant, elf, elm, end, ensign, enter, enterprise, entertain, entrance, epoch, exercise, exit, extra

Medial: bed, bell, bet, dead, deck, fed, fell, head, led, men, mend, met, red, said, sell, set, stead, tell, tent, well, west, when, whence, yell
Final: Does not appear in this position in English.

6. Read these word pairs aloud:

Easy to contrast:
[ɛ-i] bed-bead, dead-deed, etch-each, fed-feed, led-lead, men-mean, met-meat, red-read, set-seat, wreck-reek
[ɛ-ɑ] head-hod, Ned-nod, net-not, pet-pot, red-rod, said-sod, set-sot, shed-shod, wed-wad, wreck-rock
[ɛ-u] bed-booed, Ben-boon, bet-boot, bread-brood, fed-food, met-moot, red-rude, said-sued, shed-shooed, wed-wooed

Difficult to contrast:
[ɛ-ɪ] bed-bid, bet-bit, dell-dill, etch-itch, fell-fill, head-hid, lead-lid, met-mitt, red-rid, set-sit
[ɛ-eɪ] bell-bail, Ben-bane, bet-bait, dell-dale, fed-fade, fell-fail, met-mate, pet-pate, red-raid, wreck-rake
[ɛ-æ] bed-bad, beg-bag, Ben-ban, bet-bat, head-had, led-lad, met-mat, pet-pat, set-sat, wreck-rack
[ɛ-ʌ] bed-bud, Ben-bun, dell-dull, dead-dud, deck-duck, egg-ugh, met-mutt, net-nut, pep-pup, pet-putt

Sentence Practice

7. Read these sentences aloud:

The red-headed ensign said, "My friend, Ed, is dead and buried."
"Edit any extra," says Ned, editor of the sensational *Sentinel.*
Engineer Ethelbert wrecked the express at the end of Elm Street.
Red led men to the heifer which fell in the dell.
"Ready, Geoffrey?" Debby elfishly enquired.

PHONETIC [æ] DIACRITIC ă

	KEY WORD	VOCAL FOLDS	VELUM
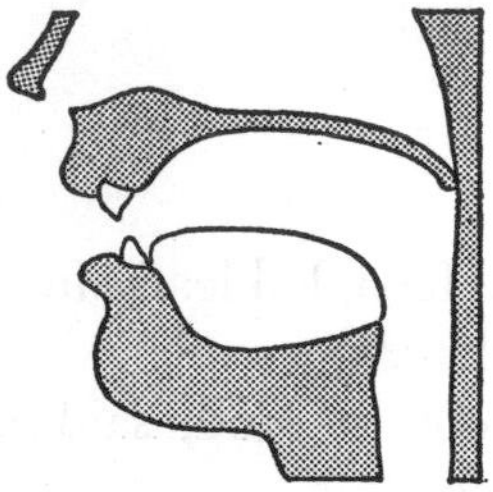	*bat*	Vibrating	Raised

DEVIATIONS

Learn to recognize each of the following deviations in the production of [æ]. *Eliminate from your speech all of those deviations which are not representative of the best speech in your region.*

1. Substitution of [ɪ] so that *can* sounds like [kɪn].
2. Substitution of [ɛ] so that *bag* sounds like [bɛg].
3. Substitution of [ɑ] so that *ant* sounds like [ɑnt].
4. Substitution of [ʌ] so that *rat* sounds like [rʌt].
5. Addition of [ə] so that *bad* sounds like [bæəd].
6. Nasalized production of [æ]—most likely to occur in a word such as *man*.

EXERCISES

Sound Practice

1. Articulate a series of staccato [æ] sounds.
2. Articulate these vowel pairs: *Easy to contrast:* [æ-i] [æ-ɪ] [æ-u]
   Difficult to contrast: [æ-ɛ] [æ-ɑ] [æ-ʌ]

Syllable Practice

3. Articulate these syllables: [mæ] [læ] [bæ] [dæ] [gæ]
   [æm] [æl] [æb] [æd] [æg]
   [mæm] [læl] [bæb] [dæd] [gæg]
4. Articulate these syllable pairs:

   Easy to contrast: [mæ-mi] [mæ-mɪ] [mæ-mu]

TECHNICAL DESCRIPTION	MOUTH	LIPS	TONGUE
Low front vowel	Open noticeably more than for [ɛ]	Unrounded	Tip behind lower front teeth, front arched just slightly toward hard palate, lower than for [ɛ]. No contact with upper molars. Tongue lax

[æm-im] [æm-ɪm] [æm-um]
[mæm-mim] [mæm-mɪm] [mæm-mum]

Difficult to contrast: [mæ-mɛ] [mæ-mɑ] [mæ-mʌ]
[æm-ɛm] [æm-ɑm] [æm-ʌm]
[mæm-mɛm] [mæm-mɑm] [mæm-mʌm]

Repeat by substituting [l], [b], [d], and [g] for [m].

Word Practice

5. Read these words aloud:

Initial: act, actual, Adam, add, after, Allen, altitude, altruism, am, ample, anchor, and, animal, ant, antler, anthem, anvil, apple, apt, as, ash, at, Athens, avarice

Medial: band, bat, fad, graduate, had, haggle, hat, lack, landing, lad, mat, mattress, pat, path, rack, sack, sallow, Sally, sang, sat, satire, Saturday, tack, talisman

Final: [æ] seldom appears in this position.

6. Read these word pairs aloud:

Easy to contrast:

[æ-i] at-eat, bam-beam, fad-feed, had-heed, lack-leak, mat-meat, rack-reek, sack-seek, sap-seep, sat-seat

[æ-ɪ] at-it, bag-big, bat-bit, fat-fit, grad-grid, hat-hit, pat-pit, Sally-silly, sang-sing, sat-sit

[æ-u] bad-booed, ban-boon, bam-boom, bat-boot, cat-coot, hat-hoot, mat-moot, pal-pool, sad-sued, shad-shooed

Difficult to contrast:

[æ-ɛ] bad-bed, ban-Ben, bat-bet, had-head, ham-hem, lad-led, mat-met, pat-pet, rack-wreck, sat-set

[æ-ɑ] add-odd, cad-cod, cam-calm, cat-cot, lack-lock, pad-pod, rat-rot, sad-sod, sat-sot, tack-tock

[æ-ʌ] bad-bud, bag-bug, ban-bun, bank-bunk, cam-come, cat-cut, lack-luck, pat-putt, rat-rut, Sam-sum

Sentence Practice

7. Read these sentences aloud:

Apple Annie, clad in plaid, crammed the shad in an antiquated bag.
Sad Sam lacked a hatrack in the shack.
Scratch the match on the latch.

Back Vowels

PHONETIC [ɑ] DIACRITIC ä

	KEY WORD	VOCAL FOLDS	VELUM
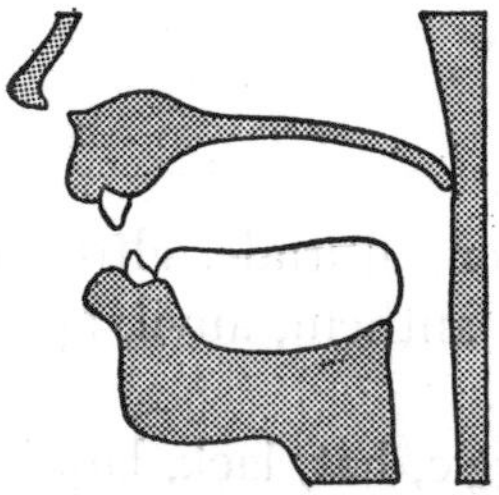	*father*	Vibrating	Raised

DEVIATIONS

Learn to recognize each of the following deviations in the production of [ɑ]. *Eliminate from your speech all of those deviations which are not representative of the best speech in your region.*

1. Substitution of [æ] so that *palm* sounds like [pæm].
2. Substitution of [ɔ] so that *don* sounds like [dɔn].

Adam sang an anthem from the "Anvil Chorus."
Pack the snack in the black sack, Mac, and we'll stack it on the yak.

PHONETIC [a] DIACRITIC ȧ

Refer to the vowel diagram and you will see that this vowel lies midway between [æ] and [ɑ]. Say *at,* then *ah,* then try to make a sound that lies between these two, allowing your lowered tongue to hump up in the middle rather than toward the front or toward the back.

Relatively few Americans (and these mostly Easterners) use this sound, whereas Europeans use it frequently. Those Americans who do use it will say words like *ask, bath,* and *dance* with this sound.

TECHNICAL DESCRIPTION	MOUTH	LIPS	TONGUE
Low back vowel	Open wide	Open wide, unrounded	Tip behind lower front teeth, back low, almost flat and relaxed

3. Substitution of [ʌ] so that *cot* sounds like [kʌt].
4. Addition of [ə] so that *don* sounds like [dɑən].
5. Addition of [r] so that *wash* sounds like [wɑrʃ].
6. Nasalized production of [ɑ]—most likely to occur in a word such as *Mom.*

EXERCISES

Sound Practice

1. Articulate a series of staccato [ɑ] sounds.
2. Articulate these vowel pairs: *Easy to contrast:* [ɑ-i] [ɑ-ɛ] [ɑ-u]
   Difficult to contrast: [ɑ-æ] [ɑ-ɔ] [ɑ-ʌ]

Syllable Practice

3. Articulate these syllables: [mɑ] [lɑ] [bɑ] [dɑ] [gɑ]
   [ɑm] [ɑl] [ɑb] [ɑd] [ɑg]
   [mɑm] [lɑl] [bɑb] [dɑd] [gɑg]

4. Articulate these syllable pairs:

   Easy to contrast: [mɑ-mi] [mɑ-mɛ] [mɑ-mu]
   [ɑm-im] [ɑm-ɛm] [ɑm-um]
   [mɑm-mim] [mɑm-mɛm] [mɑm-mum]

   Difficult to contrast: [mɑ-mæ] [mɑ-mɔ] [mɑ-mʌ]
   [ɑm-æm] [ɑm-ɔm] [ɑm-ʌm]
   [mɑm-mæm] [mɑm-mɔm] [mɑm-mʌm]

   Repeat by substituting [l], [b], [d], and [g] for [m].

Word Practice

5. Read these words aloud:

   Initial: alms, aria, ark, obstacle, obstinate, octopus, odd, odyssey, ominous, on, onyx, opera, opportune, optimist, osmosis, oxide

   Medial: balm, bar, car, cod, cot, dock, palm, pod, rock, scarf, shark, snarl, sot, swan, wan, yard

   Final: ah, aha, bah, bourgeois, fa, faux pas, ha, haha, huzzah, la, mamba, Panama, schwa, shah, spa, Utah

6. Read these word pairs aloud:

Easy to contrast:
[ɑ-i] bomb-beam, hot-heat, lock-leak, mock-meek, psalm-seem, rod-reed, rock-reek, sock-seek, sop-seep, sot-seat
[ɑ-ɛ] dock-deck, don-den, hod-head, knock-neck, not-net, rock-wreck, rod-red, sot-set, wad-wed, want-went
[ɑ-u] bomb-boom, cod-cooed, cop-coop, cot-coot, hop-hoop, lop-loop, rod-rude, shod-shooed, sop-soup, wand-wound

Difficult to contrast:
[ɑ-æ] calm-cam, cod-cad, cot-cat, lock-lack, odd-add, pod-pad, rot-rat, sod-sad, sot-sat, tock-tack
[ɑ-ɔ] cod-cawed, cot-caught, nod-gnawed, not-naught, odd-awed, pod-pawed, rot-wrought, sod-sawed, sot-sought, tock-talk
[ɑ-ʌ] balm-bum, calm-come, cot-cut, dock-duck, lock-luck, not-nut, Psalm-sum, rot-rut, sob-sub, wan-one

Sentence Practice

7. Read these sentences aloud:

Father was calm as he threw the bomb on the dock.
The sergeant socked the guard for dropping the rock on his cot.
The pod will rot if left on the rock.
Oddly, the ominous octopus remained calm.
The operator heard Tom sing the aria from his heart.

PHONETIC [ɒ] DIACRITIC ŏ

Refer to the vowel diagram and you will see that [ɒ] lies between [ɑ] and [ɔ]. Say *father*, then *ought*. Isolate the vowel sounds, then try to say the sound that lies between. The back of your tongue should hump up slightly as it moves from [ɑ] through [ɒ] to [ɔ].

This sound is found mostly in Eastern New England, the [ɒ] being the pronunciation of *o* in words like *off, froth, loss,* and of *a* in words like *watch*.

PHONETIC [ɔ] DIACRITIC ô

	KEY WORD	VOCAL FOLDS	VELUM
	awl	Vibrating	Raised

DEVIATIONS

Learn to recognize each of the following deviations in the production of [ɔ]. *Eliminate from your speech all of those deviations which are not representative of the best speech in your region.*

1. Substitution of [ɑ] so that *talk* sounds like [tɑk].
2. Substitution of [oʊ] so that *saw* sounds like [soʊ].
3. Substitution of [ʊ] so that *fall* sounds like [fʊl].
4. Substitution of [ʌ] so that *call* sounds like [kʌl].
5. Addition of [ə] so that *ought* sounds like [ɔət].
6. Addition of [r] so that *law* sounds like [lɔr].
7. Nasalized production of [ɔ]—most likely to occur in a word such as *gnawed.*

EXERCISES

Sound Practice

1. Articulate a series of staccato [ɔ] sounds.
2. Articulate these vowel pairs:
   Easy to contrast: [ɔ-ɪ] [ɔ-ɛ] [ɔ-u]
   Difficult to contrast: [ɔ-ɑ] [ɔ-oʊ] [ɔ-ʊ] [ɔ-ʌ]

Syllable Practice

3. Articulate these syllables: [mɔ] [lɔ] [bɔ] [dɔ] [gɔ]
   [ɔm] [ɔl] [ɔb] [ɔd] [ɔg]
   [mɔm] [lɔl] [bɔb] [dɔd] [gɔg]

TECHNICAL DESCRIPTION	MOUTH	LIPS	TONGUE
Low back vowel	Open slightly less than for [ɑ]	Slightly rounded, tensed, and slightly protruded	Tip behind lower front teeth, back arched slightly toward soft palate

4. Articulate these syllable pairs:

Easy to contrast: [mɔ-mi] [mɔ-mɛ] [mɔ-mu]
[ɔm-im] [ɔm-ɛm] [ɔm-um]
[mɔm-mim] [mɔm-mɛm] [mɔm-mum]

Difficult to contrast:
[mɔ-mɑ] [mɔ-moʊ] [mɔ-mʊ] [mɔ-mʌ]
[ɔm-ɑm] [ɔm-oʊm] [ɔm-ʊm] [ɔm-ʌm]
[mɔm-mɑm] [mɔm-moʊm] [mɔm-mʊm] [mɔm-mʌm]

Repeat by substituting [l], [b], [d], and [g] for [m].

Word Practice

5. Read these words aloud:

Initial: all, alter, auction, audience, auditor, ought, August, author, auto, autumn, awe, awed, awesome, awful, off, often
Medial: applaud, ball, bought, call, caught, fall, fought, gnawed, haul, naught, ought, sauce, sawed, song, sought, thought
Final: caw, claw, craw, draw, flaw, gnaw, jaw, law, paw, raw, saw, Shaw, slaw, straw, taw, thaw

6. Read these word pairs aloud:

Easy to contrast:
[ɔ-i] bought-beat, fall-feel, fought-feet, gnaw-knee, law-lea, naught-neat, ought-eat, Paul-peel, saw-see, sought-seat

[ɔ-ɛ] audible-edible, audit-edit, ball-bell, bought-bet, fall-fell, gnawed-Ned, laud-led, naught-net, sawed-said, sought-set

[ɔ-u] bought-boot, call-cool, caught-coot, draw-drew, fall-fool, lawn-loon, loss-loose, Paul-pool, saw-sue, taught-toot

Difficult to contrast:

[ɔ-ɑ] awed-odd, caught-cot, gnawed-nod, naught-not, pawed-pod, sawed-sod, sought-sot, talk-tock, wrought-rot

[ɔ-oʊ] awed-owed, bought-boat, caught-coat, fall-foal, gnawed-node, Maude-mowed, naught-note, Saul-soul, sawed-sowed, wrought-wrote

[ɔ-ʊ] balk-book, ball-bull, cawed-could, fall-full, fought-foot, hawk-hook, Paul-pull, sought-soot, talk-took, wall-wool

[ɔ-ʌ] bought-but, call-cull, caught-cut, cawed-cud, gall-gull, haul-hull, maul-mull, naught-nut, song-sung, wrought-rut

Sentence Practice

7. Read these sentences aloud:

Paul authored the awful song.
The Mohawk found a tomahawk on the sidewalk.

PHONETIC [ʊ] DIACRITIC o͝o

KEY WORD	VOCAL FOLDS	VELUM
foot	Vibrating	Raised

DEVIATIONS

Learn to recognize each of the following deviations in the production of [ʊ]. *Eliminate from your speech all of those deviations which are not representative of the best speech in your region.*

1. Substitution of [ɔ] so that *pull* sounds like [pɔl].
2. Substitution of [oʊ] so that *full* sounds like [foʊl].

The Autumn Auto Auction was held in August.
Gawky Claude talked on a squawky walkie-talkie.
All for naught, Shaw sought the sauce he had bought.

PHONETIC [o] DIACRITIC ō

As in the case of [e], the pure vowel [o] seldom occurs in stressed syllables in American speech. Ordinarily the [ʊ] element is added and the sound becomes the diphthong [oʊ] when it occurs in the stressed position in a word such as *go*. When it occurs in an unstressed position, as in the word *obey*, the [ʊ] element usually is omitted.

Use of the pure vowel [o] in both the stressed and unstressed positions is typical of English spoken with a Spanish dialect. Since [o] and [oʊ] may be interchanged without confusion of meaning, the sound referred to as the long *o* is considered in the next chapter under diphthongs.

TECHNICAL DESCRIPTION	MOUTH	LIPS	TONGUE
High back vowel	Open slightly less than for [ɔ]	More round and more protruded than for [ɔ]	Tip behind lower front teeth, back arched higher toward soft palate than for [ɔ]; lax

3. Substitution of [u] so that *cook* sounds like [kuk].
4. Substitution of [ʌ] so that *crook* sounds like [krʌk].
5. Addition of [ə] so that *look* sounds like [lʊək].
6. Nasalized production of [ʊ]—most likely to occur in a word such as *nook.*

EXERCISES

Sound Practice

1. Articulate a series of staccato [ʊ] sounds.
2. Articulate these vowel pairs:

   Easy to contrast: [ʊ-i] [ʊ-ɛ] [ʊ-ɑ]
   Difficult to contrast: [ʊ-ɔ] [ʊ-oʊ] [ʊ-u] [ʊ-ʌ]

Syllable Practice

3. Articulate these syllables: [mʊ] [lʊ] [bʊ] [dʊ] [gʊ]
   [ʊm] [ʊl] [ʊb] [ʊd] [ʊg]
   [mʊm] [lʊl] [bʊb] [dʊd] [gʊg]

4. Articulate these syllable pairs:

   Easy to contrast: [mʊ-mi] [mʊ-mɛ] [mʊ-mɑ]
   [ʊm-im] [ʊm-ɛm] [ʊm-ɑm]
   [mʊm-mim] [mʊm-mɛm] [mʊm-mɑm]

   Difficult to contrast:
   [mʊ-mɔ] [mʊ-moʊ] [mʊ-mu] [mʊ-mʌ]
   [ʊm-ɔm] [ʊm-oʊm] [ʊm-um] [ʊm-ʌm]
   [mʊm-mɔm] [mʊm-moʊm] [mʊm-mum] [mʊm-mʌm]

   Repeat by substituting [l], [b], [d], and [g] for [m].

Word Practice

5. Read these words aloud:

   Initial: Almost never appears in this position.
   Medial: book, bookish, booklet, brook, bull, bullet, bully, bush, Butch, cook, cooking, could, crook, crooked, cushion, foot, forsook, full, fuller, good, hood, hook, hooked, look, looking, mistook, nook, overlook, partook, pull, pullet, pulley, push, put, pud-

ding, rook, shook, should, sooty, stood, sugar, undertook, woman, wood, wooden, wool, woolen

Final: Never appears in this position.

6. Read these word pairs aloud:

Easy to contrast:

[ʊ-i] book-beak, crook-creak, foot-feet, full-feel, hood-heed, look-leak, pull-peel, rook-reek, shook-sheik, took-teak

[ʊ-ɛ] book-beck, bull-bell, full-fell, hood-head, nook-neck, put-pet, rook-wreck, should-shed, stood-stead, wool-well

[ʊ-ɑ] could-cod, crook-crock, hood-hod, look-lock, nook-knock, put-pot, rook-rock, shook-shock, should-shod, took-tock

Difficult to contrast:

[ʊ-ɔ] book-balk, bull-ball, could-cawed, foot-fought, full-fall, hook-hawk, pull-Paul, pulled-palled, took-talk, wool-wall

[ʊ-oʊ] brook-broke, bull-bowl, could-code, crook-croak, full-foal, hood-hoed, hooks-hoax, pulled-poled, should-showed, stood-stowed

[ʊ-u] could-cooed, full-fool, fuller-fooler, fullish-foolish, look-Luke, pull-pool, pulled-pooled, pulling-pooling, should-shooed, wood-wooed

[ʊ-ʌ] book-buck, booking-bucking, could-cud, crooks-crux, look-luck, hook-Huck, put-putt, shook-shuck, stood-stud, took-tuck

Sentence Practice

7. Read these sentences aloud:

The crook mistook the brook for a nook.
Look, you could put your foot on the hood and push!
The woman is sitting on a cushion, looking at a book.
The bully shook his fist at Butch, who stood with his foot on the pulley.
You could pull the basket of wool if you would.

PHONETIC [u] DIACRITIC o͞o

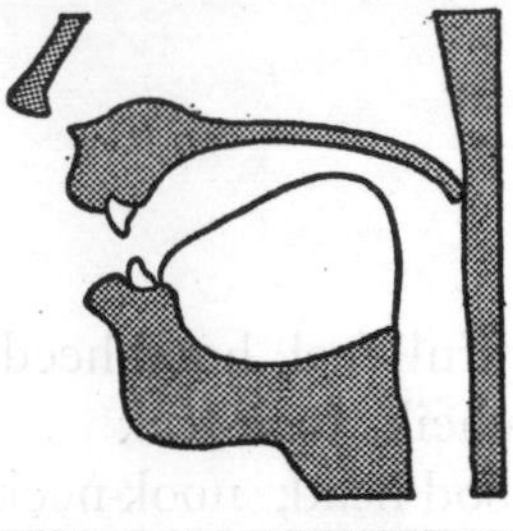

KEY WORD	VOCAL FOLDS	VELUM
shoe	Vibrating	Raised

DEVIATIONS

Learn to recognize each of the following deviations in the production of [u]. *Eliminate from your speech all of those deviations which are not representative of the best speech in your region.*

1. Substitution of [ʊ] so that *fool* sounds like [fʊl].
2. Substitution of [ʌ] so that *cool* sounds like [kʌl].
3. Substitution of [ju] so that *moot* sounds like [mjut].
4. Addition of [ə] so that *fool* sounds like [fuəl].
5. Nasalized production of [u]—most likely to occur in a word such as *moon.*

EXERCISES

Sound Practice

1. Articulate a series of staccato [u] sounds.
2. Articulate these vowel pairs: *Easy to contrast:* [u-i] [u-ɛ] [u-ɑ]
   Difficult to contrast: [u-ʊ] [u-ʌ] [u-ju]

Syllable Practice

3. Articulate these syllables: [mu] [lu] [bu] [du] [gu]
   [um] [ul] [ub] [ud] [ug]
   [mum] [lul] [bub] [dud] [gug]
4. Articulate these syllable pairs:

   Easy to contrast: [mu-mi] [mu-mɛ] [mu-mɑ]
   [um-im] [um-ɛm] [um-ɑm]
   [mum-mim] [mum-mɛm] [mum-mɑm]

TECHNICAL DESCRIPTION	MOUTH	LIPS	TONGUE
High back vowel	Nearly closed	Rounded and protruded with small opening	Tip behind lower front teeth, back arched high toward soft palate; tense

Difficult to contrast: [mu-mʊ] [mu-mʌ] [mu-mju]
[um-ʊm] [um-ʌm] [um-jum]
[mum-mʊm] [mum-mʌm] [mum-mjum]

Repeat by substituting [l], [b], [d], and [g] for [m].

Word Practice

5. Read these words aloud:

Initial: Seldom appears in this position.
Medial: boom, boost, booth, brute, cool, coop, fool, loop, loot, moon, prove, recruit, room, roost, Ruth, shoot, snoop, stoop, swoop, toot, tooth, truth, whoop, youth
Final: bamboo, bugaboo, canoe, caribou, cashew, construe, coo, crew, do, drew, flew, glue, kangaroo, moo, shoe, slew, tattoo, through, too, true, unto, who, woo, zoo

6. Read these word pairs aloud:

Easy to contrast:
[u-i] booed-bead, boom-beam, boot-beat, loon-lean, moot-meat, pool-peel, rude-reed, soon-seen, soup-seep, wound-weaned
[u-ɛ] booed-bed, boon-Ben, boot-bet, brood-bread, fool-fell, food-fed, moot-met, rude-red, shooed-shed, wooed-wed
[u-ɑ] boom-bomb, cooed-cod, coop-cop, coot-cot, hoop-hop, loot-lot, rude-rod, shoed-shod, soup-sop, wound-wand
Difficult to contrast:
[u-ʊ] cooed-could, fool-full, fooler-fuller, foolish-fullish, Luke-look, pool-pull, pooled-pulled, pooling-pulling, shoed-should, wooed-would

[u-ʌ] booed-bud, boom-bum, boon-bun, cool-cull, coot-cut, hoot-hut, moot-mutt, school-skull, soon-sun, soup-sup

[u-ju] boot-butte, cooed-cued, coot-cute, do-due, food-feud, fool-fuel, moo-mew, moot-mute, who-hue, whose-hues

Sentence Practice

7. Read these sentences aloud:

Central Vowels

PHONETIC [ʌ] DIACRITIC ŭ

	KEY WORD	VOCAL FOLDS	VELUM
	sum	Vibrating	Raised

The vowel sound [ʌ] frequently is substituted for other sounds in American speech. It should be noted that this sound occurs only in stressed syllables. The exercises in this section will help you distinguish between this and other sounds.

Sound Practice

1. Articulate a series of staccato [ʌ] sounds.
2. Articulate these vowel pairs:

   Easy to contrast: [ʌ-i]
   Difficult to contrast: [ʌ-ɪ] [ʌ-eɪ] [ʌ-ɛ] [ʌ-æ] [ʌ-ɑ] [ʌ-ɔ] [ʌ-oʊ] [ʌ-ʊ] [ʌ-u] [ʌ-ɝ]

Syllable Practice

3. Articulate these syllables: [mʌ] [lʌ] [bʌ] [dʌ] [gʌ]

Would you woo the lady with the tattoo at the zoo?
Sue didn't know what to tell Lue to do.
Hugh dropped the glue on the flue.
Ruth was rude to the youthful recruit.
The crew threw a loop through the bamboo hoop.

TECHNICAL DESCRIPTION	MOUTH	LIPS	TONGUE
Mid-central vowel	Open somewhat	Open, relaxed, unrounded	Tip behind lower front teeth, middle raised slightly toward the palate; lax

[ʌm] [ʌl] [ʌb] [ʌd] [ʌg]
[mʌm] [lʌl] [bʌb] [dʌd] [gʌg]

4. Articulate these syllable pairs:

Easy to contrast: [mʌ-mi] [ʌm-im] [mʌm-mim]
Difficult to contrast:
[mʌ-mɪ] [mʌ-meɪ] [mʌ-mɛ] [mʌ-mæ] [mʌ-mɑ] [mʌ-mɔ] [mʌ-moʊ] [mʌ-mʊ] [mʌ-mu] [mʌ-mɝ]
[ʌm-ɪm] [ʌm-eɪm] [ʌm-ɛm] [ʌm-æm] [ʌm-ɑm] [ʌm-ɔm] [ʌm-oʊm] [ʌm-ʊm] [ʌm-um] [ʌm-ɝm]
[mʌm-mɪm] [mʌm-meɪm] [mʌm-mɛm] [mʌm-mæm] [mʌm-mɑm] [mʌm-mɔm] [mʌm-moʊm] [mʌm-mʊm] [mʌm-mum] [mʌm-mɝm]

Repeat by substituting [l], [b], [d], and [g] for [m].

Word Practice

5. Read these words aloud:

Initial: onion, other, oven, ugh, ugly, ulcer, ulster, ultimate, ultra, umber, umbrage, umpire, unctious, under, undulate, unguent, up, upper, upward, us, usher, utter, utterance

Medial: bud, chug, cuff, cup, dull, dug, Dutch, gulf, gull, gum, hunt, judge, mud, muff, mug, plug, rough, run, skull, spun, stun, sup, thud, tough

Final: Never appears in this position.

6. Read these word pairs aloud:

Easy to contrast:

[ʌ-i] bun-bean, crumb-cream, dull-deal, luck-leak, mull-meal, mutt-meat, nut-neat, one-wean, sum-seem, sup-seep

Difficult to contrast:

[ʌ-ɪ] bud-bid, cull-kill, cut-kit, gull-gill, hull-hill, mull-mill, nut-knit, putt-pit, rug-rig, sung-sing

[ʌ-eɪ] dull-dale, dumb-dame, gull-gale, gum-game, gun-gain, hull-hail, mull-mail, mum-maim, skull-scale, sum-same

[ʌ-ɛ] bud-bed, bun-Ben, duck-deck, dud-dead, dull-dell, mutt-met, nut-net, pup-pep, putt-pet, ugh-egg

[ʌ-æ] bud-bad, bug-bag, bun-ban, come-cam, cut-cat, luck-lack, nut-gnat, putt-pat, rut-rat, sum-Sam [ʌ-ɑ] bum-balm, come-calm, cut-cot, duck-dock, luck-lock, nut-not, one-wan, rut-rot, sum-psalm, sup-sop

[ʌ-ɔ] but-bought, cull-call, cut-caught, gull-gall, hull-haul, mud-Maud, mull-maul, nut-naught, rut-wrought, sung-song

[ʌ-oʊ] bud-bowed, chuck-choke, cluck-cloak, crux-croaks, cud-code, gull-goal, rub-robe, rug-rogue, sculled-scold, struck-stroke

[ʌ-ʊ] buck-book, bucking-booking, crux-crooks, cud-could, Huck-hook, luck-look, putt-put, shuck-shook, stud-stood, tuck-took

[ʌ-u] bud-booed, bum-boom, bun-boon, cull-cool, cut-coot, hut-hoot, mutt-moot, skull-school, sun-soon, sup-soup

[ʌ-ɝ] bud-bird, cull-curl, cut-curt, gull-girl, hull-hurl, putt-pert, spun-spurn, stun-stern, thud-third, tough-turf

Sentence Practice

7. Read these sentences aloud:

Much of the flood comes under the hutch.
"Courage," said the rough thug, as he wiped the blood from the rug.
On a hunch, the gang had drunk punch at lunch.
"Don't snub the grub at the club," said the sub.
Bud had brushed, rubbed, and scrubbed his cuff to remove the mud.

PHONETIC [ə] DIACRITIC ŭ

It has been noted that the foregoing vowel sound [ʌ] occurs only in stressed syllables, as in the word *sum*. The vowel sound [ə], on the other hand, never occurs in a stressed position but is always in an unaccented syllable, as in the word *arena*. It is also used by some speakers who drop their *r*'s in the unaccented last syllable of words like *father* or *horror*.

[ə] is often referred to as the *schwa* or neutral vowel. In the words listed below note how many different vowel letters are used to represent this sound. In fact, all vowels are at times articulated as [ə]. If you were to analyze connected speech, you would find the schwa used more frequently than any other vowel. For example, connecting words like *to, and, or* get very little stress in rapid speech, and the vowels may become [ə], regardless of how they are articulated in words in isolation.

Most of the words which follow would be pronounced with a schwa in connected speech. However, when they are pronounced in isolation, some people will use a more definite vowel sound for the unaccented vowel. As you practice these words, try to determine which ones are given the value of [ə], and which the value of another vowel.

Word Practice

1. Read these words aloud:

Initial: abandon, about, above, absurd, abuse, abyss, occasion, accost, account, across, adore, advance, advise, affect, around
Medial: accident, astronomy, beneficent, economy, Elizabethan, emanate, equivalent, Genesis, grenadier, guillotine, heliotrope, holocaust, horoscope, immature, impeccable, mischievous
Final: arena, Australia, Austria, bacteria, barracuda, cinema, data, Lena, petunia, pizza, pneumonia, Prussia, Rebecca, regatta, Riviera, Sahara

Sentence Practice

2. Read these sentences aloud:

It's absurd to abuse or accuse immature Rebecca.
Take my advice and abandon the attack on Austria.
Mischievous Lena took the occasion to see the regatta on the Riviera.
The accident occurred on Heliotrope across from the arena.
He amassed an equivalent amount and added it to his account.

PHONETIC [ɝ] DIACRITIC ûr

KEY WORD	VOCAL FOLDS	VELUM
bird	Vibrating	Raised

PHONETIC [ɜ] DIACRITIC û

KEY WORD	VOCAL FOLDS	VELUM
bird	Vibrating	Raised

Word Practice

1. Read these words aloud:

   Initial: Earl, early, earn, earnest, earning, earthen, earthly, erg, Erwin, err, erstwhile, irk, urban, urchin, urge
   Medial: birch, bird, curt, curve, dirt, heard, hurt, mirth, perch, purse, search, verse, word, work, worse, worth
   Final: blur, burr, confer, cur, defer, fur, her, incur, infer, prefer, purr, sir, slur, spur, stir, were

This sound frequently stands alone in syllables without other vowel sounds accompanying it. It is used only in stressed syllables and only by those speakers who do not drop their r's.

TECHNICAL DESCRIPTION	MOUTH	LIPS	TONGUE
Mid-central vowel with [r] coloring	Somewhat open	Unrounded, somewhat tense	Front raised and often curled back slightly toward hard palatc (retroflex)

This sound occurs only in stressed syllables where no vowel follows it in the same syllable, and is used only by those speakers who drop their r's.

TECHNICAL DESCRIPTION	MOUTH	LIPS	TONGUE
Mid-central vowel without [r] coloring	Somewhat open	Slightly rounded, tense	Tip behind lower front teeth, humped in the middle. Sides of back part of tongue touch upper molars

Sentence Practice

2. Read these sentences aloud:

Sir, you infer with a slur that to err is a curse, yet I prefer to aver that an insult is worse.
The bird perched in the birch was searching for worms.
The urchin searched earnestly for the right word.
The early bird's advice was spurned and as a result the worm had turned.
He irked his girl by writing worthless verse and going about with an empty purse.

PHONETIC [ɚ] DIACRITIC ẽr

This sound is used only in unstressed syllables and bears the same relation to [ɝ] as [ə] does to [ɜ]. That is to say, those who do not drop their *r*'s will give the *r* sound of [ɚ] to unaccented syllables that they would articulate as [ɝ] if accented; whereas those who drop their *r*'s will use the [ə] phoneme for the same unaccented syllables. (See page 111.)

Pronounce the following words. Do you use [ɚ] or [ə] on the unaccented syllables?

Word Practice

1. Read these words aloud: actor, arbiter, better, blinker, brighter, brother, catcher, cleaner, chorister, cover, crooner, darker, drier, father, fatter, fewer, flatterer, greener, harbinger, barrier, idolater, kindlier, lighter, mother, neater, over, prettier, sewer, skimmer, shorter, silver, sinker, sister, slimmer, sliver, smoother, sooner, stranger, summer, swimmer, taller, thinner, under, viewer, weaker, weather, wetter, winter

Sentence Practice

2. Read these sentences aloud:

Sooner or later the swimmer will see the blinker.
My brother will never be a major league catcher.
Summer weather encourages swimmers to enjoy the water.
Put the cover over the silver, father, it will stay cleaner and brighter.
In just one summer the player grew taller, stronger, and heavier.

9. *Improving* DIPHTHONG SOUND ARTICULATION

test your diphthong sound articulation

Read the following words and sentences aloud while your instructor evaluates your diphthong sound articulation.

[ɪ] DIPHTHONGS

[eɪ] ā (EXPLANATION AND EXERCISES, PP. 164-66.)

1. Aid, ail, aim, bail, main, gate, nail, day, may, way
   I'm grateful that today is payday, since I have a skating date with Kay.

[ɑɪ] ī (EXPLANATION AND EXERCISES, PP. 166-69.)

2. I, ire, ide, bide, dial, mine, size, sigh, tie, my
   The jet flyer died last night because he tried to fly too high.

[ɔɪ] oi (EXPLANATION AND EXERCISES, PP. 170-72.)

3. Oil, ointment, oyster, boil, voice, noise, coin, toy, boy, soy
   You may enjoy the noise of a boy and his toy but it annoys me.

[ʊ] DIPHTHONGS

[ɑʊ] ou (EXPLANATION AND EXERCISES, PP. 172-75.)

4. Out, owl, our, noun, cowl, town, found, row, now, bough
   I found out how to rouse everyone in town by shouting loudly.

[ou] ō (EXPLANATION AND EXERCISES, PP. 176-78.)

5. Oat, ode, old, bowl, dome, goat, moan, tow, dough, low
   The lonely old goat herder towed his load down the dusty road.

*Name*____	***Rating***
Student produces the following diphthong sounds accurately.	
1. [eɪ]	____
2. [ɑɪ]	____
3. [ɔɪ]	____
4. [ɑʊ]	____
5. [oʊ]	____
Total	____

Rating: It is suggested that the student be scored on a 5 to 1 point scale, 5 being used to indicate an excellent and 1 a poor rating.

Introduction Diphthong sounds have certain characteristics in common. The first of the two vowel elements is always stressed. The word *ate,* for example, includes the sounds [e] and [ɪ] blended into the diphthong [eɪ]. When you say the word *ate* correctly, you use greater force and you spend more time in producing the [e] portion of the diphthong than you do in producing the [ɪ] portion. You will find the same relationship in the word *bide,* which blends the sounds [ɑ] and [ɪ] into the diphthong [ɑɪ]; in the word *voice,* which blends the sounds [ɔ] and [ɪ] into the diphthong [ɔɪ]; in the word *how,* which blends the sounds [ɑ] and [ʊ] into the diphthong [ɑʊ]; and in the word *oat,* which blends the sounds [o] and [ʊ] into the diphthong [oʊ].

The diphthongs [oʊ] and [eɪ] are frequently shortened to the vowels [o] and [e] when they occur in unstressed syllables. Listen to the *a* in *chaotic.* You will probably not hear the [ɪ] phoneme at all. Say *obey* and *Ohio.* The first *o* in each word is unaccented and therefore there is no movement from [o] to [ʊ]. But wherever [e] or [o] receive stress in a word, they are almost invariably diphthongized to [eɪ] and [oʊ].

A second characteristic that diphthongs have in common is that tongue movement is always upward from the first to the second element.

The third common characteristic is that the mouth opening becomes smaller as the second element of the diphthong is produced.

A diphthong may be described as a combination of two vowel sounds occurring in the same syllable and blending continuously from one vowel to the other without interruption.

DIPHTHONG PRODUCTION Two diagrams have been included in order to assist you in visualizing how diphthongs are produced.

These illustrations indicate the relative tongue positions and the movement of the tongue in the mouth for the production of the five basic diphthong sounds in General American speech.

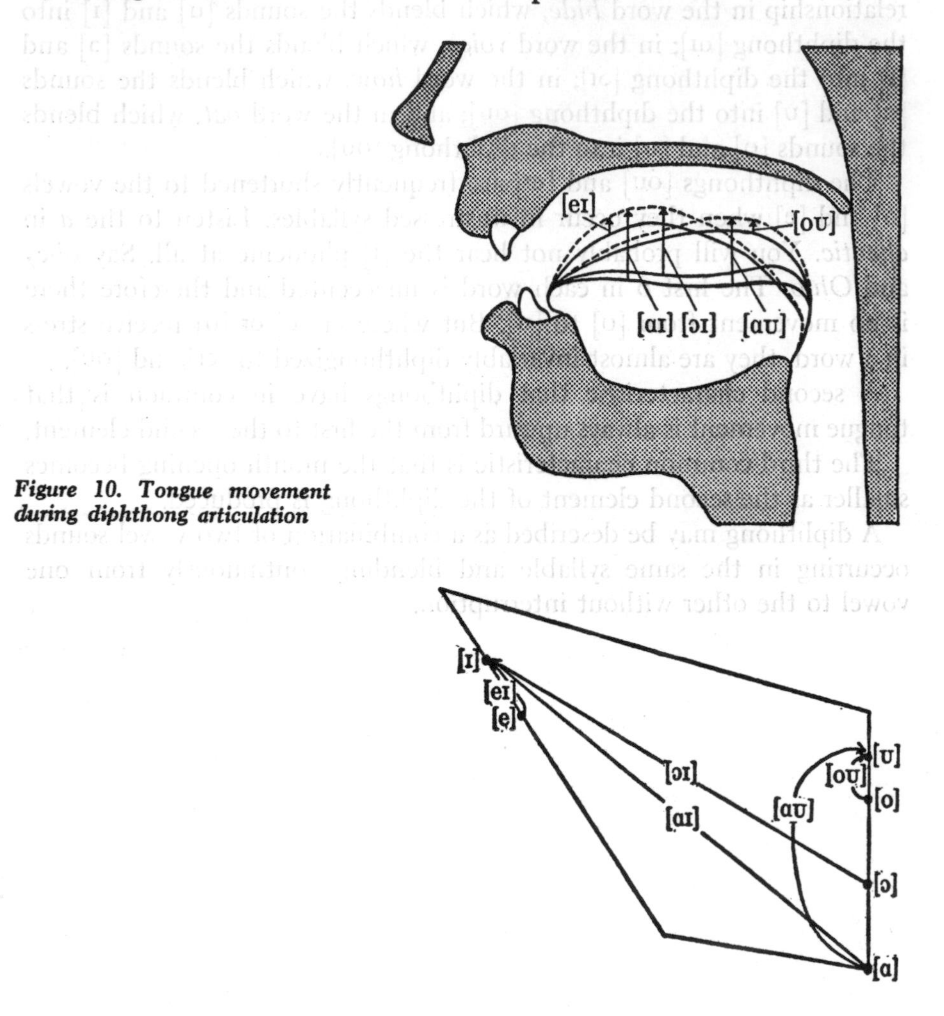

Figure 10. Tongue movement during diphthong articulation

It will be noted that the tongue moves toward the position of the [ɪ] for the second element of three of these diphthong sounds, [eɪ], [ɑɪ], and [ɔɪ]. These are known as the [ɪ] *diphthongs.*

It can also be seen that the tongue moves toward the position of the [ʊ] sound for the second element of two of these diphthong sounds, [ɑʊ] and [oʊ]. These are known as the [ʊ] *diphthongs.*

These five diphthongs are not the only ones which can be produced. Other vowels may be blended continuously in rapid succession without interruption in the same syllable. Some Americans use the diphthong [æʊ] rather than [ɑʊ], for example, and pronounce the word *house* as [hæʊs]. Still others use the diphthong [ɜʊ] or [ʌʊ] and pronounce the word as [hɜʊs] or [hʌʊs].

It is also possible to link three vowels together to produce what are called *triphthongs.* This is illustrated by speakers who pronounce *my* as [mɑɪə], rather than as [mɑɪ]. In some regions of the country it is normal to triphthongize words such as *fire* [fɑɪə].

You should avoid certain common errors in diphthong production:

1. Omission of the second element of the diphthong. This error is apparent in the speech of those who pronounce the word *boil* as if it were *ball.* It may result from carelessness.

2. Overstressing of the first element. Here a distortion of the diphthong is created by prolonging the first element excessively. To correct this fault the speaker should listen carefully to those who produce the sound properly.

3. Substitution of another sound for the required one. The person who pronounces *boil* as if it were *bile* is making this error. He should identify the substitution and establish correct habits in diphthong production.

4. Addition of other sounds to the required one. Where the addition of the extra element is not acceptable, the speaker should concentrate upon eliminating the unwanted element.

5. Nasalization of the required sound. This distortion occurs when the velum is lowered, allowing air to escape through the nose during diphthong production.

[ɪ] *Diphthongs*

PHONETIC [eɪ] DIACRITIC ā

	KEY WORD	VOCAL FOLDS	VELUM
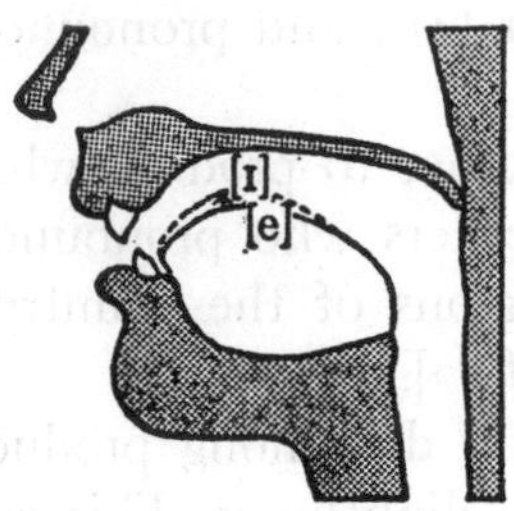	*ate*	Vibrating	Raised

DEVIATIONS

Learn to recognize each of the following deviations in the production of [eɪ]. ***Eliminate from your speech all of those deviations which are not representative of the best speech in your region.***

1. Omission of [ɪ] so that *may* sounds like [me].
2. Overstressing of [e] so that *bail* sounds like [be͡e͡eɪl].
3. Substitution of [ɛɪ] so that *aid* sounds like [ɛɪd].
4. Substitution of [ɛ] so that *fail* sounds like [fɛl].
5. Substitution of [ɑɪ] so that *ail* sounds like [ɑɪl].
6. Substitution of [ʌ] so that *bail* sounds like [bʌl].
7. Addition of [ə] so that *gate* sounds like [geɪət].
8. Addition of [r] so that *day* sounds like [deɪr].
9. Nasalized production of [eɪ]—most likely to occur in a word such as *main.*

EXERCISES

Sound Practice

1. Articulate a series of staccato [e] sounds.
   Articulate a series of staccato [ɪ] sounds.
   Alternately articulate [e] and [ɪ].
   Articulate a series of staccato [eɪ] sounds.
2. Articulate these sound pairs: *Easy to contrast:* [eɪ-ɔɪ] [eɪ-ɑʊ] [eɪ-oʊ]
   Difficult to contrast: [eɪ-ɛ] [eɪ-ɑɪ] [eɪ-ʌ]

TECHNICAL DESCRIPTION	MOUTH	LIPS	TONGUE
[ɪ] diphthong	Open slightly less than for [ɛ], closing during production to position for [ɪ]	Drawn back and open slightly less than for [ɛ], closing during production to position for [ɪ]	Tip behind lower front teeth, arched toward hard palate slightly higher than for [ɛ], moving upward during production to position for [ɪ]

Syllable Practice

3. Articulate these syllables: [meɪ] [leɪ] [beɪ] [deɪ] [geɪ]
[eɪm] [eɪl] [eɪb] [eɪd] [eɪg]
[meɪm] [leɪl] [beɪb] [deɪd] [geɪg]

4. Articulate these syllable pairs:

Easy to contrast: [meɪ-mɔɪ] [meɪ-mɑʊ] [meɪ-moʊ]
[eɪm-ɔɪm] [eɪm-ɑʊm] [eɪm-oʊm]
[meɪm-mɔɪm] [meɪm-mɑʊm] [meɪm-moʊm]

Difficult to contrast: [meɪ-mɛ] [meɪ-mɑɪ] [meɪ-mʌ]
[eɪm-ɛm] [eɪm-ɑɪm] [eɪm-ʌm]
[meɪm-mɛm] [meɪm-mɑɪm] [meɪm-mʌm]

Repeat by substituting [l], [b], [d], and [g] for [m].

Word Practice

5. Read these words aloud:

Initial: Abe, able, ace, ache, acorn, acre, age, aid, ail, aileron, ailment, aim, aitch, ape, Asia, ate

Medial: babe, bail, base, dale, daze, face, fade, gauge, great, pail, raid, rain, safe, same, tape, veil

Final: bay, day, dray, fray, gay, hay, jay, may, neigh, pay, ray, say, stay, stray, they, weigh

6. Read these word pairs aloud:

Easy to contrast:

[eɪ-ɔɪ] bail-boil, bays-boys, cane-coin, fail-foil, Jane-join, lane-loin, pays-poise, rail-roil, sail-soil, tale-toil

[eɪ-ɑʊ] bays-boughs, date-doubt, fail-foul, gauge-gouge, gain-gown, gait-gout, late-lout, pate-pout, raise-rouse, rate-rout

[eɪ-oʊ] cake-coke, cane-cone, gate-goat, lame-loam, pail-pole, rain-roan, raise-rose, rate-wrote, sail-sole, steak-stoke

Difficult to contrast:

[eɪ-ɛ] bail-bell, bane-Ben, bait-bet, dale-dell, fade-fed, fail-fell, mate-met, pate-pet, raid-red, rake-wreck

[eɪ-ɑɪ] bait-bite, braid-bride, dale-dial, fail-file, main-mine, mate-might, raid-ride, strafe-strife, tame-time, trail-trial

PHONETIC [ɑɪ] DIACRITIC ī*

	KEY WORD	VOCAL FOLDS	VELUM
	bide	Vibrating	Raised

DEVIATIONS

Learn to recognize each of the following deviations in the production of [ɑɪ]. *Eliminate from your speech all of those deviations which are not representative of the best speech in your region.*

1. Omission of [ɪ] so that *I* sounds like [ɑ].
2. Overstressing of [ɑ] so that *sigh* sounds like [sɑ͡ɑ͡ɑɪ].

* Many speakers produce this diphthong by combining the vowels [a] and [ɪ]. Therefore, the symbol [aɪ] is often used to represent this sound.

[eɪ-ʌ] dale-dull, dame-dumb, gale-gull, game-gum, gain-gun, hail-hull, mail-mull, maim-mum, scale-skull, same-sum

Sentence Practice

7. Read these sentences aloud:

Signal the mail train to beware of the raid on the main line.
Set the sail, Dale, and take plenty of bait.
Nate had a fishing date with Kate but he was late.
They wailed because they were late to the sale.
Ray was a gay blade with no aches, pains, or ailments.

TECHNICAL DESCRIPTION	MOUTH	LIPS	TONGUE
[ɪ] diphthong	Open in position for [ɑ], closing during production to position for [ɪ]	Open wide and unrounded in position for [ɑ], closing during production to position for [ɪ]	Tip behind lower front teeth, back low, flat, and relaxed in position for [ɑ], front arches toward hard palate during production to position for [ɪ]

3. Substitution of [eɪ] so that *I* sounds like [eɪ].
4. Substitution of [ɔɪ] so that *tie* sounds like [tɔɪ].
5. Substitution of [ʌ] so that *my* sounds like [mʌ].
6. Addition of [ə] so that *size* sounds like [sɑɪəz].
7. Addition of [r] so that *I* sounds like [ɑɪr].
8. Nasalized production of [ɑɪ]—most likely to occur in a word such as *mine.*

EXERCISES

Sound Practice

1. Articulate a series of staccato [ɑ] sounds.
   Articulate a series of staccato [ɪ] sounds.
   Alternately articulate [ɑ] and [ɪ].
   Articulate a series of staccato [ɑɪ] sounds.
2. Articulate these sound pairs:

   Easy to contrast: [ɑɪ-ɑʊ] [ɑɪ-oʊ]
   Difficult to contrast: [ɑɪ-eɪ] [ɑɪ-ɑ] [ɑɪ-ɔɪ] [ɑɪ-ʌ]

Syllable Practice

3. Articulate these syllables: [mɑɪ] [lɑɪ] [bɑɪ] [dɑɪ] [gɑɪ]
   [ɑɪm] [ɑɪl] [ɑɪb] [ɑɪd] [ɑɪg]
   [mɑɪm] [lɑɪl] [bɑɪb] [dɑɪd] [gɑɪg]
4. Articulate these syllable pairs:

   Easy to contrast: [mɑɪ-mɑʊ] [mɑɪ-moʊ]
   [ɑɪm-ɑʊm] [ɑɪm-oʊm]
   [mɑɪm-mɑʊm] [mɑɪm-moʊm]

   Difficult to contrast:
   [mɑɪ-meɪ] [mɑɪ-mɑ] [mɑɪ-mɔɪ] [mɑɪ-mʌ]
   [ɑɪm-eɪm] [ɑɪm-ɑm] [ɑɪm-ɔɪm] [ɑɪm-ʌm]
   [mɑɪm-meɪm] [mɑɪm-mɑm] [mɑɪm-mɔɪm] [mɑɪm-mʌm]

   Repeat by substituting [l], [b], [d], and [g] for [m].

Word Practice

5. Read these words aloud:

   Initial: aisle, eye, ice, icicle, Ida, ides, idle, ion, ire, iris, iron, irony, island, item, ivory, ivy

Medial: bite, crime, dice, died, file, fine, hire, kite, like, line, nice, rhyme, ripe, tide, tile, tire

Final: buy, cry, die, dry, fry, my, pie, ply, pry, shy, sigh, sty, tie, try, vie, why

6. Read these word pairs aloud:

Easy to contrast:

[aɪ-aʊ] bite-bout, cried-crowd, file-foul, fined-found, lice-louse, lied-loud, plied-plowed, pride-proud, tine-town, vied-vowed

[aɪ-oʊ] bite-boat, dime-dome, file-foal, kite-coat, lied-load, line-loan, rhyme-roam, ripe-rope, side-sewed, tied-toad

Difficult to contrast:

[aɪ-eɪ] bite-bait, bride-braid, dial-dale, file-fail, mine-main, might-mate, ride-raid, strife-strafe, time-tame, trial-trail

[aɪ-ɑ] dike-dock, dine-Don, hide-hod, kite-cot, like-lock, ride-rod, shied-shod, site-sot, tyke-tock, wind-wand

[aɪ-ɔɪ] bile-boil, buys-boys, file-foil, lied-Lloyd, line-loin, pies-poise, ties-toys, tile-toil, vice-voice, vied-void

[aɪ-ʌ] crime-crumb, dial-dull, died-dud, dime-dumb, dine-done, height-hut, might-mutt, mile-mull, rhyme-rum, tine-ton

Sentence Practice

7. Read these sentences aloud:

Ida felt it a crime that Hiram should stride down the aisle with Eileen.

It's time to buy a nice limeade for a dime.

The tired tyke cried when Kyle tied a line to his kite.

Mike set the time of the crime at nine on the night of the ninth.

The shy guy was hired, grew tired, got fired, found his car mired, became ired, stopped looking for work, and retired.

PHONETIC [ɔɪ] DIACRITIC oi

	KEY WORD	VOCAL FOLDS	VELUM
	voice	Vibrating	Raised

DEVIATIONS

Learn to recognize each of the following deviations in the production of [ɔɪ]. *Eliminate from your speech all of those deviations which are not representative of the best speech in your region.*

1. Omission of [ɪ] so that *boil* sounds like [bɔl].
2. Overstressing of [ɔ] so that *boy* sounds like [bɔ͡ɔ͡ɔɪ].
3. Substitution of [ɑɪ] so that *oil* sounds like [ɑɪl].
4. Substitution of [ɝ] so that *oyster* sounds like [ɝstɚ].
5. Addition of [ə] so that *boil* sounds like [bɔɪəl].
6. Addition of [r] so that *boy* sounds like [bɔɪr].
7. Nasalized production of [ɔɪ]—most likely to occur in a word such as *noise.*

EXERCISES

Sound Practice

1. Articulate a series of staccato [ɔ] sounds.
   Articulate a series of staccato [ɪ] sounds.
   Alternately articulate [ɔ] and [ɪ].
   Articulate a series of staccato [ɔɪ] sounds.
2. Articulate these sound pairs: *Easy to contrast:* [ɔɪ-eɪ] [ɔɪ-ɑʊ] [ɔɪ-oʊ]
   Difficult to contrast: [ɔɪ-ɑɪ] [ɔɪ-ɔ] [ɔɪ-ɝ]

TECHNICAL DESCRIPTION	MOUTH	LIPS	TONGUE
[ɪ] diphthong	Open in position for [ɔ], closing during production to position for [ɪ]	Slightly rounded and slightly protruded in position for [ɔ], closing during production to position for [ɪ]	Tip behind lower front teeth, back arched slightly toward soft palate in position for [ɔ], front arches toward hard palate during production to position for [ɪ]

Syllable Practice

3. Articulate these syllables: [mɔɪ] [lɔɪ] [bɔɪ] [dɔɪ] [gɔɪ]
   [ɔɪm] [ɔɪl] [ɔɪb] [ɔɪd] [ɔɪg]
   [mɔɪm] [lɔɪl] [bɔɪb] [dɔɪd] [gɔɪg]

4. Articulate these syllable pairs:

   Easy to contrast: [mɔɪ-meɪ] [mɔɪ-maʊ] [mɔɪ-moʊ]
   [ɔɪm-eɪm] [ɔɪm-aʊm] [ɔɪm-oʊm]
   [mɔɪm-meɪm] [mɔɪm-maʊm] [mɔɪm-moʊm]

   Difficult to contrast: [mɔɪ-maɪ] [mɔɪ-mɔ] [mɔɪ-mɝ]
   [ɔɪm-aɪm] [ɔɪm-ɔm] [ɔɪm-ɝm]
   [mɔɪm-maɪm] [mɔɪm-mɔm] [mɔɪm-mɝm]

   Repeat by substituting [l], [b], [d], and [g] for [m].

Word Practice

5. Read these words aloud:

   Initial: oil, oilcloth, oiler, oilskin, oilstone, oily, ointment, oyster

   Medial: boil, boiler, boys, broil, choice, coil, coin, foil, join, joint, joist, Lloyd, loin, moist, noise, poise, point, royal, soil, spoil, roil, toys, voice, void

   Final: ahoy, alloy, annoy, boy, coy, decoy, deploy, destroy, employ, enjoy, envoy, joy, Roy, soy, toy, Troy

6. Read these word pairs aloud:

Easy to contrast:

[ɔɪ-eɪ] boil-bail, boys-bays, coin-cane, foil-fail, join-Jane, loin-lane, poise-pays, roil-rail, soil-sail, toil-tale

[ɔɪ-ɑʊ] alloyed-allowed, boys-boughs, coil-cowl, foil-fowl, Hoyle-howl, joist-joust, Lloyd-loud, royal-rowel, toil-towel, voile-vowel

[ɔɪ-oʊ] boil-bowl, coil-coal, coin-cone, foil-foal, Lloyd-load, loin-loan, moist-most, noise-nose, poise-pose, toil-toll

Difficult to contrast:

[ɔɪ-ɑɪ] boil-bile, boys-buys, foil-file, Lloyd-lied, loin-line, poise-pies, toys-ties, toil-tile, voice-vice, void-vied

[ʊ] *Diphthongs*

PHONETIC [ɑʊ] DIACRITIC **ou***

	KEY WORD	VOCAL FOLDS	VELUM
	how	Vibrating	Raised

DEVIATIONS

Learn to recognize each of the following deviations in the production of [ɑʊ]. *Eliminate from your speech all of those deviations which are not representative of the best speech in your region.*

1. Omission of [ʊ] so that *out* sounds like [ɑt].
2. Overstressing of [ɑ] so that *town* sounds like [tɑ͡ɑ͡ɑʊn].

* Many speakers produce this diphthong by combining the vowels [a] and [ʊ]. Therefore, the symbol [aʊ] is often used to represent this sound.

[ɔɪ-ɔ] boil-ball, broil-brawl, coil-call, foil-fall, Hoyle-hall, joint-jaunt, Lloyd-laud, noise-gnaws, poise-pause, toil-tall
[ɔɪ-ɝ] adjoin-adjourn, boil-burl, boys-burrs, coif-kerf, coil-curl, foil-furl, Hoyle-hurl, loin-learn, poise-purrs, voice-verse

Sentence Practice

7. Read these sentences aloud:

The toiling boys will soon return from the noisy joint on the point.
Flip a coin, Roy; you have a choice of oysters or poi.
The coy duck was overjoyed at the sight of the decoy.
The noisy boys enjoyed their toys, until Lloyd got annoyed.
The noise was choice outside the joint in which Boyd was employed.

TECHNICAL DESCRIPTION	MOUTH	LIPS	TONGUE
[ʊ] diphthong	Open in position for [ɑ], closing during production to position for [ʊ]	Open and rounded in position for [ɑ], closing during production to position for [ʊ]	Tip behind lower front teeth, back low, flat, and relaxed in position for [ɑ], arches toward soft palate during production to position for [ʊ]

3. Substitution of [æʊ] so that *now* sounds like [næʊ].
4. Substitution of [u] so that *out* sounds like [ut].
5. Substitution of [ʌ] so that *noun* sounds like [nʌn].
6. Addition of [ə] so that *cowl* sounds like [kɑʊəl].
7. Addition of [r] so that *now* sounds like [nɑʊr].
8. Nasalized production of [ɑʊ]—most likely to occur in a word such as *noun.*

EXERCISES

Sound Practice

1. Articulate a series of staccato [ɑ] sounds.
   Articulate a series of staccato [ʊ] sounds.
   Alternately articulate [ɑ] and [ʊ].
   Articulate a series of staccato [ɑʊ] sounds.
2. Articulate these sound pairs:

   Easy to contrast: [ɑʊ-eɪ] [ɑʊ-ɑɪ] [ɑʊ-oʊ]
   Difficult to contrast: [ɑʊ-æ] [ɑʊ-ɑ] [ɑʊ-u] [ɑʊ-ʌ]

Syllable Practice

3. Articulate these syllables: [mɑʊ] [lɑʊ] [bɑʊ] [dɑʊ] [gɑʊ]
   [ɑʊm] [ɑʊl] [ɑʊb] [ɑʊd] [ɑʊg]
   [mɑʊm] [lɑʊl] [bɑʊb] [dɑʊd] [gɑʊg]
4. Articulate these syllable pairs:

   Easy to contrast: [mɑʊ-meɪ] [mɑʊ-mɑɪ] [mɑʊ-moʊ]
   [ɑʊm-eɪm] [ɑʊm-ɑɪm] [ɑʊm-oʊm]
   [mɑʊm-meɪm] [mɑʊm-mɑɪm] [mɑʊm-moʊm]

   Difficult to contrast:
   [mɑʊ-mæ] [mɑʊ-mɑ] [mɑʊ-mu] [mɑʊ-mʌ]
   [ɑʊm-æm] [ɑʊm-ɑm] [ɑʊm-um] [ɑʊm-ʌm]
   [mɑʊm-mæm] [mɑʊm-mɑm] [mɑʊm-mum] [mɑʊm-mʌm]

   Repeat by substituting [l], [b], [d], and [g] for [m].

Word Practice

5. Read these words aloud:

   Initial: hourglass, ouch, ounce, our, ouster, out, outcast, outdo, outdoor, outfit, outgo, outlay, outlet, outline, outlook, owlish

Medial: bower, cloud, clown, cower, doubt, down, flower, foul, house, louse, mouse, mouth, proud, rout, south, towel

Final: allow, avow, bow, brow, chow, cow, endow, how, now, plow, pow-wow, prow, row, scow, sow, vow

6. Read these word pairs aloud:

Easy to contrast:

[ɑʊ-ɑɪ] boughs-bays, doubt-date, foul-fail, gouge-gauge, gout-gate, gown-gain, lout-late, pout-pate, rouse-raise, rout-rate

[ɑʊ-eɪ] bout-bite, crowd-cried, foul-file, found-find, loud-lied, louse-lice, plowed-plied, proud-pried, town-tine, vowed-vied

[ɑʊ-oʊ] boughs-bows, cowl-coal, crowd-crowed, doubt-dote, foul-foal, gout-goat, loud-load, rouse-rose, rout-wrote, town-tone

Difficult to contrast:

[ɑʊ-æ] bowed-bad, bout-bat, cloud-clad, couch-catch, cowed-cad, loud-lad, plowed-plaid, pout-pat, rout-rat, town-tan

[ɑʊ-ɑ] cloud-clod, cowed-cod, cower-car, down-don, gout-got, lout-lot, pound-pond, pout-pot, rout-rot, tower-tar

[ɑʊ-u] bout-boot, bowed-booed, cow-coo, cowl-cool, foul-fool, growl-gruel, lout-loot, louse-loose, mouse-moose, rouse-ruse

[ɑʊ-ʌ] bowed-bud, cowl-cull, dowel-dull, down-done, found-fund, gown-gun, howl-hull, pout-putt, rout-rut, town-ton

7. Read these sentences aloud:

There's a mouse in the house, get it out.
An hour after the shower the flower stood proudly by the tower.
The lout pouted about the house.
The clown gave a loud shout at the hound he found lying down.
Brown was proud of his snowplow.

PHONETIC [ou] DIACRITIC ō

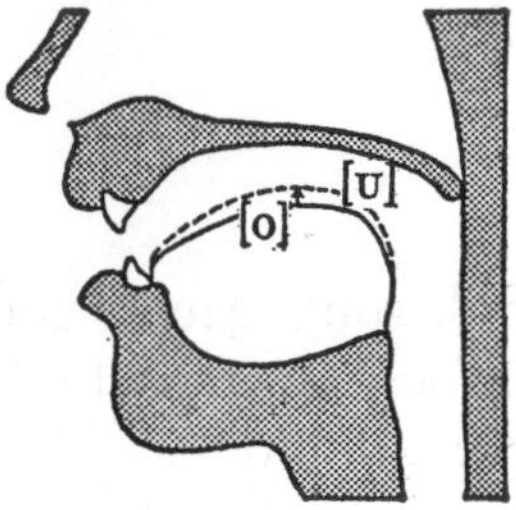

	KEY WORD	VOCAL FOLDS	VELUM
[o] [u]	*oat*	Vibrating	Raised

DEVIATIONS

Learn to recognize each of the following deviations in the production of [oʊ]. *Eliminate from your speech all of those deviations which are not representative of the best speech in your region.*

1. Omission of [ʊ] so that *goat* sounds like [got].
2. Overstressing of [o] so that *bowl* sounds like [bo͡o͡oʊl].
3. Substitution of [ɔ] so that *old* sounds like [ɔld].
4. Substitution of [ʊ] so that *oat* sounds like [ʊt].
5. Substitution of [ʌ] so that *old* sounds like [ʌld].
6. Addition of [ə] so that *bowl* sounds like [boʊəl].
7. Addition of [r] so that *low* sounds like [loʊr].
8. Nasalized production of [oʊ]—most likely to occur in a word such as *moan.*

EXERCISES

Sound Practice

1. Articulate a series of staccato [o] sounds.
   Articulate a series of staccato [ʊ] sounds.
   Alternately articulate [o] and [ʊ].
   Articulate a series of staccato [oʊ] sounds.
2. Articulate these sound pairs:

   Easy to contrast: [oʊ-eɪ] [oʊ-ɑɪ] [oʊ-ɑʊ].
   Difficult to contrast: [oʊ-ɔ] [oʊ-ʊ] [oʊ-ʌ]

TECHNICAL DESCRIPTION	MOUTH	LIPS	TONGUE
[ʊ] diphthong	Open slightly less than for [ɔ], closing during production to position for [ʊ]	Rounded and slightly more protruded than for [ɔ], closing during production to position for [ʊ]	Tip behind lower front teeth, back arched toward soft palate, slightly higher than for [ɔ], moving upward during production to position for [ʊ]

Syllable Practice

3. Articulate these syllables: [moʊ] [loʊ] [boʊ] [doʊ] [goʊ]
   [oʊm] [oʊl] [oʊb] [oʊd] [oʊg]
   [moʊm] [loʊl] [boʊb] [doʊd] [goʊg]
4. Articulate these syllable pairs:

   Easy to contrast: [moʊ-meɪ] [moʊ-maɪ] [moʊ-maʊ]
   [oʊm-eɪm] [oʊm-aɪm] [oʊm-aʊm]
   [moʊm-meɪm] [moʊm-maɪm] [moʊm-maʊm]
   Difficult to contrast: [moʊ-mɔ] [moʊ-mʊ] [moʊ-mʌ]
   [oʊm-ɔm] [oʊm-ʊm] [oʊm-ʌm]
   [moʊm-mɔm] [moʊm-mʊm] [moʊm-mʌm]

   Repeat by substituting [l], [b], [d], and [g] for [m].

Word Practice

5. Read these words aloud:

   Initial: oaf, oak, oat, oath, ochre, ode, ogre, ohm, old, only, opal, open, over, owe, own, ozone
   Medial: boat, coat, coke, hold, loaf, loam, loan, loath, rope, soap, sold, stoke, stone, toad, told, wrote
   Final: crow, dough, foe, go, grow, hoe, low, mow, no, sew, slow, snow, stow, throw, toe, woe

6. Read these word pairs aloud:

Easy to contrast:

[oʊ-eɪ] coke-cake, cone-cane, goat-gate, loam-lame, pole-pail, roan-rain, rose-raise, sole-sail, stoke-steak, wrote-rate

[oʊ-ɑɪ] boat-bite, coat-kite, dome-dime, foal-file, load-lied, loan-line, roam-rhyme, rope-ripe, sewed-side, toad-tide

[oʊ-ɑʊ] bows-boughs, coal-cowl, crowed-crowd, dote-doubt, foal-foul, goat-gout, load-loud, rose-rouse, tone-town, wrote-rout

Difficult to contrast:

[oʊ-ɔ] boat-bought, coat-caught, foal-fall, load-laud, loan-lawn, nose-gnaws, scold-scald, sewed-sawed, toll-tall, wrote-wrought

[oʊ-ʊ] bowl-bull, broke-brook, code-could, croak-crook, foal-full, hoed-hood, hoax-hooks, poled-pulled, showed-should, stowed-stood

[oʊ-ʌ] bowed-bud, choke-chuck, cloak-cluck, croaks-crux, code-cud, goal-gull, robe-rub, rogue-rug, scold-sculled, stroke-struck

Sentence Practice

7. Read these sentences aloud:

Go slow, Joe, you're stepping on my toe.
The roan has been roaming too far from home.
Rose was told there was no way to avoid growing old.
Opal broke her oath and wrote a note about her mother's stroke.
That load of coke and coal won't be sold.

10. Improving CONSONANT SOUND ARTICULATION

test your consonant sound articulation

Read the following words and sentences aloud while your instructor evaluates your consonant sound articulation.

PLOSIVES

[p] p (EXPLANATION AND EXERCISES, PP. 192-94.)

1. Ripping, rapid, wrapping, nap, grasp, pliers, open, apt, gap, hemp
   A competent employee is prized and amply paid by an employer.

[b] b (EXPLANATION AND EXERCISES, PP. 192-96.)

2. Rubbed, submarine, bat, tub, bulb, lobbed, ramble, bell, crib, blurb
   The boy stumbled on the lumber, tumbled backwards and broke a rib.

[t] t (EXPLANATION AND EXERCISES, PP. 196-99.)

3. Water, bottle, batter, tree, true, wait, mutter, rattle, debt, east
   Tony the waiter went for water, but coffee was what we wanted.

[d] d (EXPLANATION AND EXERCISES, PP. 196-201.)

4. Middle, bidder, fading, drip, dog, ladle, had, find, window, grandstand

Don wouldn't admit that his dairy had driven him deeper and deeper into debt.

[k] k (EXPLANATION AND EXERCISES, PP. 202-04.)

5. Coat, accident, can, come, like, picture, backing, car, cat, basked
   A weakness of Californians is that they like to claim they can bask in the clean, clear sunshine every week.

[g] g (EXPLANATION AND EXERCISES, PP. 202-06.)

6. Goal, trigger, glad, guess, beg, finger, great, green, forget, hungry
   In his eagerness to find a snug bed, the ragged beggar forgot his hunger.

NASALS

[m] m (EXPLANATION AND EXERCISES, PP. 206-08.)

7. My, foam, seem, came, somewhere, loom, something, hammer, am, empty
   Something tells me my memory may seem uncommon.

[m̩] 'm (EXPLANATION AND EXERCISES, P. 209.)

8. Chasm, criticism, egoism, heroism, optimism, prism, realism, spasm, truism, witticism
   His criticism of my patriotism is prompted by egoism or barbarism, not altruism.

[n] n (EXPLANATION AND EXERCISES, PP. 210-12.)

9. Sun, sign, token, window, panel, fine, train, noun, down, animal
   Don insisted he had never been warned to stay only until midnight.

[n̩] 'n (EXPLANATION AND EXERCISES, P. 213.)

10. Batten, button, chosen, cotton, dozen, fatten, kitten, prison, rotten, season
    My cousin has a dozen Persian kittens.

[ŋ] ng (EXPLANATION AND EXERCISES, PP. 214-16.)

11. Thing, bring, strength, singer, king, going, running, banging, wringer, hanging
    The lanky Mr. Long was angered by the banging and clanging coming from the skating rink.

FRICATIVES

[f] f (EXPLANATION AND EXERCISES, PP. 216-19.)

12. Fine, fleet, fly, after, careful, safe, wolf, different, gulf, surface
    It isn't safe for you to have a different rifle until you find out how to be careful.

[v] v (EXPLANATION AND EXERCISES, PP. 216-20.)

13. Vest, vat, veteran, saved, strived, valve, twelve, shelve, culvert, starves
    The veteran braved the violent river to save Vivian.

[s] s (EXPLANATION AND EXERCISES, PP. 220-23.)

14. Sing, sway, small, suspect, mister, gets, grasps, kiss, lisps, trusts
    It is said, "Slips of lips sank several ships."

[z] z (EXPLANATION AND EXERCISES, PP. 220-25.)

15. Zest, fuzzy, please, zebra, hazard, because, zero, pleasant, buzzes, sleeves
    The zoo refuses to keep zebras because none survives the freezing, subzero winters.

[θ] th (EXPLANATION AND EXERCISES, PP. 226-28.)

16. Ether, truth, thought, think, teeth, sixth, nothing, month, moth, three
    Both authors think thoughtless youth has no faith in truth.

[ð] t̶h̶ (EXPLANATION AND EXERCISES, PP. 226-30.)

17. Writhe, smooth, that, either, weather, they, wreathed, brother, bathe, these

Neither this brother nor the other will bother to soothe either father or mother.

[ʃ] sh (EXPLANATION AND EXERCISES, PP. 230-33.)

18. Fission, shake, short, crash, usher, brushing, washer, diction, anxious, show
    She showed tension initially but it diminished when she took an ocean vacation.

[ʒ] zh (EXPLANATION AND EXERCISES, PP. 230-35.)

19. Measure, derision, prestige, rouge, seizure, garage, regime, invasion, beige, pleasure
    Through an unusual delusion he envisions a life of immeasurable pleasure.

[h] h (EXPLANATION AND EXERCISES, PP. 236-37.)

20. Haven, behave, heat, behead, home, mishap, house, behalf, hire, inhabit
    He's unhappy, Harry, hand him his hat.

SEMIVOWELS

[r] r (EXPLANATION AND EXERCISES, PP. 238-40.)

21. Red, trial, pry, hear, very, bright, trial, there, dried, barrel
    She remains near tears, for she's made no real progress in reducing.

[l] l (EXPLANATION AND EXERCISES, PP. 240-43.)

22. Tell, like, silly, play, film, mail, lied, yellow, climb, elm
    Silently the hull of the old sailing sloop rolled over and gradually slipped lower and lower.

[l̩] 'l (EXPLANATION AND EXERCISES, P. 243.)

23. Battle, fable, kennel, kettle, metal, panel, riddle, table, vessel, whittle

He whittled on the middle of the table while he related the fable of the battle for the castle.

GLIDES

[ʍ] hw (EXPLANATION AND EXERCISES, PP. 244-46.)

24. Whale, awhile, whether, elsewhere, which, somewhat, where, bull-whip, when, flywheel
    Why do you whittle while White whispers?

[w] w (EXPLANATION AND EXERCISES, PP. 244-48.)

25. Word, awake, water, away, was, unwind, wear, twelve, wish, always
    Anyway, he's always aware of the worth of words.

[j] y (EXPLANATION AND EXERCISES, PP. 248-50.)

26. Yet, lawyer, yeast, onion, yesterday, vineyard, yak, million, yours, genial
    A year from yesterday you and your young companion were lost in the canyon.

[ju] ū (EXPLANATION AND EXERCISES, P. 251.)

27. Unify, unique, unit, useful, youth, abuse, beauty, news, due, retinue
    Unify the youth and you will have performed a useful new duty.

COMBINATIONS

[tʃ] ch (EXPLANATION AND EXERCISES, PP. 252-55.)

28. Etching, chain, matching, chair, scratch, rich, pitcher, much, question, literature
    He watched cheerfully as each child munched a cheese sandwich.

[dʒ] j (EXPLANATION AND EXERCISES, PP. 252-56.)

29. Edger, cage, judge, jester, jump, age, ledger, danger, cringe, stringent
    Jerry just broke his jaw jumping from the bridge.

*Name*____

Student produces the following consonant sounds accurately:

	Rating
1. [p]	____
2. [b]	____
3. [t]	____
4. [d]	____
5. [k]	____
6. [g]	____
7. [m]	____
8. [m̩]	____
9. [n]	____
10. [n̩]	____
11. [ŋ]	____
12. [f]	____
13. [v]	____
14. [s]	____
15. [z]	____
16. [θ]	____
17. [ð]	____
18. [ʃ]	____
19. [ʒ]	____
20. [h]	____
21. [r]	____
22. [l]	____
23. [l̩]	____
24. [ʍ]	____
25. [w]	____
26. [j]	____
27. [ju]	____
28. [tʃ]	____
29. [dʒ]	____
Total	____

Rating: It is suggested that the student be scored on a 5 to 1 point scale, 5 being used to indicate an excellent and 1 a poor rating.

Introduction The way we articulate consonants determines to a great extent how easily we are understood. That is not to say that speech is clear no matter what happens to the vowels; but only that, of the two, consonants can make our speech more distinct. Therefore, clear articulation of the consonants of American speech is central to effective communication.

There is a second reason for improving your production of consonants. The person who produces speech sounds carelessly inevitably gives the impression that he takes little trouble with other things. If you would clothe your thoughts in such a way as to attract your listeners, you should pay particular attention to your use of consonants.

A consonant differs from a vowel in that it is a speech sound which is produced by some blockage, restriction, or audible friction at some point in the breath channel, and which may or may not include vocal fold vibration. A vowel, as you will recall, is always voiced, that is, produced by vocal fold vibration, unless it is whispered. There is relatively little blockage in its production, and it has a sonority, whereas the consonant is mostly made up of noise elements (irregular vibrations). It is not possible, however, to distinguish consonants from vowels in terms of absolutely distinct characteristics. As we will see, some consonants have vowel-like qualities, and, as you know, some vowels are produced with some restriction of the outflowing breath.

Consonant Production

A chart has been included in order to assist you in understanding how consonant sounds are related (page 189). In comparing consonants it is helpful to consider each sound from three points of view. Consonants may be described according to their acoustical characteristics, the place of their articulation, and according to whether or not the vocal folds vibrate during their production.

Acoustically, a consonant sound may be described as plosive, nasal, fricative, semivowel, glide, or combination.

A *plosive* is a consonant sound produced by closing the breath channel completely, building up air pressure, and quickly releasing the impounded air. The plosives are [p], [b], [t], [d], [k], and [g].

A *nasal* is a consonant sound produced by lowering the velum, blocking the oral breath channel, and directing the air stream through the nose. The nasals are [m], [n], and [ŋ].

A *fricative* is a consonant sound produced by restricting the breath channel at some point so that audible friction results. The fricatives are [f], [v], [θ], [ð], [s], [z], [ʃ], [ʒ], and [h].

A *semivowel* is a consonant sound produced with the breath channel sufficiently open so that the sound has acoustic qualities resembling a vowel. The semivowels are [r] and [l].

A *glide* is a consonant sound produced with the articulators in motion during production, resulting in a continuous change in acoustic quality. The glides are [ʍ], [w], and [j].

A *combination* is a consonant sound produced by articulating certain plosive and fricative sounds in such rapid succession that they are merged into a single sound unit. The combinations are [tʃ] and [dʒ].

Classified according to their place of articulation, sounds may be designated as bilabial, labiodental, lingua-dental, lingua-alveolar, lingua-palatal, lingua-velar, and glottal.

A *bilabial* sound is so designated because the two lips are used in its articulation. The bilabial sounds are [p], [b], [m], [ʍ], and [w].

Labiodental sounds have this classification because the lower lip is in contact with the upper teeth during their production. The labiodental sounds are [f] and [v].

Lingua-dentals are thus identified because of their characteristic contact between the tongue and upper teeth. The lingua-dental sounds are [θ] and [ð].

The term *lingua-alveolar* refers to the fact that the tongue is in close proximity to the upper gum ridge as the sounds are produced. The lingua-alveolar sounds are [t], [d], [n], [s], [z], and [l].

Lingua-palatal sounds are so called because of the relationship between the tongue and hard palate during articulation. The lingua-palatal sounds are [ʃ], [ʒ], [r], [j], [tʃ], and [dʒ].

Lingua-velar sounds are those in which the back of the tongue contacts the soft palate during production. The lingua-velar sounds are [k], [g], and [ŋ].

The *glottal* sound is produced with the vocal folds open slightly and not vibrating, producing audible friction as the air stream passes through the glottis. The glottal sound is [h].

In addition to their acoustical characteristics and the place of their articulation, consonant sounds may be further described according to whether or not the vocal folds vibrate during their production. From this point of view they may be described as *voiced* (indicating that the vocal folds are in vibration), or *voiceless* (indicating an absence of vocal

CONSONANT CHART

		Bilabial *(two lips)*	Labio-dental *(lip-teeth)*	Lingua-dental *(tongue-teeth)*	Lingua-alveolar *(tongue-gum-ridge)*	Lingua-palatal *(tongue-hard palate)*	Lingua-velar *(tongue-soft palate)*	Glottal *(vocal folds)*
Plosives	*Voiceless*	[p]			[t]		[k]	
	Voiced	[b]			[d]		[g]	
Nasals	*Voiced*	[m]			[n]		[ŋ]	
Fricatives	*Voiceless*		[f]	[θ]	[s]	[ʃ]		[h]
	Voiced		[v]	[ð]	[z]	[ʒ]		
Semivowels	*Voiced*				[l]	[r]		
Glides	*Voiceless*	[ʍ]						
	Voiced	[w]				[j]		
Combinations	*Voiceless*					[tʃ]		
	Voiced					[dʒ]		

fold vibration). Some of the consonants are produced with the articulators in exactly the same position, the difference in their sounds depending on whether or not the vocal folds are vibrating. For example, to make the sounds [b] and [p], the position of the articulators is exactly the same. However, the [b] is made with the vocal folds vibrating, whereas the [p] is unvoiced. Put your finger on your Adam's apple and feel the vibration as you produce the sound of [b] in saying *bad.* Now say *pad.* Until you start to say the *a,* your vocal folds will not vibrate in saying *pad.* Compare the [d] and [t] in *dad* and *tad,* the [g] and [k] in *gold* and *cold,* [v] and [f] in *vile* and *file.* In the lists of consonants which follow, see which voiced and voiceless consonants can be paired in this way by being produced with the articulators in the same position. Not all of them can.

The voiced consonant sounds are [b], [d], [g], [m], [n], [ŋ], [v], [ð], [z], [ʒ], [l], [r], [w], [j], and [dʒ]. The voiceless consonant sounds are [p], [t], [k], [f], [θ], [s], [ʃ], [h], [ʍ], and [tʃ].

We found, in discussing vowels, that there may be more than one way of shaping the oral cavity for the production of each vowel sound. A great variety of positions of the tongue, lips, and mouth can be used to produce a sound recognizable as one and the same vowel. No such latitude is found in the articulation of consonants, although even here some variation is possible. Therefore, in the exercises which follow, you should pay particular attention to the position of the articulators for each consonant, since in each case it will indicate how the consonant should be produced.

There are certain common errors to watch for in articulating consonants. Careful and respected speakers in any part of this country seldom make the following errors:

1. Consonant articulation that is not clear. This results in lazy speech. The articulators move sluggishly and are often in the wrong position for the production of many consonants. Words are often misunderstood, and the listener has to strain to catch their meaning. If this is a weakness in your own speech, the exercises which follow should do a great deal to remedy the fault.

2. Overprecise articulation. This is less common, but it is just as offensive as slovenly articulation. There is a danger that in practicing words in isolation your speech may tend to become too precise. Make sure, as you practice full sentences, that your words are clear and yet flow together naturally, that no particular word is articulated so pre-

cisely as to make it stand apart from the rest, unless of course you intend a rhetorical effect.

3. Substitution of one consonant for another. Certain substitutions that are frequently made will be discussed under the individual consonants.

4. Omission of a consonant, such as the first *r* in *library*.

5. Addition of other sounds to the required consonant.

Plosives

PHONETIC [p] DIACRITIC p

KEY WORD		VOCAL FOLDS	VELUM
[p]	*peep*	Not vibrating	Raised
[b]	*bib*	Vibrating	

DEVIATIONS for [p]

1. Substitution of [b] so that *play* sounds like [bleɪ].
2. Substitution of [m] so that *open* sounds like ['oumən].
3. Substitution of [f] so that *mapped* sounds like [mæft].
4. Addition of [ə] so that *cap* sounds like ['kæpə].
5. Omission of [p] so that *rasp* sounds like [ræs].
6. Insufficient pressure in production. This sound distortion is the result of insufficient closure of the lips so that air pressure does not build up to produce the required explosion.
7. Excessive pressure in production. This sound distortion occurs when the lips are pressed together so tightly that the resultant sound is too explosive.

EXERCISES for [p]

Sound Practice

1. Articulate a series of staccato [p] sounds.
2. Articulate these sound pairs: *Easy to contrast:* [p-t] [p-k] [p-n]
   Difficult to contrast: [p-b] [p-m] [p-f]

Syllable Practice

3. Articulate these syllables: [pi] [paɪ] [poʊ] [pʌm]
   [ip] [aɪp] [oʊp] [ʌp]
   [pip] [paip] [poʊp] [pʌp]

PHONETIC [b] DIACRITIC ḃ

TECHNICAL DESCRIPTION	MOUTH	LIPS	TONGUE
Bilabial plosive consonant	Closed	Pressed firmly together, impounding the column of air under pressure until released suddenly	Neutral

4. Articulate these syllable pairs:

   Easy to contrast: [ip-it] [ip-ik] [ip-in]
   [pi-ti] [pi-ki] [pi-ni]
   [ipi-iti] [ipi-iki] [ipi-ini]
   Difficult to contrast: [ip-ib] [ip-im] [ip-if]
   [pi-bi] [pi-mi] [pi-fi]
   [ipi-ibi] [ipi-imi] [ipi-ifi]

   Repeat by substituting [ɑɪ], [oʊ], and [ʌ] for [i].

Word Practice

5. Read these words aloud:

   Initial: pad, pack, pat, peat, peck, pet, pit, purse
   Medial: aperture, coupon, open, opera, opposite, optic, rapid, upon
   Final: cap, cup, dip, gap, lip, map, rip, top
   Special [p] *combinations:* play, please, culprit, help, slept, supped, clamp, hemp, pray, price, carp, harp, bumped, slumped, clasped, grasped, gasp, hasp, splash, splice, spry, sprout, leaps, props

6. Read these word pairs aloud:

   Easy to contrast:
   [p-t] pack-tack, pear-tare, prowl-trowel, sipper-sitter, supper-Sutter, supple-subtle, upper-utter, cap-cat, cup-cut, pup-putt
   [p-k] pat-cat, pleat-cleat, pride-cried, mopped-mocked, open-oaken, sapped-sacked, wrapped-wracked, lap-lack, nap-knack, rap-rack

[p-n] pat-gnat, pet-net, purse-nurse, capped-canned, mapped-manned, sipper-sinner, supped-sunned, grip-grin, pup-pun, tap-tan

Difficult to contrast:

[p-b] pad-bad, peak-beak, pear-bear, mopped-mobbed, rapid-rabid, ripping-ribbing, sups-subs, lop-lob, nap-nab, sop-sob

[p-m] pad-mad, peal-meal, pill-mill, open-omen, seeped-seamed, stepped-stemmed, wrapped-rammed, dip-dim, lip-limb, slap-slam

[p-f] pad-fad, peal-feel, pill-fill, dipper-differ, lapping-laughing, supper-suffer, wrapped-raft, cap-calf, cup-cuff, tip-tiff

Sentence Practice

7. Read these sentences aloud:

The porter mopped off the top of his cap.
Pete had plenty of potatoes but no apple pie.
Pert Penelope playfully plowed the potato patch.
Pearl pleaded with Paul to put down his pipe.
Pat awoke from a nap, ate a pear, dropped the core, flopped on the floor, and slept some more.

DEVIATIONS for [b]

1. Substitution of [p] so that *robed* sounds like [roʊpt].
2. Substitution of [m] so that *sunburn* sounds like ['sʌnmɚn].
3. Substitution of [v] so that *boat* sounds like [voʊt].
4. Addition of [ə] so that *tribe* sounds like ['traɪbə].
5. Omission of [b] so that *clamber* sounds like ['klæmɚ].
6. Insufficient pressure in production. This sound distortion is the result of insufficient closure of the lips, so that air pressure does not build up to produce the required explosion.
7. Excessive pressure in production. This sound distortion occurs when the lips are pressed together so tightly that the resultant sound is too explosive.

EXERCISES for [b]

Sound Practice

1. Articulate a series of staccato [b] sounds.
2. Articulate these sound pairs: *Easy to contrast:* [b-d] [b-g] [b-n]
   Difficult to contrast: [b-p] [b-m] [b-v]

Syllable Practice

3. Articulate these syllables: [bi] [bɑɪ] [boʊ] [bʌm]
   [ib] [ɑɪb] [oʊb] [ʌb]
   [ibi] [ɑɪbɑɪ] [oʊboʊ] [ʌbʌ]
4. Articulate these syllable pairs:

   Easy to contrast: [ib-id] [ib-ig] [ib-in]
   [bi-di] [bi-gi] [bi-ni]
   [ibi-idi] [ibi-igi] [ibi-ini]
   Difficult to contrast: [ib-ip] [ib-im] [ib-iv]
   [bi-pi] [bi-mi] [bi-vi]
   [ibi-ipi] [ibi-imi] [ibi-ivi]

   Repeat by substituting [ɑɪ], [oʊ], and [ʌ] for [i].

Word Practice

5. Read these words aloud:

   Initial: bad, back, bat, bead, bet, book, bought, bundle
   Medial: dauber, ebbing, fibbing, grubbing, ribbing, robbing, rubbing, stabbing
   Final: cab, crib, fib, rib, rub, stab, tab, tub
   Special [b] *combinations:* blast, blimp, blouse, blue, bulb, bulbous, Elbe, elbow, daubed, nabbed, robed, rubbed, break, brother, brown, brute, barb, carbon, proverb, verb, curbed, disturbed, garbed, perturbed

6. Read these word pairs aloud:

   Easy to contrast:
   [b-d] bay-day, bell-dell, bet-debt, cubs-cuds, dubs-duds, ribs-rids, subs-suds, cab-cad, curb-curd, rib-rid

[b-g] ball-gall, bill-gill, bowl-goal, ebbing-egging, rabid-ragged, ribs-rigs, tubbing-tugging, rub-rug, tab-tag, tub-tug

[b-n] bat-gnat, bell-knell, bite-night, dubs-duns, robes-roans, rubbing-running, subbing-sunning, cab-can, tab-tan, tub-ton

Difficult to contrast:

[b-p] bad-pad, beak-peak, bear-pear, mobbed-mopped, rabid-rapid, ribbing-ripping, subs-sups, lob-lop, nab-nap, sob-sop

[b-m] bad-mad, bet-met, bill-mill, bobs-bombs, cabs-cams, ribs-rims, subs-sums, dub-dumb, rub-rum, tab-tam

[b-v] base-vase, bat-vat, berry-very, dubs-doves, rabble-ravel, ribber-river, robes-roves, cab-calve, curb-curve, dub-dove

PHONETIC [t] DIACRITIC t

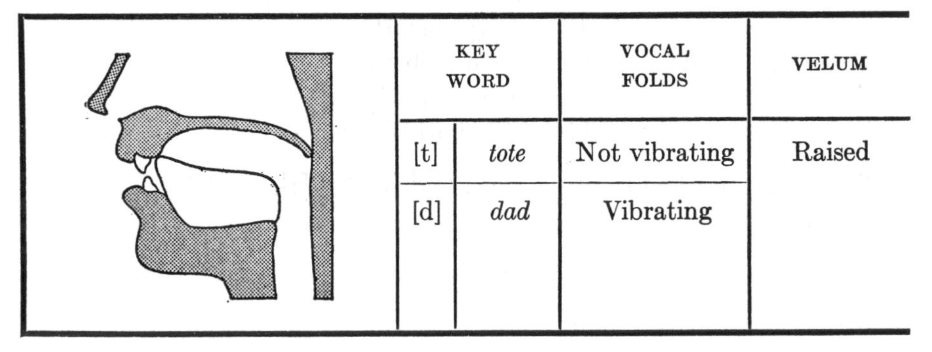

KEY WORD		VOCAL FOLDS	VELUM
[t]	*tote*	Not vibrating	Raised
[d]	*dad*	Vibrating	

DEVIATIONS for [t]

1. Substitution of [d] so that *fatter* sounds like ['fædɚ].
2. Substitution of [n] so that *bitter* sounds like ['bɪnɚ].
3. Substitution of [s] so that *water* sounds like ['wɑsɚ].
4. Substitution of [θ] so that *trip* sounds like [θrɪp].
5. Substitution of [k] so that *best* sounds like [bɛsk].
6. Substitution of the glottal stop [ʔ] so that *bottle* sounds like ['bɑʔl̩].*
7. Addition of [ə] so that *get* sounds like ['gɛtə].

* This sound is actually a plosive sound produced by the vocal folds being pressed together firmly, impounding the column of air under pressure, then releasing it suddenly with an explosive sound. This sound should never be used in General American speech.

Sentence Practice

7. Read these sentences aloud:

Bob's bulldog broke into the bookstore and browsed through the Browning collection.

Burt worked like a beaver getting beetles for bait but the balky fish wouldn't bite.

From the bottom of the baseball stadium came the belligerent bellow, "Hey, Bub, I'll break your back if you boot that ball."

Billy bundled the baby into her bed and picked up a book.

Babs bought balloons for the baby, a ball for Betty and a bobsled for the boys.

PHONETIC [d] DIACRITIC d

TECHNICAL DESCRIPTION	MOUTH	LIPS	TONGUE
Lingua-alveolar plosive consonant	Nearly closed	Neutral	Tip pressed firmly against upper gum-ridge; sides pressed firmly against upper teeth, impounding the column of air under pressure, released suddenly

8. Omission of [t] so that *kept* sounds like [kɛp].
9. Dentalization of [t]. This sound distortion, common among Europeans speaking English, is the result of pressing the tongue against upper teeth rather than against upper gum-ridge.
10. Insufficient pressure in production. This sound distortion is the result of insufficient contact between tongue and gum-ridge so that air pressure does not build up to produce the required explosion.
11. Excessive pressure in production. This sound distortion occurs when the tongue is pressed against the upper gum-ridge so tightly that the resultant sound is too explosive.

EXERCISES for [t]

Sound Practice

1. Articulate a series of staccato [t] sounds.
2. Articulate these sound pairs:

   Easy to contrast: [t-p] [t-b] [t-m]
   Difficult to contrast: [t-d] [t-n] [t-s] [t-θ] [t-k]

Syllable Practice

3. Articulate these syllables: [ti] [taɪ] [toʊ] [tʌm]
   [it] [aɪt] [oʊt] [ʌt]
   [iti] [aɪtaɪ] [oʊtoʊ] [ʌtʌ]
4. Articulate these syllable pairs:

   Easy to contrast: [it-ip] [it-ib] [it-im]
   [ti-pi] [ti-bi] [ti-mi]
   [iti-ipi] [iti-ibi] [iti-imi]
   Difficult to contrast: [it-id] [it-in] [it-is] [it-iθ] [it-ik]
   [ti-di] [ti-ni] [ti-si] [ti-θi] [ti-ki]
   [iti-idi] [iti-ini] [iti-isi] [iti-iθi] [iti-iki]

   Repeat by substituting [aɪ], [oʊ], and [ʌ] for [i].

Word Practice

5. Read these words aloud:

   Initial: tack, tap, tell, test, toast, top, took, turn
   Medial: beating, dating, flitting, floating, getting, goats, greets, rooting
   Final: bat, beat, cot, hat, met, put, sat, sought
   Special [t] *combinations:* trail, tree, twine, twirl, eighth, lots, stray, fished, wished, filched, battle, pert, slept, wrapped, unkempt, raft, stuffed, bent, balked, stalked, melt, tilt, first, last

6. Read these word pairs aloud:

   Easy to contrast:
   [t-p] tack-pack, tear-pear, trowel-prowl, sitter-sipper, subtle-supple, Sutter-supper, utter-upper, cat-cap, cut-cup, putt-pup
   [t-b] tall-ball, tell-bell, till-bill, cats-cabs, cuts-cubs, rattle-rabble, rots-robs, curt-curb, fit-fib, rut-rub

[t-m] tail-mail, tie-my, toast-most, cats-cams, cuts-comes, gates-games, sitter-simmer, rat-ram, seat-seem, tight-time

Difficult to contrast:

[t-d] tale-dale, tie-die, tip-dip, beating-beading, goats-goads, rating-raiding, sights-sides, bet-bed, right-ride, sat-sad

[t-n] tale-nail, tap-nap, took-nook, batting-banning, boats-bones, rating-raining, sighting-signing, cat-can, gate-gain, pat-pan

[t-s] tale-sail, tap-sap, tie-sigh, getting-guessing, greeting-greasing, patting-passing, rating-racing, curt-curse, let-less, right-rice

[t-θ] tank-thank, taught-thought, tree-three, eater-ether, mitts-myths, pity-pithy, rootless-ruthless, boat-both, debt-death, dirt-dearth

[t-k] tall-call, tap-cap, teen-keen, batting-backing, mates-makes, pats-packs, rating-raking, bat-back, debt-deck, light-like

Sentence Practice

7. Read these sentences aloud:

Tom stood on tip-toe to reach a carton of tomatoes.

"Tell me, Tim, was it two minutes of ten or ten minutes of two when you quit?"

To tell the truth, Sutter has a rating as a first-rate eater.

Ted and Theresa took turns teasing the cat.

He put a light bet on a horse named Kate who got started late, bumped a mate, tried to tempt fate and broke the pate of her jockey, Nate.

DEVIATIONS for [d]

1. Substitution of [t] so that *had* sounds like [hæt].
2. Substitution of [n] so that *bad* sounds like [bæn].
3. Substitution of [z] so that *dog* sounds like [zɑg].
4. Substitution of [ð] so that *drip* sounds like [ðrɪp].
5. Substitution of [g] so that *doubt* sounds like [gaʊt].
6. Substitution of the glottal stop [ʔ] so that *middle* sounds like ['mɪʔl̩]. (See footnote to chart on [t] and [d] in this chapter.)
7. Addition of [ə] so that *bid* sounds like ['bɪdə].
8. Omission of [d] so that *find* sounds like [faɪn].
9. Dentalization of [d]. This sound distortion, common among Euro-

peans speaking English, is the result of pressing the tongue against upper teeth rather than against upper gum-ridge.

10. Insufficient pressure in production. This sound distortion is the result of insufficient contact between tongue and gum-ridge so that air pressure does not build up to produce the required explosion.
11. Excessive pressure in production. This sound distortion occurs when the tongue is pressed against the upper gum ridge so tightly that the resultant sound is too explosive.

EXERCISES for [d]

Sound Practice

1. Articulate a series of staccato [d] sounds.
2. Articulate these sound pairs:

   Easy to contrast: [d-b] [d-p] [d-m]
   Difficult to contrast: [d-t] [d-n] [d-z] [d-ð] [d-g]

Syllable Practice

3. Articulate these syllables: [di] [daɪ] [doʊ] [dʌm]
   [id] [aɪd] [oʊd] [ʌd]
   [idi] [aɪdaɪ] [oʊdoʊ] [ʌdʌ]
4. Articulate these syllable pairs:

   Easy to contrast: [id-ib] [id-ip] [id-im]
   [di-bi] [di-pi] [di-mi]
   [idi-ibi] [idi-ipi] [idi-imi]
   Difficult to contrast: [id-it] [id-in] [id-iz] [id-ið] [id-ig]
   [di-ti] [di-ni] [di-zi] [di-ði] [di-gi]
   [idi-iti] [idi-ini] [idi-izi] [idi-iði] [idi-igi]

   Repeat by substituting [ɑɪ], [oʊ], and [ʌ] for [i].

Word Practice

5. Read these words aloud:

   Initial: dale, date, deep, desk, dill, dip, do, down
   Medial: grading, greedy, lady, maiden, midnight, reading, shady, wedding

Final: Bud, clad, deed, head, hid, made, sad, said

Special [d] *combinations:* draw, dwell, width, words, rouged, caged, urged, fiddle, filmed, dabbed, scrubbed, curved, saved, bathed, writhed, canned, lend, gigged, banged, failed, skilled, lard, scarred, hazed

6. Read these word pairs aloud:

Easy to contrast:

[d-b] dale-bail, day-bay, die-buy, cads-cabs, bids-bibs, rods-robs, wedding-webbing, tried-tribe, rod-rob, sod-sob

[d-p] dale-pail, day-pay, die-pie, addle-apple, cads-caps, reading-reaping, suds-sups, hid-hip, mad-map, sad-sap

[d-m] day-may, die-my, dale-mail, cads-cams, ridding-rimming, shading-shaming, suds-sums, clad-clam, lid-limb, tied-time

Difficult to contrast:

[d-t] dale-tail, die-tie, dip-tip, beading-beating, bides-bites, goads-goats, sides-sights, bed-bet, ride-right, sad-sat

[d-n] dale-nail, die-nigh, dip-nip, grades-grains, paddle-panel, raiding-raining, sides-signs, died-dine, pad-pan, seed-seen

[d-z] deal-zeal, dip-zip, do-zoo, grading-grazing, lady-lazy, raiding-razing, riding-rising, hid-his, seed-seize, sighed-size

[d-ð] dare-their, den-then, dense-thence, fodder-father, ladder-lather, reads-wreathes, riding-writhing, bayed-bathe, tied-tithe, sued-soothe

[d-g] dale-gale, dole-goal, down-gown, bedding-begging, buddy-buggy, lads-lags, rids-rigs, bid-big, did-dig, lead-league

Sentence Practice

7. Read these sentences aloud:

Being good he understood, and being bad made him sad, but being bold left him cold.

He agreed to concede if he could be freed.

Dale's dad died in the stampede for gold.

Buddy drove the sedan down the grade and rolled it over the ledge.

Did Donald do this dastardly deed?

PHONETIC [k] DIACRITIC k

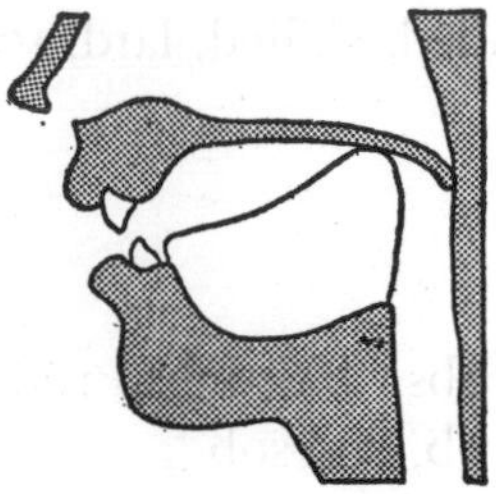

KEY WORD		VOCAL FOLDS	VELUM
[k]	*kick*	Not vibrating	Raised
[g]	*gag*	Vibrating	

DEVIATIONS for [k]

1. Substitution of [g] so that *tacking* sounds like ['tægɪŋ].
2. Substitution of [ŋ] so that *stacking* sounds like ['stæŋɪŋ].
3. Substitution of [t] so that *cat* sounds like [tæt].
4. Substitution of [s] so that *come* sounds like [sʌm].
5. Addition of [ə] so that *back* sounds like ['bækə].
6. Omission of [k] so that *masked* sounds like [mæst].
7. Insufficient pressure in production. This sound distortion is the result of insufficient contact between tongue and velum so that air pressure does not build up to produce the required explosion.
8. Excessive pressure in production. This sound distortion occurs when the back of the tongue is pressed against the soft palate so tightly that the resultant sound is too explosive.

EXERCISES for [k]

Sound Practice

1. Articulate a series of staccato [k] sounds.
2. Articulate these sound pairs:

   Easy to contrast: [k-p] [k-b] [k-m]
   Difficult to contrast: [k-g] [k-n] [k-t] [k-s]

Syllable Practice

3. Articulate these syllables: [ki] [kɑɪ] [koʊ] [kʌm]

PHONETIC [g] DIACRITIC g

TECHNICAL DESCRIPTION	MOUTH	LIPS	TONGUE
Lingua-velar plosive consonant	Open halfway	Neutral	Tip behind lower front teeth, back arched and pressed firmly against soft palate, impounding the column of air under pressure, released suddenly

[ik] [aɪk] [oʊk] [ʌk]
[iki] [aɪkaɪ] [oʊkoʊ] [ʌkʌ]

4. Articulate these syllable pairs:

Easy to contrast: [ik-ip] [ik-ib] [ik-im]
[ki-pi] [ki-bi] [ki-mi]
[iki-ipi] [iki-ibi] [iki-imi]
Difficult to contrast: [ik-ig] [ik-in] [ik-it] [ik-is]
[ki-gi] [ki-ni] [ki-ti] [ki-si]
[iki-igi] [iki-ini] [iki-iti] [iki-isi]

Repeat by substituting [aɪ], [oʊ], and [ʌ] for [i].

Word Practice

5. Read these words aloud:

Initial: call, can, cat, cod, come, cull, keep, kit
Medial: balking, boxing, brooks, cheeks, lacks, raking, seeking, thinking
Final: deck, lack, like, mock, oak, stake, streak, stroke
Special [k] *combinations:* claw, clue, crew, quiet, asked, basked, corrects, deflects, asks, tusks, bunks, skunks, disc, scheme, scream, prank, think, bilk, silk, arc, lurk, excuse, banked, thanked

6. Read these word pairs aloud:

Easy to contrast:
[k-p] cat-pat, cleat-pleat, cried-pride, mocked-mopped, oaken-

open, sacked-sapped, wracked-wrapped, lack-lap, knack-nap, tack-tap

[k-b] call-ball, kill-bill, kite-bite, bakes-babes, rocker-robber, stacking-stabbing, tacking-tabbing, bark-barb, rick-rib, stuck-stub

[k-m] cute-mute, keel-meal, kill-mill, making-maiming, seeking-seeming, stacker-stammer, streaks-streams, lack-lamb, like-lime, rack-ram

Difficult to contrast:

[k-g] clean-glean, cot-got, kill-gill, lacks-lags, picks-pigs, sacked-sagged, tacking-tagging, knack-nag, leak-league, rack-rag

[k-ŋ] backing-banging, bricks-brings, clicking-clinging, picks-pings, sticks-stings, amuck-among, rack-rang, slack-slang, struck-strung, thick-thing

[k-t] call-tall, cap-tap, keen-teen, backing-batting, makes-mates, packs-pats, raking-rating, back-bat, deck-debt, like-light

[k-s] cat-sat, coal-soul, kale-sail, braking-bracing, raked-raced, seeking-ceasing, spiking-spicing, like-lice, peak-peace, rake-race

Sentence Practice

7. Read these sentences aloud:

Call Kenneth, Catherine; the kite is stuck in the top of the big oak.
Rick, the detective, asked the crew for some clue as to the trunk hidden under the bunk.
"Excuse me for thinking you were trying to bilk me," exclaimed the thankful banker.
He lacked the knack of keeping his cat away from the codfish.
Katrinka thought Kit would commend her for her cleverness.

DEVIATIONS for [g]

1. Substitution of [k] so that *dog* sounds like [dɑk].
2. Substitution of [ŋ] so that *rugged* sounds like ['rʌŋɪd].
3. Substitution of [d] so that *grew* sounds like [dru].
4. Substitution of [z] so that *get* sounds like [zɛt].
5. Addition of [ə] so that *peg* sounds like ['pɛgə].
6. Omission of [g] so that *exact* sounds like [ɛ'zækt].
7. Insufficient pressure in production. This sound distortion is the re-

sult of insufficient contact between tongue and velum so that air pressure does not build up to produce the required explosion.

8. Excessive pressure in production. This sound distortion occurs when the back of the tongue is pressed against the soft palate so tightly that the resultant sound is too explosive.

EXERCISES for [g]

Sound Practice

1. Articulate a series of staccato [g] sounds.
2. Articulate these sound pairs:

   Easy to contrast: [g-b] [g-p] [g-m]
   Difficult to contrast: [g-k] [g-ŋ] [g-d] [g-z]

Syllable Practice

3. Articulate these syllables: [gi] [gɑɪ] [goʊ] [gʌm]
   [ig] [ɑɪg] [oʊg] [ʌg]
   [igi] [ɑɪgɑɪ] [oʊgoʊ] [ʌgʌ]
4. Articulate these syllable pairs:

   Easy to contrast: [ig-ib] [ig-ip] [ig-im]
   [gi-bi] [gi-pi] [gi-mi]
   [igi-ibi] [igi-ipi] [igi-imi]
   Difficult to contrast: [ig-ik] [ig-iŋ] [ig-id] [ig-iz]
   [gi-ki] [gi-ŋi] [gi-di] [gi-zi]
   [igi-iki] [igi-iŋi] [igi-idi] [igi-izi]

   Repeat by substituting [ɑɪ], [oʊ], and [ʌ] for [i].

Word Practice

5. Read these words aloud:

   Initial: gas, gauge, gay, gaze, geese, go, gust, guy
   Medial: aghast, again, against, ago, agree, egress, forget, forgive
   Final: bag, beg, big, brag, fog, keg, lag, stag
   Special [g] *combinations:* glass, glimpse, glue, grand, great, grew, bagged, lagged, rigged, tugged, begs, exact, hugs, pigs, tags, argue, burgh, organ, anguish, finger, language, angle, single, tingle

6. Read these word pairs aloud:

Easy to contrast:

[g-b] gall-ball, gill-bill, goal-bowl, egging-ebbing, ragged-rabid, rigs-ribs, tugging-tubbing, rug-rub, tag-tab, tug-tub

[g-p] gay-pay, gear-pier, gig-pig, lagging-lapping, ragged-rapid, sagged-sapped, trigger-tripper, gag-gap, lag-lap, pug-pup

[g-m] gale-male, gill-mill, goal-mole, hugging-humming, rags-rams, rigs-rims, trigger-trimmer, lag-lamb, rug-rum, tag-tam

Difficult to contrast:

[g-k] glean-clean, gill-kill, got-cot, lags-lacks, pigs-picks, sagged-sacked, tagging-tacking, league-leak, nag-knack, rag-rack

[g-ŋ] bags-bangs, logging-longing, pigs-pings, rigs-rings, rugs-rungs, brig-bring, gag-gang, sag-sang, slag-slang, tag-tang

Nasals

PHONETIC [m] DIACRITIC m

	KEY WORD	VOCAL FOLDS	VELUM
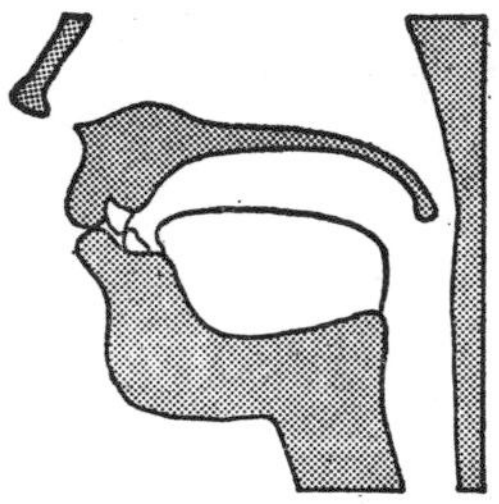	*maimed*	Vibrating	Lowered

DEVIATIONS

1. Substitution of [b] so that *me* sounds like [bi].
2. Substitution of [n] so that *some* sounds like [sʌn].
3. Substitution of [ŋ] so that *some* sounds like [sʌŋ].
4. Addition of [ə] so that *him* sounds like [ˈhɪmə].
5. Omission of [m] so that *elm* sounds like [ɛl].

EXERCISES

Sound Practice

1. Articulate a series of staccato [m] sounds.

[g-d] gale-dale, goal-dole, gown-down, begging-bedding, buggy-buddy, lags-lads, rigs-rids, big-bid, dig-did, league-lead
[g-z] gander-zander, goose-Zeus, guest-zest, bigness-business, bug-buzz, dug-does, fig-fizz, hag-has, jag-jazz, rogue-rose

Sentence Practice

7. Read these sentences aloud:

Gladys, go get gas at the green garage.
His language was anguished as he argued against his grandfather.
Gus, go get the geese, and don't forget to feed the pigs.
Gail glued the picture against the green glass.
The guests gave Gussie gorgeous gifts.

TECHNICAL DESCRIPTION	MOUTH	LIPS	TONGUE
Bilabial nasal consonant	Nearly closed	Pressed lightly together	Neutral

2. Articulate these sound pairs: *Easy to contrast:* [m-t] [m-d] [m-k]
Difficult to contrast: [m-b] [m-n] [m-ŋ]

Syllable Practice

3. Articulate these syllables: [mi] [mɑɪ] [moʊ] [mʌm]
[im] [ɑɪm] [oʊm] [ʌm]
[imi] [ɑɪmɑɪ] [oʊmoʊ] [ʌmʌ]
4. Articulate these syllable pairs:

Easy to contrast: [im-it] [im-id] [im-ik]
[mi-ti] [mi-di] [mi-ki]
[imi-iti] [imi-idi] [imi-iki]

Difficult to contrast: [im-ib] [im-in][im-iŋ]
[mi-bi] [mi-ni] [mi-ŋi]
[imi-ibi] [imi-ini] [imi-iŋi]

Repeat by substituting [ɑɪ], [oʊ], and [ʌ] for [i].

Word Practice

5. Read these words aloud:

Initial: many, may, meek, more, mouse, move, mule, my
Medial: among, coming, common, lemon, roamed, summons, surmise, swimming
Final: come, home, lamb, loom, seem, tame, time, tomb
Special [m] *combinations:* lamp, limp, tramp, slumped, stomped, trumped, framed, rhymed, roomed, mumps, romps, sums, tombs, smash, smile, smirk, elm, film, overwhelm, arm, firm, form, alarmed, stormed

6. Read these word pairs aloud:

Easy to contrast:
[m-t] male-tale, my-tie, most-toast, cams-cats, comes-cuts, games-gates, simmer-sitter, ram-rat, seem-seat, time-tight
[m-d] male-dale, may-day, my-die, cams-cads, rimming-ridding, shaming-shading, sums-suds, clam-clad, limb-lid, time-tide
[m-k] meal-keel, mill-kill, mute-cute, maiming-making, seeming-seeking, stammer-stacker, streams-streaks, lamb-lack, lime-like, ram-rack

Difficult to contrast:
[m-b] mad-bad, met-bet, mill-bill, bombs-bobs, cams-cabs, rims-ribs, sums-subs, dumb-dub, rum-rub, tam-tab
[m-n] mat-gnat, met-net, my-nigh, coming-cunning, games-gains, roams-roans, simmer-sinner, dumb-done, rum-run, time-tine
[m-ŋ] brimming-bringing, hams-hangs, rimming-ringing, rums-rungs, simmer-singer, hum-hung, ram-rang, slam-slang, slim-sling, tam-tang

Sentence Practice

7. Read these sentences aloud:

Many men remember Maude, the meek timid mule.

Mabel remembers the millstream lined with many elms.
Slim Sam, the home run slammer, hummed each time he came smilingly to the plate.
It seemed a shame that Mary was so slow in recovering from the mumps.
"Smile, don't smirk, Martha," Matilda remarked.

PHONETIC [m̩] DIACRITIC 'm

Typically in American speech, in every syllable of every word is included a vowel sound or vowel-like sound. There are cases, however, in which certain consonant sounds stand alone as the only sound in a syllable. In the word *chasm*, for example, there is only one vowel sound, [æ], although there are two syllables. In this instance a syllabic *m* (indicated as [m̩]) is the only sound in the second syllable. The exercises in this section will assist you in producing speech which distinguishes between the syllabic [m̩] and other sounds.

Word Practice

1. Read these words aloud: altruism, atheism, barbarism, cataclysm, chasm, criticism, egoism, enthusiasm, heroism, monotheism, mysticism, optimism, organism, patriotism, plagiarism, prism, protoplasm, realism, schism, solecism, syllogism, spasm, truism, witticism

Sentence Practice

2. Read these sentences aloud:

A criticism of his enthusiasm is that it is more egoism than altruism.
That witticism is the result of plagiarism and is not a true syllogism although it is an example of realism.
His patriotism and heroism are the result of his eternal optimism.
The schism is as wide as a chasm and will develop into a cataclysm.
He has run the gamut from atheism through mysticism to monotheism.

PHONETIC [n] DIACRITIC n

	KEY WORD	VOCAL FOLDS	VELUM
	noon	Vibrating	Lowered

DEVIATIONS

1. Substitution of [d] so that *knees* sounds like [diz].
2. Substitution of [m] so that *months* sounds like [mʌmθs].
3. Substitution of [ŋ] so that *branch* sounds like [bræŋtʃ].
4. Substitution of [ð] so that *land* sounds like [læðd].
5. Substitution of [l] so that *went* sounds like [wɛlt].
6. Addition of [ə] so that *green* sounds like ['grinə].
7. Omission of [n] so that *pint* sounds like [paɪt].

EXERCISES

Sound Practice

1. Articulate a series of staccato [n] sounds.
2. Articulate these sound pairs:

   Easy to contrast: [n-p] [n-b]
   Difficult to contrast: [n-d] [n-m] [n-ŋ] [n-θ] [n-l]

Syllable Practice

3. Articulate these syllables: [ni] [naɪ] [noʊ] [nʌm]
   [in] [aɪn] [oʊn] [ʌn]
   [ini] [aɪnaɪ] [oʊnoʊ] [ʌnʌ]
4. Articulate these syllable pairs:

   Easy to contrast: [in-ip] [in-ib]

TECHNICAL DESCRIPTION	MOUTH	LIPS	TONGUE
Lingua-alveolar nasal consonant	Nearly closed	Neutral	Tip pressed lightly against upper gum-ridge, sides pressed lightly against upper teeth, blocking the air passage

[ni-pi] [ni-bi]
[ini-ipi] [ini-ibi]

Difficult to contrast: [in-id] [in-im] [in-iŋ] [in-iθ] [in-il]
[ni-di] [ni-mi] [ni-ŋi] [ni-θi] [ni-li]
[ini-idi] [ini-imi] [ini-iŋi] [ini-iθi] [ini-ili]

Repeat by substituting [ɑɪ], [oʊ], and [ʌ] for [i].

Word Practice

5. Read these words aloud:

Initial: nap, neither, net, never, new, no, none, now
Medial: anew, anon, any, endure, only, under, uniform, until
Final: been, can, ran, scan, son, ton, train, wan
Special [n] *combinations:* bunch, launch, ranch, ferns, lawns, pins, engine, revenge, hand, wind, stunt, tent, labyrinth, month, hunts, rants, barn, horn, warn, dance, mince, rents, snipe, snoop

6. Read these word pairs aloud:

Easy to contrast:

[n-p] gnat-pat, net-pet, nurse-purse, canned-capped, manned-mapped, sinner-sipper, sunned-supped, grin-grip, pun-pup, tan-tap

[n-b] gnat-bat, knell-bell, night-bite, duns-dubs, roans-robes, running-rubbing, sunning-subbing, can-cab, tan-tab, ton-tub

Difficult to contrast:

[n-d] nail-dale, nigh-die, nip-dip, grains-grades, panel-paddle, raining-raiding, signs-sides, dine-died, pan-pad, seen-seed

[n-m] gnat-mat, net-met, nigh-my, cunning-coming, gains-games, roans-roams, sinner-simmer, done-dumb, run-rum, tine-time

[n-ŋ] hand-hanged, pins-pings, runs-rungs, sinner-singer, wind-winged, ban-bang, ran-rang, sun-sung, tan-tang, ton-tongue

[n-θ] gnaw-thaw, nigh-thigh, numb-thumb, den-death, feigns-faiths, ferns-firths, groans-growths, ban-bath, loan-loath, ran-wrath

[n-l] net-let, nigh-lie, night-light, cutting-culling, gains-gales, raining-railing, roans-rolls, grin-grill, pin-pill, seen-seal

Sentence Practice

7. Read these sentences aloud:

The colonel's son donned the uniform of his rank.
None of the lawn under that bunch of ferns gets any sun.
Nan and Nick danced under the moonlight until one in the morning.
None of the nurses knew of the new rule which banned them from staying out after midnight.
Nat nailed the new sign on the door of the diner.

PHONETIC [n̩] DIACRITIC 'n

These exercises will assist you in improving your articulation of the syllabic [n̩].

Word Practice

1. Read these words aloud: batten, bitten, brighten, button, chosen, christen, cotton, cousin, dozen, fatten, gotten, kitten, lighten, mizzen, moisten, Persian, prison, reason, resin, rosin, rotten, season, smitten, treason

Sentence Practice

2. Read these sentences aloud:

His cousin had chosen to christen a dozen kittens.
That cotton will brighten the coming season.
The reason that resin was chosen was to keep the wood from getting rotten.
The Persian was smitten when he was sent to prison on a charge of treason.
Batten the hatches, secure the mizzenmast, lighten the cargo, this is the season for storms without reason.

PHONETIC [ŋ] DIACRITIC ng

KEY WORD	VOCAL FOLDS	VELUM
singing	Vibrating	Lowered

DEVIATIONS

1. Substitution of [g] so that *sing* sounds like [sɪg].
2. Substitution of [m] so that *thinker* sounds like ['θɪmkɚ].
3. Substitution of [n] so that *coming* sounds like ['kʌmɪn].
4. Addition of [g] so that *ringer* sounds like ['rɪŋgɚ].
5. Addition of [k] so that *king* sounds like [kɪŋk].
6. Addition of [ə] so that *long* sounds like ['lɑŋə].
7. Omission of [ŋ] so that *hungry* sounds like ['hʌgrɪ].

EXERCISES

Sound Practice

1. Articulate a series of staccato [ŋ] sounds.
2. Articulate these sound pairs: *Easy to contrast:* [ŋ-p] [ŋ-b] [ŋ-t]
   Difficult to contrast: [ŋ-g] [ŋ-m] [ŋ-n]

Syllable Practice

3. Articulate these syllables: [ŋi] [ŋɑɪ] [ŋoʊ] [ŋʌm]
   [iŋ] [ɑɪŋ] [oʊŋ] [ʌŋ]
   [iŋi] [ɑɪŋɑɪ] [oʊŋoʊ] [ʌŋʌ]
4. Articulate these syllable pairs:

   Easy to contrast: [iŋ-ip] [iŋ-ib] [iŋ-it]
   [ŋi-pi] [ŋi-bi] [ŋi-ti]
   [iŋi-ipi] [iŋi-ibi] [iŋi-iti]

TECHNICAL DESCRIPTION	MOUTH	LIPS	TONGUE
Lingua-velar nasal consonant	Open half way	Neutral	Tip behind lower front teeth, back arched and pressed firmly against soft palate, blocking the air passage

Difficult to contrast: [iŋ-ig] [iŋ-im] [iŋ-in]
[ŋi-gi] [ŋi-mi] [ŋi-ni]
[iŋi-igi] [iŋi-imi] [iŋi-ini]

Repeat by substituting [ɑɪ], [oʊ], and [ʌ] for [i].

Word Practice

5. Read these words aloud:

Medial: banging, belonging, clanging, clinging, flinging, longing, ringing, singing, springing, stringing, thronging, wronging
Final: among, hang, rang, rung, slang, sling, song, strung, swing, tang, thing, wing
Special [ŋ] *combinations:* hanged, longed, pinged, winged, drink, pink, rank, anger, finger, stronger, jingle, single, wrangle, blanked, ranked, winked, banks, rinks, spanks, length, strength, brings, fangs, lungs

6. Read these word pairs aloud:

Easy to contrast:
[ŋ-p] clanged-clapped, flinger-flipper, ringer-ripper, singer-sipper, slinger-slipper, cling-clip, rang-rap, slang-slap, string-strip, tang-tap
[ŋ-b] gangs-gabs, ringing-ribbing, rungs-rubs, tangs-tabs, tongues-tubs, clung-club, hung-hub, slang-slab, stung-stub, sung-sub
[ŋ-t] bangs-bats, flinging-flitting, rung-ruts, sings-sits, tangs-tats, fling-flit, hung-hut, rang-rat, slang-slat, sling-slit

Difficult to contrast:

[ŋ-g] bangs-bags, longing-logging, pings-pigs, rings-rigs, rungs-rugs, bring-brig, gang-gag, sang-sag, slang-slag, tang-tag

[ŋ-m] bringing-brimming, hangs-hams, ringing-rimming, rungs-rums, singer-simmer, hung-hum, rang-ram, slang-slam, sling-slim, tang-tam

[ŋ-n] hanged-hand, pings-pins, rungs-runs, singer-sinner, winged-wind, bang-ban, rang-ran, sung-sun, tang-tan, tongue-ton

Fricatives

PHONETIC [f] DIACRITIC f

KEY WORD		VOCAL FOLDS	VELUM
[f]	*fife*	Not vibrating	Raised
[v]	*vivid*	Vibrating	

DEVIATIONS for [f]

1. Substitution of [v] so that *fast* sounds like [væst].
2. Substitution of [p] so that *after* sounds like ['æptɚ].
3. Substitution of [θ] so that *fifteen* sounds like ['fiθtin].
4. Addition of [ə] so that *flip* sounds like [fə'lɪp].
5. Omission of [f] so that *twelfth* sounds like [twɛlθ].
6. Excessive pressure in production. This sound distortion occurs when the lower lip is pressed against the upper teeth so tightly that there is excessive audible friction in the resultant sound.

Sentence Practice

7. Read these sentences aloud:

A good ping pong player spends hours batting a ball.
In becoming a singer she had sung song after song.
The wrangler was angered by the length of time it was taking for the branding.
Slang rings from the tongues of members of that gang.
His father spanked him for singing jingles, clanging kettles, and banging bottles.

PHONETIC [V] DIACRITIC V

TECHNICAL DESCRIPTION	MOUTH	LIPS	TONGUE
Labiodental fricative consonant	Nearly closed	Lower lip is pressed lightly against upper teeth	Neutral

EXERCISES for [f]

Sound Practice

1. Articulate a series of staccato [f] sounds.
2. Articulate these sound pairs: *Easy to contrast:* [f-t] [f-k] [f-ʃ]
   Difficult to contrast: [f-v] [f-p] [f-θ]

Syllable Practice

3. Articulate these syllables: [fi] [fɑɪ] [foʊ] [fʌm]

[if] [aɪf] [oʊf] [ʌf]
[ifi] [aɪfaɪ] [oʊfoʊ] [ʌfʌ]

4. Articulate these syllable pairs:

Easy to contrast: [if-it] [if-ik] [if-iʃ]
[fi-ti] [fi-ki] [fi-ʃi]
[ifi-iti] [ifi-iki] [ifi-iʃi]
Difficult to contrast: [if-iv] [if-ip] [if-iθ]
[fi-vi] [fi-pi] [fi-θi]
[ifi-ivi] [ifi-ipi] [ifi-iθi]

Repeat by substituting [aɪ], [oʊ], and [ʌ] for [i].

Word Practice

5. Read these words aloud:

Initial: fat, father, feet, few, fight, fist, foolish, for
Medial: afar, affect, effect, confide, confound, effete, effort, often
Final: cough, laugh, life, muff, proof, roof, rough, staff
Special [f] *combinations:* flow, flee, flew, aft, laughed, left, diphtheria, fifth, naphtha, staffs, stuffs, fray, frost, froze, self, shelf, sulphur, curfew, surf, camphor, emphatic, triumph, spherical, sphincter

6. Read these word pairs aloud:

Easy to contrast:
[f-t] fat-tat, feel-teal, fight-tight, cuffs-cuts, grief-greet, puffing-putting, roofing-rooting, beef-beat, calf-cat, rough-rut
[f-k] fat-cat, feel-keel, fight-kite, laughing-lacking, raft-wracked, staffing-stacking, suffer-succor, beef-beak, laugh-lack, life-like
Difficult to contrast:
[f-v] fat-vat, feel-veal, few-view, griefs-grieves, safes-saves, surfs-serves, waifs-waves, belief-believe, kerf-curve, leaf-leave
[f-p] fad-pad, feel-peel, fill-pill, differ-dipper, laughing-lapping, raft-wrapped, suffer-supper, calf-cap, cuff-cup, tiff-tip
[f-θ] fin-thin, fought-thought, free-three, laughs-laths, miffs-myths, oafs-oaths, roofless-ruthless, deaf-death, loaf-loath, sheaf-sheath

Sentence Practice

7. Read these sentences aloud:

Father laughed often after Fred's foolish efforts met with failure.

The staff often confides in that fat fellow who finds no difference between grief and laughter.
A few fought freely in behalf of the waifs.
Fern was fat and foolish enough to find self-satisfaction in stuffing herself with fine food from the frozen food shelf.
Half a loaf is often not enough to satisfy the suffering few.

DEVIATIONS for [v]

1. Substitution of [f] so that *never* sounds like ['nɛfɚ].
2. Substitution of [b] so that *seven* sounds like ['sɛbən].
3. Substitution of [ð] so that *grooves* sounds like [gruðz].
4. Substitution of [w] so that *seven* sounds like ['sɛwən].
5. Addition of [ə] so that *five* sounds like ['faɪvə].
6. Omission of [v] so that *served* sounds like [sɝd].
7. Excessive pressure in production. This sound distortion occurs when the lower lip is pressed against the upper teeth so tightly that there is excessive audible friction in the resultant sound.

EXERCISES for [v]

Sound Practice

1. Articulate a series of staccato [v] sounds.
2. Articulate these sound pairs: *Easy to contrast:* [v-d] [v-g] [v-ʒ]
   Difficult to contrast: [v-f] [v-b] [v-ð]

Syllable Practice

3. Articulate these syllables: [vi] [vɑɪ] [voʊ] [vʌm]
   [iv] [ɑɪv] [oʊv] [ʌv]
   [ivi] [ɑɪvɑɪ] [oʊvoʊ] [ʌvʌ]
4. Articulate these syllable pairs:

   Easy to contrast: [iv-id] [iv-ig] [iv-iʒ]
   [vi-di] [vi-gi] [vi-ʒi]
   [ivi-idi] [ivi-igi] [ivi-iʒi]
   Difficult to contrast: [iv-if] [iv-ib] [iv-ið]
   [vi-fi] [vi-bi] [vi-ði]
   [ivi-ifi] [ivi-ibi] [ivi-iði]

   Repeat by substituting [ɑɪ], [oʊ], and [ʌ] for [i].

Word Practice

5. Read these words aloud:

Initial: vast, vat, vein, very, view, viola, violent, violin
Medial: advent, avarice, avenue, average, every, gravel, oval, over
Final: cave, cove, dove, love, move, rave, save, shove
Special [v] *combinations:* braved, shaved, strived, weaved, curves, deserves, roves, wharves, dissolve, involve, twelve, valve, absolves, elves, evolves, resolves, larva, observe, reserve, serve, arrival, drivel, marvel, rival

6. Read these word pairs aloud:

Easy to contrast:

[v-d] veal-deal, very-dairy, view-due, curves-curds, doves-duds, raving-raiding, roves-roads, calve-cad, cove-code, grieve-greed
[v-g] vale-gale, vein-gain, vie-guy, avast-aghast, oval-ogle, over-ogre, roves-rogues, dove-dug, give-gig, love-lug
[v-ʒ] alluvian-allusion, avian-Asian, braver-brazier, clover-closure, diluvian-delusion, graver-grazier, Hoover-Hoosier, lever-leisure, over-osier, Vivian-vision

PHONETIC [s] DIACRITIC s

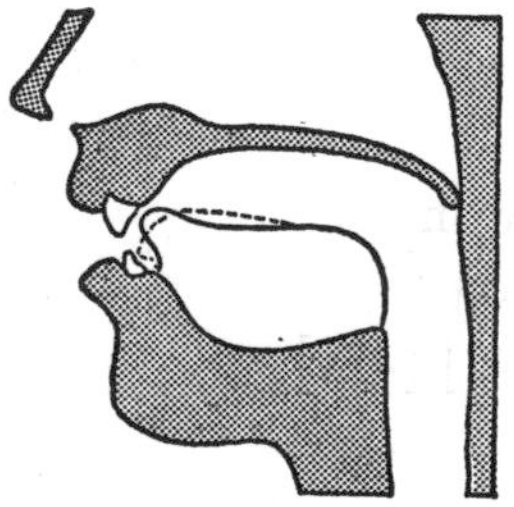

	KEY WORD		VOCAL FOLDS	VELUM
	[s]	*sauce*	Not vibrating	Raised
	[z]	*zero*	Vibrating	

DEVIATIONS for [s]

1. Substitution of [z] so that *sing* sounds like [zɪŋ].
2. Substitution of [t] so that *swing* sounds like [twɪŋ].

Difficult to contrast:

[v-f] vat-fat, veal-feel, view-few, grieves-griefs, saves-safes, serves-serfs, waves-waifs, believe-belief, curve-kerf, leave-leaf

[v-b] vase-base, vat-bat, very-berry, doves-dubs, ravel-rabble, river-ribber, roves-robes, calve-cab, curve-curb, dove-dub

[v-ð] van-than, vat-that, vie-thy, cloves-clothes, loaves-loathes, reaves-wreathes, sheaves-sheathes, clove-clothe, lave-lathe, live-lithe

Sentence Practice

7. Read these sentences aloud:

Vivian served liver to every arrival.
They strived to develop an over-all average of seventy reservations per evening.
The sign gave very valuable advice.
The doves saved the clover by devouring the larvae.
I do not believe the observations advanced by my rival.

PHONETIC [z] DIACRITIC **z**

TECHNICAL DESCRIPTION	MOUTH	LIPS	TONGUE
Lingua-alveolar fricative consonant	Nearly closed	Drawn back slightly	Grooved, so that air is directed against edge of lower teeth, tip not quite touching upper front teeth (or lower front teeth), sides pressed against upper teeth

3. Substitution of [ʃ] so that *gasoline* sounds like ['gæʃolin].
4. Substitution of [θ] so that *kiss* sounds like [kɪθ].
5. Substitution of [f] so that *last* sounds like [læft].

6. Addition of [ə] so that *sweep* sounds like [sə'wip].
7. Omission of [s] so that *months* sounds like [mʌnθ].
8. Excessive pressure in production. This sound distortion occurs when the tip of the tongue is held against the upper gum-ridge or when the middle of the tongue is raised so high toward the hard palate that there is excessive audible friction in the resultant sound.
9. Lateral production. This sound distortion occurs when the tip of the tongue is held too close to the teeth or gum-ridge so that the breath stream is diverted and audibly diffused as it escapes over one or both of the sides of the tongue.
10. Nasal omission. This sound distortion occurs when the soft palate is lowered and all or part of the breath stream is allowed to escape through the nose, producing a resulting sound resembling a snort.

EXERCISES for [s]

Sound Practice

1. Articulate a series of staccato [s] sounds.
2. Articulate these sound pairs:

Easy to contrast: [s-p] [s-k]
Difficult to contrast: [s-z] [s-t] [s-ʃ] [s-θ] [s-f]

Syllable Practice

3. Articulate these syllables: [si] [sɑɪ] [soʊ] [sʌm]
[is] [ɑɪs] [oʊs] [ʌs]
[isi] [ɑɪsɑɪ] [oʊsoʊ] ʌsʌ]
4. Articulate these syllable pairs:

Easy to contrast: [is-ip] [is-ik]
[si-pi] [si-ki]
[isi-ipi] [isi-iki]
Difficult to contrast: [is-iz] [is-it] [is-iʃ] [is-iθ] [is-if]
[si-zi] [si-ti] [si-ʃi] [si θi] [si-fi]
[isi-izi] [isi-iti] [isi-iʃi] [isi-iθi] [isi-ifi]

Repeat by substituting [ɑɪ], [oʊ], and [ʌ] for [i].

Word Practice

5. Read these words aloud:

Initial: saw, set, sister, sit, so, soap, schism, some
Medial: fasten, glassy, glossy, guessing, hasten, hustle, kissing, listen
Final: cross, gloss, lease, moss, place, race, sluice, box
Special [s] *combinations:* sphere, desk, sleeve, scrap, smile, swap, spool, rasps, svelte, stall, costs, cots, sneer, spleen, spray, strive, square, grapes, births, since, silks, else, terse, puffs

6. Read these word pairs aloud:

Easy to contrast:
[s-p] sad-pad, saw-paw, set-pet, caisson-capon, classed-clapped, last-lapped, massed-mapped, lease-leap, loose-loop, sluice-sloop
[s-k] sat-cat, sin-kin, sod-cod, kissing-kicking, last-lacked, past-packed, raced-raked, brace-break, lease-leak, lice-like
Difficult to contrast:
[s-z] seal-zeal, sink-zinc, sue-zoo, buses-buzzes, muscle-muzzle, prices-prizes, racer-razor, fuss-fuzz, lice-lies, loose-lose
[s-t] sap-tap, seal-teal, sin-tin, gracing-grating, passer-patter, racing-rating, slicing-slighting, lice-light, loose-loot, mass-mat
[s-ʃ] sad-shad, sigh-shy, sue-shoe, classed-clashed, fist-fished, last-lashed, gas-gash, mass-mash, mess-mesh
[s-θ] saw-thaw, sin-thin, sink-think, ascetic-aesthetic, answers-anthers, mossy-mothy, useful-youthful, face-faith, miss-myth, truce-truth
[s-f] sat-fat, so-foe, sin-fin, last-laughed, muscle-muffle, sister-sifter, west-weft, lease-leaf, lice-life, rice-rife

Sentence Practice

7. Read these sentences aloud:

Susybelle insists sassafras tea is insufficient nourishment for adequate sustenance.
The muscle-bound wrestler raced away from the hissing spectators.
Sue passed Spanish at last, and is the happiest lass in the class.
Sit down, sip some soup, see the soap opera, and let's gossip.
Grapes, plums, peaches, and strawberries are among the succulent fruits that herald the arrival of summer.

DEVIATIONS for [z]

1. Substitution of [s] so that *was* sounds like [wɑs].
2. Substitution of [d] so that *wins* sounds like [wɪnd].
3. Substitution of [ʒ] so that *eggs* sounds like [ɛgʒ].
4. Substitution of [ð] so that *music* sounds like ['mjuðɪk].
5. Substitution of [v] so that *dozen* sounds like ['dʌvn̩].
6. Addition of [ə] so that *loves* sounds like ['lʌvzə].
7. Omission of [z] so that *limbs* sounds like [lɪm].
8. Excessive pressure in production. This sound distortion occurs when the tip of the tongue is held against the upper gum-ridge or when the middle of the tongue is raised so high toward the hard palate that there is excessive audible friction in the resultant sound.
9. Lateral production. This sound distortion occurs when the tip of the tongue is held too close to the teeth or gum-ridge so that the breath stream is diverted and unduly diffused as it escapes over one or both of the sides of the tongue.
10. Nasal emission. This sound distortion occurs when the soft palate is lowered and all or part of the breath stream is allowed to escape through the nose, producing a resulting sound resembling a voiced snort.

EXERCISES for [z]

Sound Practice

1. Articulate a series of staccato [z] sounds.
2. Articulate these sound pairs:

   Easy to contrast: [z-b] [z-g]
   Difficult to contrast: [z-s] [z-d] [z-ʒ] [z-ð] [z-v]

Syllable Practice

3. Articulate these syllables: [zi] [zɑɪ] [zoʊ] [zʌm]
   [iz] [ɑɪz] [oʊz] [ʌz]
   [izi] [ɑɪzɑɪ] [oʊzoʊ] [ʌzʌ]
4. Articulate these syllable pairs:

   Easy to contrast: [iz-ib] [iz-ig] [zi-bi] [zi-gi] [izi-ibi] [izi-igi]
   Difficult to contrast: [iz-is] [iz-id] [iz-iʒ] [iz-ið] [iz-iv]
   [zi-si] [zi-di] [zi-ʒi] [zi-ði] [zi-vi]
   [izi-isi] [izi-idi] [izi-iʒi] [izi-iði] [izi-ivi]

Repeat by substituting [ɑɪ], [oʊ], and [ʌ] for [i].

Word Practice

5. Read these words aloud:

Initial: zebra, zero, zest, zip, zircon, zither, zodiac, zoology
Medial: easy, grazing, hazy, housing, lazy, pleasing, raising, squeezing
Final: bees, buzz, does, ease, is, phase, smells, trees
Special [z] *combinations:* crazed, dazed, tabs, tubs, brads, dudes, weds, digs, lags, kills, sales, bums, tombs, bans, tons, sings, tongues, cares, furs, stirs, wreathes, writhes, roves, starves

6. Read these word pairs aloud:

Easy to contrast:
[z-b] czar-bar, zest-best, zone-bone, dazzle-dabble, drizzle-dribble, fizzed-fibbed, rosin-robin, does-dub, jazz-jab, prose-probe
[z-g] zest-guest, Zeus-goose, zircon-gherkin, cruiser-Krueger, dazzle-daggle, easel-eagle, hazard-haggard, buzz-bug, does-dug

Difficult to contrast:
[z-s] zeal-seal, zinc-sink, zoo-sue, buzzes-buses, muzzle-muscle, prizes-prices, razor-racer, fuzz-fuss, lies-lice, lose-loose
[z-d] zeal-deal, zip-dip, zoo-do, grazing-grading, lazy-lady, raising-raiding, rising-riding, his-hid, seize-seed, size-side
[z-ʒ] Caesar-seizure, Caesar's-seizures, closer-closure, composer-composure, glazer-glazier, ruses-rouges, bays-beige, Cortez-cortege, ruse-rouge
[z-ð] zee-thee, closing-clothing, rising-writhing, teasing-teething, whizzer-whither, wizard-withered, bays-bathe, breeze-breathe
[z-v] Zane-vein, zeal-veal, zest-vest, braised-braved, closer-clover, daisy-Davy, raising-raving, does-dove, ease-eve, has-have

Sentence Practice

7. Read these sentences aloud:

The lazy zebra raised his head to avoid antagonizing the buzzing bees in the tops of the trees.
Buzz dazzled the dudes by playing jazz on the zither.
Zero on one's composition is no prize, Zelma.
The gun muzzle was dazzling in the drizzle.
Zanzibar, the wizard, produced a lizard.

PHONETIC [θ] DIACRITIC th

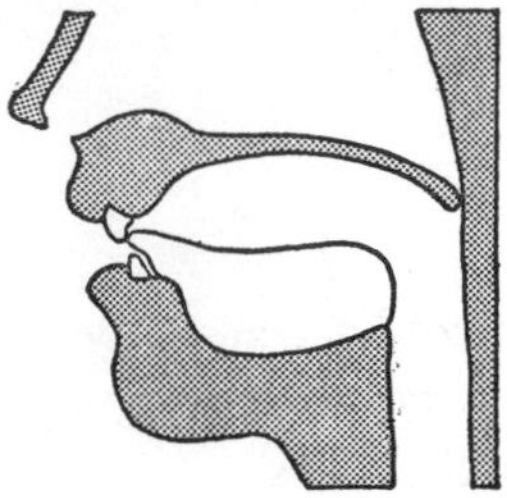

	KEY WORD		VOCAL FOLDS	VELUM
	[θ]	*thought*	Not vibrating	Raised
	[ð]	*that*	Vibrating	

DEVIATIONS for [θ]

1. Substitution of [ð] so that *moth* sounds like [mɔð].
2. Substitution of [f] so that *mouth* sounds like [mauf].
3. Substitution of [t] so that *thought* sounds like [tɔt].
4. Substitution of [s] so that *thank* sounds like [sæŋk].
5. Addition of [ə] so that *thread* sounds like [θə'rɛd].
6. Omission of [θ] so that *deaths* sounds like [dɛs].
7. Excessive pressure in production. This sound distortion occurs when the teeth are held against the tongue so tightly that there is excessive audible friction in the resultant sound.

EXERCISES for [θ]

Sound Practice

1. Articulate a series of staccato [θ] sounds.
2. Articulate these sound pairs:

   Easy to contrast: [θ-p] [θ-k]
   Difficult to contrast: [θ-ð] [θ-f] [θ-t] [θ-s]

Syllable Practice

3. Articulate these syllables: [θi] [θaɪ] [θoʊ] [θʌm]
   [iθ] [aɪθ] [oʊθ] [ʌθ]
   [iθi] [aɪθaɪ] [oʊθoʊ] [ʌθʌ]
4. Articulate these syllable pairs:

   Easy to contrast: [iθ-ip] [iθ-ik]

PHONETIC [ð] DIACRITIC th

TECHNICAL DESCRIPTION	MOUTH	LIPS	TONGUE
Lingua-dental fricative consonant	Open slightly	Neutral	Tip touching edges or back of upper front teeth so that air is forced between tongue and teeth; sides of tongue against upper molars

[θi-pi] [θi-ki]
[iθi-ipi] [iθi-iki]

Difficult to contrast: [iθ-ið] [iθ-if] [iθ-it] [iθ-is]
[θi-ði] [θi-fi] [θi-ti] [θi-si]
[iθi-iði] [iθi-ifi] [iθi-iti] [iθi-isi]

Repeat by substituting [ɑɪ], [oʊ], and [ʌ] for [i].

Word Practice

5. Read these words aloud:

Initial: thank, thatch, theater, thick, thin, thing, think, thought
Medial: aesthetic, author, athlete, ether, ethics, ethyl, mothy, youthful
Final: birth, earth, fourth, mirth, myth, north, truth, worth
Special [θ] *combinations:* through, thrust, deaths, growths, thwart, hundredth, thousandth, diphtheria, diphthong, fifths, twelfths, filth, health, warmth, length, strengths, labyrinth, month, tenths, depth, mirth, worth, births, girths

6. Read these word pairs aloud:

Easy to contrast:
[θ-p] thin-pin, think-pink, thump-pump, ethics-epics, healthful-helpful, lathing-lapping, growths-gropes, truth-troop, wrath-wrap, wreath-reap
[θ-k] thick-kick, thing-king, thought-caught, deaths-decks, lathing-lacking, myths-mix, wraiths-rakes, bath-back, path-pack, teeth-teak

Difficult to contrast:

[θ-ð] thigh-thy, ether-either, lather-lather, Blythe-blithe, loath-loathe, mouth (*n.*)-mouth (*v.*), sooth-soothe, sheath-sheathe, teeth-teethe, wreath-wreathe

[θ-f] thin-fin, thought-fought, thrill-frill, throws-froze, author-offer, lathing-laughing, myths-miffs, death-deaf, loath-loaf, oath-oaf

[θ-t] thank-tank, thought-taught, three-tree, ether-eater, myths-mitts, pithy-pity, ruthless-rootless, both-boat, death-debt, dearth-dirt

[θ-s] thaw-saw, thin-sin, think-sink, aesthetic-ascetic, anthers-answers, mothy-mossy, youthful-useful, faith-face, myth-miss, truth-truce

Sentence Practice

7. Read these sentences aloud:

The three thoughtless thespians thwarted the author.
To get the authentic measure of a man's worth take the depth of his faith and the warmth of his mirth.
Think through the ethics of the thing.
Was the tenth answer three-fourths, three-fifths, or five-sixths of one one-hundredth?
They threw in thoughts of little worth which brought forth mirth.

DEVIATIONS for [ð]

1. Substitution of [θ] so that *breathe* sounds like [briθ].
2. Substitution of [v] so that *brother* sounds like ['brʌvɚ].
3. Substitution of [t] so that *father* sounds like ['fɑtɚ].
4. Substitution of [d] so that *father* sounds like ['fɑdɚ].
5. Substitution of [z] so that *other* sounds like ['ʌzɚ].
6. Addition of [ə] so that *writhe* sounds like ['wraɪðə].
7. Omission of [ð] so that *mother* sounds like ['mʌɚ].
8. Excessive pressure in production. This sound distortion occurs when the teeth are held against the tongue so tightly that there is excessive audible friction in the resultant sound.

EXERCISES for [ð]

Sound Practice

1. Articulate a series of staccato [ð] sounds.
2. Articulate these sound pairs:

   Easy to contrast: [ð-b] [ð-g]
   Difficult to contrast: [ð-θ] [ð-v] [ð-d] [ð-z] [ð-l]

Syllable Practice

3. Articulate these syllables: [ði] [ðaɪ] [ðoʊ] [ðʌm]
   [ið] [aɪð] [oʊð] [ʌð]
   [iði] [aɪðaɪ] [oʊðoʊ] [ʌðʌ]
4. Articulate these syllable pairs:

   Easy to contrast: [ið-ib] [ið-ig]
   [ði-bi] [ði-gi]
   [iði-ibi] [iði-igi]
   Difficult to contrast: [ið-iθ] [ið-iv] [ið-id] [ið-iz] [ið-il]
   [ði-θi] [ði-vi] [ði-di] [ði-zi] [ði-li]
   [iði-iθi] [iði-ivi] [iði-idi] [iði-izi] [iði-ili]

   Repeat by substituting [aɪ], [oʊ], and [ʌ] for [i].

Word Practice

5. Read these words aloud:

   Initial: than, them, there, these, they, this, those, though
   Medial: father, feather, gather, neither, rather, smoother, weather, wither
   Final: bathe, breathe, clothe, loathe, seethe, soothe, teethe, wreathe
   Special [ð] *combinations:* bathed, bequeathed, mouthed, seethed, sheathed, smoothed, soothed, wreathed, breathes, clothes, enwreathes, lathes, loathes, swathes, teethes, tithes, either, father, feather, lather, neither, other, rather, tether

6. Read these word pairs aloud:

   Easy to contrast:
   [ð-b] than-ban, there-bear, these-bees, they-bay, though-bow, baths-Babs, loathes-lobes, tither-Tiber, weather-Weber, bathe-babe

[ð-g] they-gay, those-goes, though-go, thus-Gus, thy-guy, baths-bags, either-eager, lather-lagger, tither-tiger, with-wig

Difficult to contrast:

[ð-θ] thy-thigh, either-ether, lather-lather, blithe-Blythe, loathe-loath, mouth (*v.*)-mouth (*n.*), soothe-sooth, sheathe-sheath, teethe-teeth, wreathe-wreath

[ð-v] than-van, that-vat, thy-vie, clothes-cloves, loathes-loaves, wreathes-reaves, sheathes-sheaves, clothe-clove, lathe-lave, lithe-live

[ð-d] there-dare, they-day, though-dough, breathes-breeds, loathes-loads, seethes-seeds, writhing-riding, bathe-bayed, soothe-sued, wreathe-read

[ð-z] thee-Zee, clothing-closing, teething-teasing, whither-whizzer, withered-wizard, writing-rising, bathe-bays, breathe-breeze, seethe-seize, tithe-ties

PHONETIC [ʃ] DIACRITIC sh

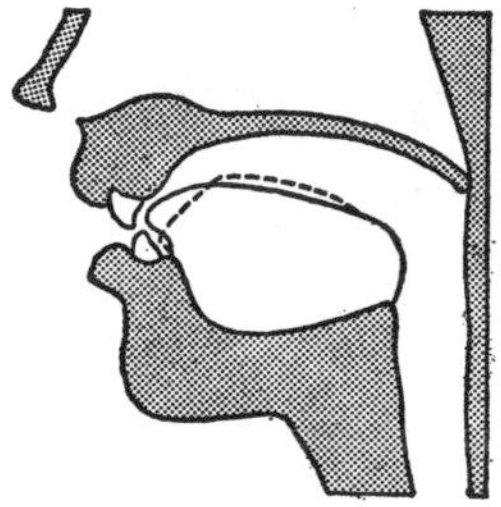

KEY WORD		VOCAL FOLDS	VELUM
[ʃ]	*sheep*	Not vibrating	Raised
[ʒ]	*vision*	Vibrating	

DEVIATIONS for [ʃ]

1. Substitution of [ʒ] so that *wishes* sounds like ['wɪʒəz].
2. Substitution of [s] so that *sheep* sounds like [sip].
3. Substitution of [t] so that *shelf* sounds like [tɛlf].
4. Substitution of [θ] so that *shop* sounds like [θop].
5. Substitution of [tʃ] so that *shoe* sounds like [tʃu].
6. Addition of [ə] so that *fish* sounds like ['fɪʃə].
7. Omission of [ʃ] so that *position* sounds like [po'zɪən].
8. Excessive pressure in production. This sound distortion occurs when the tongue position reduces the size of the required opening, and there is excessive audible friction in the resulting sound.

[ð-l] there-lair, thine-line, though-low, scathing-scaling, seethes-seals, tithing-tiling, wreathes-reels, bathe-bail, teethe-teal, with-will

Sentence Practice

7. Read these sentences aloud:

Residents of certain geographical locations have difficulty in saying *this, them, these,* and *those.*
Father loathes gathering in the clothes.
The mother soothed the teething baby.
We shall have weather, whether or not.
Neither father nor mother had a brother.

PHONETIC [ʒ] DIACRITIC zh

TECHNICAL DESCRIPTION	MOUTH	LIPS	TONGUE
Lingua-palatal fricative	Nearly closed	Protruded slightly	Flattened and raised toward hard palate, tip farther back from upper front teeth (or lower front teeth) than for [s], sides pressed against upper teeth

9. Lateral production. This sound distortion occurs when the tongue is held in such a way that the breath stream is diverted and escapes over one or both of the sides of the tongue.

EXERCISES for [ʃ]

Sound Practice

1. Articulate a series of staccato [ʃ] sounds.
2. Articulate these sound pairs:

Easy to contrast: [ʃ-p] [ʃ-k]
Difficult to contrast: [ʃ-ʒ] [ʃ-s] [ʃ-t] [ʃ-θ] [ʃ-tʃ]

Syllable Practice

3. Articulate these syllables: [ʃi] [ʃɑɪ] [ʃoʊ] [ʃʌm]
   [iʃ] [ɑɪʃ] [oʊʃ] [ʌʃ]
   [iʃi] [ɑɪʃɑɪ] [oʊʃoʊ] [ʌʃʌ]
4. Articulate these syllable pairs:

   Easy to contrast: [iʃ-ip] [iʃ-ik]
   [ʃi-pi] [ʃi-ki]
   [iʃi-ipi] [iʃi-iki]

   Difficult to contrast: [iʃ-iʒ] [iʃ-is] [iʃ-it] [iʃ-iθ] [iʃ-itʃ]
   [ʃi-ʒi] [ʃi-si] [ʃi-ti] [ʃi-θi] [ʃi-tʃi]
   [iʃi-iʒi] [iʃi-isi] [iʃi-iti] [iʃi-iθi] [iʃi-itʃi]

   Repeat by substituting [ɑɪ], [oʊ], and [ʌ] for [i].

Word Practice

5. Read these words aloud:

   Initial: shall, shawl, shine, shoe, shop, shovel, show, shower
   Medial: ashen, bishop, cushion, motion, ocean, pension, tension, usher
   Final: crash, crush, fish, fresh, mesh, mush, push, thrush
   Special [ʃ] *combinations:* shrank, shrapnel, shred, shrew, shrewd, shrill, shrimp, shrine, shrunk, shroud, shrub, shrug, cashed, clashed, crashed, crushed, fished, leashed, meshed, rushed, slashed, smashed, squashed, swished

6. Read these word pairs aloud:

   Easy to contrast:
   [ʃ-p] shall-pal, share-pear, shine-pine, lasher-lapper, ocean-open, slashing-slapping, usher-upper, cash-cap, dish-dip, trash-trap
   [ʃ-k] share-care, shawl-call, shoal-coal, crashed-cracked, lasher-lacquer, ocean-oaken, slasher-slacker, hash-hack, leash-leak, trash-track

   Difficult to contrast:
   [ʃ-ʒ] Aleutian-allusion, Aleutians-allusions, Confucian-confusion, dilution-delusion, dilutions-delusions, glacier-glazier, glaciers-glaziers, leasher-leisure, mesher-measure, ruche-rouge

[ʃ-s] shad-sad, shy-sigh, shoe-sue, clashed-classed, fished-fist, lashed-last, leashed-least, gash-gas, mash-mass, mesh-mess
[ʃ-t] shawl-tall, shoe-too, shop-top, fishing-fitting, lasher-latter, musher-mutter, usher-utter, hash-hat, mesh-met, push-put
[ʃ-θ] shank-thank, pshaw-thaw, shin-thin, shrew-threw, shrill-thrill, lasher-lather, hash-hath, harsh-hearth, lash-lath, rash-wrath
[ʃ-tʃ] share-chair, shoe-chew, shop-chop, cashing-catching, dishes-ditches, lashing-latching, mashing-matching, hash-hatch, leash-leach, mush-much

Sentence Practice

7. Read these sentences aloud:

She shouted that the ocean's motion was crushing the ship.
The shoeshine boy set up shop outside the fresh fish market.
"You shall share the shrimp," the shrewish fishwife shouted.
The shiftless usher got a demotion instead of a promotion.
Show Sharon a shawl, shrieked Shirley.

DEVIATIONS for [ʒ]

1. Substitution of [ʃ] so that *vision* sounds like ['vɪʃən].
2. Substitution of [z] so that *division* sounds like [də'vɪzən].
3. Substitution of [d] so that *prestige* sounds like [prɛ'stid].
4. Substitution of [ð] so that *casual* sounds like ['kæðjuəl].
5. Substitution of [j] so that *decision* sounds like [dɪ'sɪjən].
6. Substitution of [dʒ] so that *rouge* sounds like [rudʒ].
7. Addition of [ə] so that *garage* sounds like [gə'rɑʒə].
8. Omission of [ʒ] so that *derision* sounds like [dɪ'rɪən].
9. Excessive pressure in production. This sound distortion occurs when the tongue position reduces the size of the required opening and there is excessive audible friction in the resulting sound.
10. Lateral production. This sound distortion occurs when the tongue is held in such a way that the breath stream is diverted and escapes over one or both of the sides of the tongue.

EXERCISES for [ʒ]

Sound Practice

1. Articulate a series of staccato [ʒ] sounds.
2. Articulate these sound pairs:

   Easy to contrast: [ʒ-b [ʒ-g]
   Difficult to contrast: [ʒ-ʃ] [ʒ-z] [ʒ-d] [ʒ-ð] [ʒ-j] [ʒ-dʒ]

Syllable Practice

3. Articulate these syllables: [ʒi] [ʒaɪ] [ʒoʊ] [ʒʌm]
   [iʒ] [aɪʒ] [oʊʒ] [ʌʒ]
   [iʒi] [aɪʒaɪ] [oʊʒoʊ] [ʌʒʌ]
4. Articulate these syllable pairs:

   Easy to contrast: [iʒ-ib] [iʒ-ig]
   [ʒi-bi] [ʒi-gi]
   [iʒi-ibi] [iʒi-igi]

   Difficult to contrast:
   [iʒ-iʃ] [iʒ-iz] [iʒ-id] [iʒ-ið] [iʒ-ij] [iʒ-idʒ]
   [ʒi-ʃi] [ʒi-zi] [ʒi-di] [ʒi-ði] [ʒi-ji] [ʒi-dʒi]
   [iʒi-iʃi] [iʒi-izi] [iʒi-idi] [iʒi-iði] [iʒi-iji] [iʒi-idʒi]

   Repeat by substituting [aɪ], [oʊ], and [ʌ] for [i].

Word Practice

5. Read these words aloud:

   Initial: Does not appear in this position in English.
   Medial: aphasia, artesian, closure, cohesion, decision, derision, evasion, illusion, leisure, measure, seizure, usual
   Final: barrage, beige, camouflage, corsage, cortege, garage, massage, mirage, persiflage, prestige, rouge, sabotage

6. Read these word pairs aloud:

Easy to contrast:

[ʒ-b] beige-babe, leisure-Lieber, rouge-rube, beige-babe, leisure-Lieber, rouge-rube, beige-babe, leisure-Lieber, rouge-rube, beige-babe

[ʒ-g] leisure-leaguer, osier-ogre, leisure-leaguer, osier-ogre, leisure-leaguer, osier-ogre, leisure-leaguer, osier-ogre, leisure-leaguer, osier-ogre

Difficult to contrast:

[ʒ-ʃ] allusion-Aleutian, allusions-Aleutians, confusion-Confucian, delusion-dilution, delusions-dilutions, glazier-glacier, glaziers-glaciers, leisure-leasher, measure-mesher, rouge-ruche

[ʒ-z] closure-closer, composure-composer, glazier-glazer, grazier-grazer, rouges-ruses, seizure-Caesar, seizures-Caesar's, beige-bays, cortege-Cortez, rouge-ruse

[ʒ-d] azure-adder, grazier-grader, leisure-leader, osier-odor, osiers-odors, seizure-cedar, seizures-cedars, treasure-treader, beige-bayed, rouge-rude

[ʒ-ð] beige-bathe, closure-clothier, beige-bathe, closure-clothier, beige-bathe, closure-clothier, beige-bathe, closure-clothier, beige-bathe, closure-clothier

[ʒ-j] osier-oyer, osier-oyer, osier-oyer, osier-oyer, osier-oyer, osier-oyer, osier-oyer, osier-oyer, osier-oyer, osier-oyer

[ʒ-dʒ] lesion-legion, lesion-legion, lesion-legion, lesion-legion, lesion-legion, lesion-legion, lesion-legion, lesion-legion, lesion-legion, lesion-legion

Sentence Practice

7. Read these sentences aloud:

A mirage is a type of illusion.

At her leisure she used rouge to camouflage her features.

The prestige of the guards was enhanced as they stopped the impending invasion.

There is no scientific measure of the amount of leisure time which insures the best possible decisions.

The usual red corsage was replaced by a beige scarf.

PHONETIC [h] DIACRITIC h

	KEY WORD	VOCAL FOLDS	VELUM
	hat	Open slightly so that air passing through them causes some friction as in whispering	Raised

DEVIATIONS

1. Omission of [h] so that *heart* sounds like [ɑrt].
2. Guttural production. This sound distortion occurs when the back of the tongue comes in close proximity to the velum and friction results.
3. Vocalized production. This sound distortion occurs when the vocal folds vibrate during the production of this sound.
4. Breathy production. This sound distortion occurs when too much air escapes before the following vowel is made. (See Chapter 4 on tone initiation.)

EXERCISES

Sound Practice

1. Articulate a series of staccato [h] sounds.
2. Articulate these sound pairs: [h-p] [h-t] [h-k]

Syllable Practice

3. Articulate these syllables: [hi] [hɑɪ] [hoʊ] [hʌm]
[ih] [ɑɪh] [oʊh] [ʌh]
[ihi] [ɑɪhɑɪ] [oʊhoʊ] [ʌhʌ]
4. Articulate these syllable pairs: [ih-ip] [ih-it] [ih-ik]
[hi-pi] [hi-ti] [hi-ki]
[ihi-ipi] [ihi-iti] [ihi-iki]

Repeat by substituting [ɑɪ], [oʊ], and [ʌ] for [i].

TECHNICAL DESCRIPTION	MOUTH	LIPS	TONGUE
Glottal fricative consonant	In position for following sound	In position for following sound	In position for following sound

Word Practice

5. Read these words aloud:

Initial: hail, have, he, heel, hearth, heavy, him, her, hill, hit, home, house
Medial: ahead, behalf, behave, behead, grasshopper, inhale, inhabit, mohair, perhaps, prohibit, rehearse, uphold
Final: Does not appear in this position in English.

6. Articulate these words pairs:

[h-p] hacked-packed, had-pad, hail-pail, hat-pat, heel-peal, hen-pen, hit-pit, hunt-punt, hurl-pearl, hurt-pert
[h-t] hack-tack, had-tad, ham-tam, heel-teal, height-tight, hen-ten, high-tie, hock-tock, hop-top, hot-tot
[h-k] had-cad, ham-cam, hat-cat, heel-keel, height-kite, hot-cot, how-cow, hub-cub, hurl-curl, hurt-curt

Sentence Practice

7. Read these sentences aloud:

He went to the hardware store in search of a heavy garden hose.
Hail the return of the conquering hero.
His heavy heel gave him the height he needed.
Hey, Harry, hurry up and help that unhappy customer.
He helped to hasten the construction of the house on the hill.

Semivowels

PHONETIC [r] DIACRITIC r

	KEY WORD	VOCAL FOLDS	VELUM
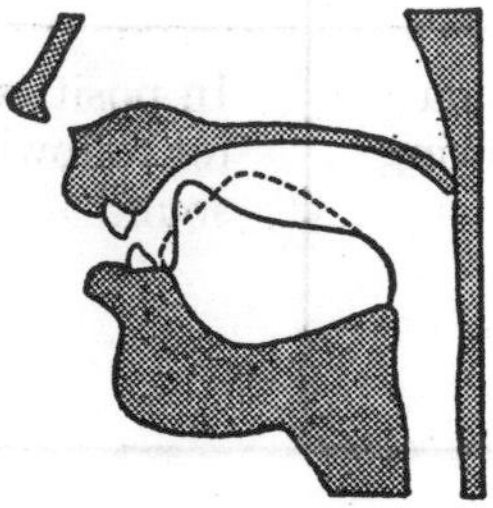	*rarer*	Vibrating	Raised

DEVIATIONS

1. Substitution of [w] so that *red* sounds like [wɛd].
2. Substitution of [l] so that *rice* sounds like [lɑɪs].
3. Insertion of [ə] so that *true* sounds like [tə'ru].
4. Addition of [ə] so that *car* sounds like ['kɑrə].
5. Retroflex production. This sound distortion occurs when the tip of the tongue is raised in the mouth and bent back excessively.
6. Uvular production. This sound distortion occurs when the back of the tongue is raised toward the uvula, causing the outgoing air stream to produce uvular vibration.
7. Flapped production. This sound distortion occurs when the tip of the tongue taps the upper gum-ridge lightly once, producing a sound similar to [d]. This is frequently found in British speech.
8. Trilled production. This sound distortion occurs when the tip of the tongue taps the upper gum-ridge lightly several times in rapid succession.

EXERCISES

Sound Practice

1. Articulate a series of staccato [r] sounds.
2. Articulate these sound pairs: *Easy to contrast:* [r-b] [r-d] [r-g]
   Difficult to contrast: [r-w] [r-l]

TECHNICAL DESCRIPTION	MOUTH	LIPS	TONGUE
Lingua-palatal semivowel consonant	Open slightly	Drawn back slightly	Broadened tip pointed upward or tip of tongue lowered and center of tongue humped toward velum, with the sides touching upper teeth

Syllable Practice

3. Articulate these syllables: [ri] [rɑɪ] [roʊ] [rʌm]
[ir] [ɑɪr] [oʊr] [ʌr]
[iri] [ɑɪrɑɪ] [oʊroʊ] [ʌrʌ]

4. Articulate these syllable pairs:

Easy to contrast: [ir-ib] [ir-id] [ir-ig]
[ri-bi] [ri-di] [ri-gi]
[iri-ibi] [iri-idi] [iri-igi]

Difficult to contrast: [ir-iw] [ir-il]
[ri-wi] [ri-li]
[iri-iwi] [iri-ili]

Repeat by substituting [ɑɪ], [oʊ], and [ʌ] for [i].

Word Practice

5. Read these words aloud:

Initial: ran, real, red, rice, right, room, rose, rut
Medial: already, arose, around, arrive, arrow, errand, every, orange
Final: (Final *r*'s and *r*'s before consonants are sometimes dropped completely in Eastern and Southern speech.) car, far, gear, hear, stare, star, stair, there
Special [r] *combinations:* carbon, card, torch, snarl, large, perform, born, spark, tarp, hearth, carve, brow, fright, thrust, sort, drop, grieve, scarce, stars, shrimp, marshal, spruce, strangle, script

6. Read these word pairs aloud:

Easy to contrast:

[r-b] ran-ban, ray-bay, right-bright, airing-ebbing, around-abound, fearing-fibbing, rearing-ribbing, far-fob, near-nib, wear-web

[r-d] ray-day, real-deal, rice-dice, airy-eddy, bearing-bedding, hairs-heads, rearing-ridding, car-cod, share-shed, wear-wed

[r-g] rate-gate, ray-gay, wrote-goat, airing-egging, bearing-begging, pairing-pegging, rearing-rigging, car-cog, dear-dig, gear-gig

Difficult to contrast:

[r-w] rail-wail, red-wed, reed-weed, reek-weak, ritch-witch, ride-wide, rig-wig, right-wight, round-wound, run-won

PHONETIC [l] DIACRITIC l

KEY WORD	VOCAL FOLDS	VELUM
lily	Vibrating	Raised

DEVIATIONS

1. Substitution of [w] so that *let* sounds like [wɛt].
2. Substitution of [j] so that *love* sounds like [jʌv].
3. Substitution of [ð] so that *village* sounds like ['vɪðɪdʒ].
4. Substitution of [r] so that *plow* sounds like [prɑʊ].
5. Insertion of [ə] before [l] so that *black* sounds like [bə'læk].
6. Addition of [ə] so that *film* sounds like ['fɪləm].
7. Omission of [l] so that *help* sounds like [hɛp].
8. Retroflex production. This sound distortion occurs when the tip of the tongue is raised in the mouth and bent back excessively.
9. Sibilant production. This sound distortion occurs when the tongue tip is too low in the mouth and the breath stream escapes over one or both sides of the tongue.

[r-l] red-led, rice-lice, ride-lied, arrive-alive, fearing-filling, fears-fills, tears-tills, near-nil, share-shell, wear-well

Sentence Practice

7. Read these sentences aloud:

Put the car in gear to overcome inertia.
The ridiculous regalia was red and orange in color.
Run around the barn, Rover.
Robert is realizing real progress in reducing.
The doctor warned her that riding horses would be a fearful risk.

TECHNICAL DESCRIPTION	MOUTH	LIPS	TONGUE
Lingua-alveolar semivowel consonant	Open slightly	Neutral	Tip touching upper gum-ridge lightly, sides lowered so that air can escape laterally, back arched downward in some cases and upward in others

EXERCISES

Sound Practice

1. Articulate a series of staccato [l] sounds.
2. Articulate these sound pairs:

Easy to contrast: [l-b] [l-d] [l-g]
Difficult to contrast: [l-w] [l-j] [l-ð [l-r]

Syllable Practice

3. Articulate these syllables: [li] [laɪ] [loʊ] [lʌm]
[il] [aɪl] [oʊl] [ʌl]
[ili] [aɪlaɪ] [oʊloʊ] [ʌlʌ]
4. Articulate these syllable pairs:

Easy to contrast: [il-ib] [il-id] [il-ig]
[li-bi] [li-di] [li-gi]
[ili-ibi] [ili-idi] [ili-igi]

Difficult to contrast: [il-iw] [il-ij] [il-ið] [il-ir]
[li-wi] [li-ji] [li-ði] [li-ri]
[ili-iwi] [ili-iji] [ili-iði] [ili-iri]

Repeat by substituting [ɑɪ], [oʊ], and [ʌ] for [i].

Word Practice

5. Read these words aloud:

Initial: lad, lamb, last, late, light, listen, long, loose
Medial: alarm, along, always, hello, pillow, silent, welcome, yellow
Final: bill, call, dwell, hall, sell, tall, well, will
Special [l] *combinations:* bulb, filled, silk, elk, mulch, bilge, pulsate, welch, elm, sulfur, kelp, stilt, health, valve, pliers, blaze, flew, close, glue, slap, tales, sleigh, splint, snarl

6. Read these word pairs aloud:

Easy to contrast:
[l-b] lad-bad, late-bait, light-bite, curls-curbs, filling-fibbing, relate-rebate, rolling-robing, bill-bib, hull-hub, well-web
[l-d] late-date, left-deft, lie-die, bells-beds, reeling-reading, railing-raiding, welling-wedding, bill-bid, sell-said, well-wed
[l-g] late-gate, let-get, lift-gift, bells-begs, gills-gigs, pills-pigs, rills-rigs, bill-big, hull-hug, will-wig

Difficult to contrast:
[l-w] late-wait, lead-weed, leap-weep, leave-weave, led-wed, ledge-wedge, left-weft, let-wet, light-wight, lit-wit
[l-j] lack-yak, lamb-yam, lank-yank, lap-yap, law-yaw, lawn-yawn, least-yeast, let-yet, lot-yacht, lung-young
[l-ð] lair-there, line-thine, low-though, scaling-scathing, seals-seethes, tiling-tithing, reels-wreathes, bale-bathe, teal-teethe, will-with
[l-r] led-red, lice-rice, lied-ride, alive-arrive, filling-fearing, fills-fears, tills-tears, nil-near, shell-share, well-wear

Sentence Practice

7. Read these sentences aloud:

The lad left the light on in the hall.
Bill led Larry to the seashore to search for shells.
The sea gull filled himself with at least three dozen shellfish.
You can lead a lamb to the liquid, to paraphrase an old saw, but you can't make him indulge.
The gobbler filled his craw with the welcome yellow kernels.

PHONETIC [l̩] DIACRITIC 'l

These exercises will assist you in improving your articulation of the syllabic [l̩].

Word Practice

1. Read these words aloud: banal, battle, camel, castle, cattle, dabble, dapple, fable, fettle, fiddle, fizzle, gobble, hackle, kennel, kernel, kettle, lable, ladle, mammal, metal, middle, missile, medal, natal, naval, nestle, nettle, nickel, paddle, panel, peddle, petal, rattle, revel, riddle, ripple, sable, settle, sizzle, table, tassel, thistle, tickle, trifle, vassal, vessel, whittle, wriggle

Sentence Practice

2. Read these sentences aloud:

The camel wriggled to the middle of the vessel.
The panel truck had a rattle.
"I'll fiddle a tune for a nickel," said the music peddler.
The vassal watched the cattle near the castle.
The contents of the kettle sizzled.

PHONETIC [ʍ] DIACRITIC hw

KEY WORD		VOCAL FOLDS	VELUM
[ʍ]	*whale*	Not vibrating	Raised
[w]	*wail*	Vibrating	

DEVIATIONS for [ʍ]

1. Substitution of [w] so that *what* sounds like [wɑt]. (However, this is becoming increasingly acceptable in American speech.)
2. Substitution of [f] so that *why* sounds like [fɑɪ].
3. Omission of [ʍ] so that *somewhat* sounds like ['sʌmɑt].

EXERCISES for [ʍ]

Sound Practice

1. Articulate a series of staccato [ʍ] sounds.
2. Articulate these sound pairs: *Easy to contrast:* [ʍ-p] [ʍ-t] [ʍ-k]
   Difficult to contrast: [ʍ-w] [ʍ-f]

Syllable Practice

3. Articulate these syllables: [ʍi] [ʍɑɪ] [ʍoʊ] [ʍʌm]
   [iʍ] [ɑɪʍ] [oʊʍ] [ʌʍ]
   [iʍi] [ɑɪʍɑɪ] [oʊʍoʊ] [ʌʍʌ]
4. Articulate these syllable pairs:

   Easy to contrast: [iʍ-ip] [iʍ-it] [iʍ-ik]

PHONETIC [w] DIACRITIC w

TECHNICAL DESCRIPTION	MOUTH	LIPS	TONGUE
Bilabial glide consonant	Open slightly as sound is initiated, changing during production to position for following sound	Rounded and protruded as sound is initiated, changing during production to position for following sound	Tip behind lower front teeth, back arched toward hard palate when sound is initiated, changing during production to position for following sound

[ʍi-pi] [ʍi-ti] [ʍi-ki]
[iʍi-ipi] [iʍi-iti] [iʍi-iki]

Difficult to contrast: [iʍ-iw] [iʍ-if]
[ʍi-wi] [ʍi-fi]
[iʍi-iwi] [iʍi-ifi]

Repeat by substituting [ɑɪ], [oʊ], and [ʌ] for [i].

Word Practice

5. Read these words aloud:

Initial: whale, what, wheel, when, where, which, whimper, whip, whisper, whistle, white, why
Medial: anywhere, awhile, awhirl, bewhiskered, bobwhite, bullwhip, elsewhere, horsewhip, meanwhile, nowhere, somewhat, somewhere
Final: Does not appear in this position.

6. Read these word pairs aloud:

Easy to contrast:
[ʍ-p] whale-pail, wheat-peat, wheel-peal, when-pen, where-pear, whet-pet, which-pitch, while-pile, whine-pine, why-pie
[ʍ-t] whale-tale, wheel-teal, wheeze-tease, when-ten, whence-tense, where-tear, while-tile, whine-tine, white-tight, why-tie

[ʍ-k] whale-kale, what-cot, wheel-keel, whelp-kelp, when-ken, where-care, whine-kine, whirr-cur, whit-kit, white-kite

Difficult to contrast:

[ʍ-w] whale-wail, what-watt, wheel-weal, where-wear, whet-wet, which-witch, while-wile, whine-wine, whirr-were, whit-wit

[ʍ-f] whale-fail, wheat-feet, wheel-feel, whence-fence, where-fair, while-file, whine-fine, whirr-fur, whit-fit, white-fight

Sentence Practice

7. Read these sentences aloud:

Where is the white whale?
Go elsewhere or I'll horsewhip you.
The bobwhite was somewhat disturbed when it was mistaken for a badminton bird.
The terms, "who," "what," "when," "where," and "why," are meaningful everywhere.
"When will you stop whining, Whiskers," whispered his master, somewhat disturbed.

DEVIATIONS for [w]

1. Substitution of [v] so that *went* sounds like [vɛnt].
2. Substitution of [l] so that *swim* sounds like [slɪm].
3. Omission of [w] so that *backward* sounds like ['backɚd].

EXERCISES for [w]

Sound Practice

1. Articulate a series of staccato [w] sounds.
2. Articulate these sound pairs: *Easy to contrast:* [w-b] [w-d] [w-g]
   Difficult to contrast: [w-v] [w-l]

Syllable Practice

3. Articulate these syllables: [wi] [waɪ] [woʊ] [wʌm]

[iw] [ɑɪw] [oʊw] [ʌw]
[iwi] [ɑɪwɑɪ] [oʊwoʊ] [ʌwʌ]

4. Articulate these syllable pairs:

   Easy to contrast: [iw-ib] [iw-id] [iw-ig]
   [wi-bi] [wi-di] [wi-gi]
   [iwi-ibi] [iwi-idi] [iwi-igi]
   Difficult to contrast: [iw-iv] [iw-il]
   [wi-vi] [wi-li]
   [iwi-ivi] [iwi-ili]

   Repeat by substituting [ɑɪ], [oʊ], and [ʌ] for [i].

Word Practice

5. Read these words aloud:

   Initial: wail, wait, warp, watt, weal, wear, were, wilt, wine, wish, wit, witch
   Medial: always, anyone, anyway, awake, aware, backward, beware, bewail, forward, onward, unwound, upward
   Final: (Does not appear in this position.)
   Special [w] *combinations:* dwarf, dwell, dwindle, language, languish, languishing, twin, twine, twirl, twist, choir, inquire, quake, quiet, squash, squeal, squeamish, sway, swindle, swirl, swoop, athwart, thwack, thwart

6. Read these word pairs aloud:

   Easy to contrast:
   [w-b] wail-bail, wait-bait, walk-balk, we-be, wear-bare, weigh-bay, well-bell, went-bent, will-bill, wilt-built
   [w-d] wail-dale, wait-date, weal-deal, wear-dare, weigh-day, well-dell, went-dent, will-dill, wine-dine, wish-dish
   [w-g] one-gun, wail-gale, wait-gait, wave-gave, way-gay, wet-get, wig-gig, will-gill, wilt-guilt, would-good
   Difficult to contrast:
   [w-v] wail-vale, waltz-vaults, wane-vein, weal-veal, wend-vend, went-vent, west-vest, wile-vile, wine-vine, worse-verse
   [w-l] wait-late, weave-leave, wed-led, wedge-ledge, weed-lead, weep-leap, weft-left, wet-let, wight-light, wit-lit

Sentence Practice

7. Read these sentences aloud:

   You waltz very well, Willie.
   Is anyone awake enough to know whether we are going forward or backward?

PHONETIC [j] DIACRITIC y

	KEY WORD	VOCAL FOLDS	VELUM
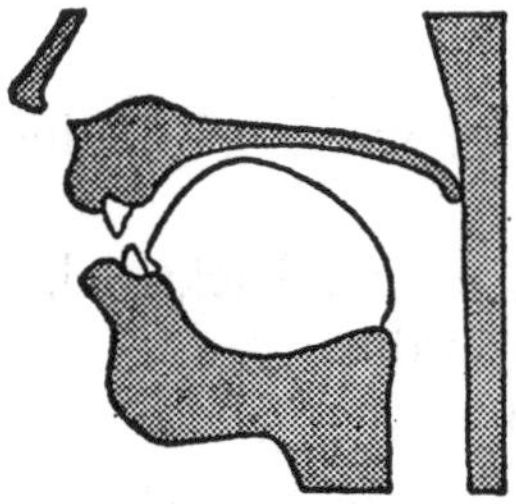	*yet*	Vibrating	Raised

DEVIATIONS

1. Substitution of [r] so that *yes* sounds like [rɛs].
2. Substitution of [l] so that *yet* sounds like [lɛt].
3. Omission of [j] so that *year* sounds like [ɪr].

EXERCISES

Sound Practice

1. Articulate a series of staccato [j] sounds.
2. Articulate these sound pairs: *Easy to contrast:* [j-b] [j-d] [j-g]
   Difficult to contrast: [j-r] [j-l]

Winnie was winsome in her wool jacket.
The swindler inquired as to the dwelling place of the rich wine merchant.
Walter wailed that the wet wood had warped.

TECHNICAL DESCRIPTION	MOUTH	LIPS	TONGUE
Lingua-palatal glide consonant	Nearly closed as sound is initiated, changing during production to position for following sound	Drawn back and tensed slightly as sound is initiated, changing during production to position for following sound	Tip behind lower front teeth, front arched high toward hard palate when sound is initiated, changing during production to position for following sound

Syllable Practice

3. Articulate these syllables: [ji] [jɑɪ] [joʊ] [jʌm]
   [ij] [ɑɪj] [oʊj] [ʌj]
   [iji] [ɑɪjɑɪ] [oʊjoʊ] [ʌjʌ]
4. Articulate these syllable pairs:

   Easy to contrast: [ij-ib] [ij-id] [ij-ig]
   [ji-bi] [ji-di] [ji-gi]
   [iji-ibi] [iji-idi] [iji-igi]

   Difficult to contrast: [ij-ir] [ij-il]
   [ji-ri] [ji-li]
   [iji-iri] [iji-ili]

   Repeat by substituting [ɑɪ], [oʊ], and [ʌ] for [i].

Word Practice

5. Read these words aloud:

Initial: yacht, yam, yank, yard, year, yeast, yellow, yes, yesterday, yield, yoke, young
Medial: beyond, canyon, companion, familiar, genius, million, onion, opinion, pavilion, spaniel, valiant, vineyard
Final: (Does not appear in this position.)

6. Read these word pairs aloud:

Easy to contrast:
[j-b] yank-bank, yard-bard, yarn-barn, yawl-ball, year-beer, yearn-burn, yeast-beast, yell-bell, yellow-bellow, yet-bet
[j-d] yacht-dot, yank-dank, yarn-darn, yawn-dawn, year-dear, yell-dell, yen-den, yet-debt, your-door, yowl-dowel
[j-g] yacht-got, yam-gam, yard-guard, yawl-gall, yaws-gauze, year-gear, years-gears, yes-guess, yet-get, your-gore
Difficult to contrast:
[j-r] yacht-rot, yam-ram, yams-rams, yank-rank, year-rear, yield-reeled, yeoman-Roman, young-rung, your-roar, yowl-rowel
[j-l] yacht-lot, yak-lack, yam-lamb, yank-lank, yap-lap, yaw-law, yawn-lawn, yeast-least, yet-let, young-lung

Sentence Practice

7. Read these sentences aloud:

The yeoman on the yacht yielded the right-of-way to the captain on the companionway.
The dog's yapping was ignored by the young boy.
The valiant Yank soldier gave his opinion.
The millionaire left the yacht.
He yearned to yell at the young man in the pavilion.

PHONETIC [ju] DIACRITIC ū

[j] is frequently combined with the vowel [u] to form a diphthong-like consonant-vowel combination in which the articulators assume the position for [j] and then move rapidly to the position for [u] without interruption of phonation. These exercises are included to assist you in improving your articulation of the consonant-vowel combination [ju].

In many parts of the country educated speakers use [u] instead of [ju] in words such as *duty, student, Tuesday.*

Word Practice

1. Read these words aloud:

Initial: unicorn, unified, uniform, unify, union, unity, unison, unique, unit, useful, useless, usurp, utilization, utilize, youth, youthful
Medial: abuse, astute, centrifuge, beauty, confuse, confusion, cute, duty, fuse, fusion, huge, music, news, student, Tuesday, views
Final: askew, barbecue, cue, curfew, due, few, hue, imbue, mew, new, pew, residue, retinue, review, view, you

Sentence Practice

2. Read these sentences aloud:

There's your cue, the curfew is due.
The youth was unique in that he utilized the opportunity to be useful.
It was the student's duty to deliver the Tuesday newspaper.
Students should review the views of astute scholars in order to avoid confusion.
The astute observer is not confused.

PHONETIC [tʃ] DIACRITIC ch

	KEY WORD		VOCAL FOLDS	VELUM
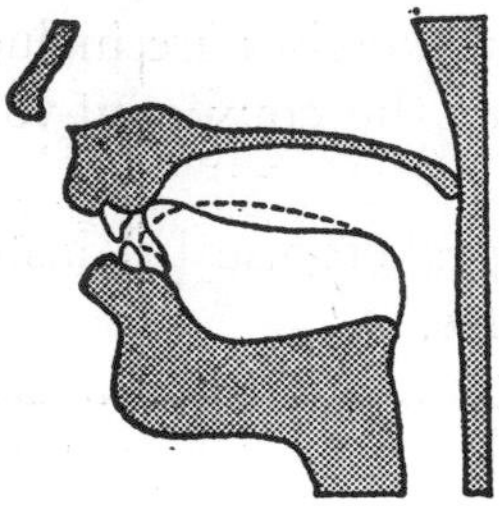	[tʃ]	*church*	Not vibrating	Raised
	[dʒ]	*judge*	Vibrating	

DEVIATIONS for [tʃ].

1. Substitution of [dʒ] so that *catch* sounds like [kædʒ].
2. Substitution of [ʃ] so that *cheap* sounds like [ʃip].
3. Substitution of [t] so that *chair* sounds like [tɛr].
4. Substitution of [θ] so that *teacher* sounds like ['tiθɚ].
5. Addition of [ə] so that *each* sounds like ['itʃə].
6. Omission of [tʃ] so that *question* sounds like ['kwɛsən].
7. Excessive pressure in production. This sound distortion occurs when the tongue position reduces the size of the required opening and there is excessive audible friction in the resulting sound.
8. Lateral production. This sound distortion occurs when the tongue is held in such a way that the breath stream is diverted and escapes over one or both of the sides of the tongue.

EXERCISES for [tʃ]

Sound Practice

1. Articulate a series of staccato [tʃ] sounds.

PHONETIC [dʒ] DIACRITIC j̇

TECHNICAL DESCRIPTION	MOUTH	LIPS	TONGUE
Lingua-palatal combination consonant	Nearly closed	Neutral as sound is initiated, becoming slightly protruded as fricative element of sound is produced	Tip pressed firmly against upper gum-ridge, sides pressed firmly against upper teeth, impounding column of air under pressure, suddenly releasing pressure and changing rapidly to position for fricative element

2. Articulate these sound pairs:

   Easy to contrast: [tʃ-p] [tʃ-k]
   Difficult to contrast: [tʃ-dʒ] [tʃ-ʃ] [tʃ-t] [tʃ-θ]

Syllable Practice

3. Articulate these syllables: [tʃi] [tʃɑɪ] [tʃoʊ] [tʃʌm]
   [itʃ] [ɑɪtʃ] [oʊtʃ] [ʌtʃ]
   [itʃi] [ɑɪtʃɑɪ] [oʊtʃoʊ] [ʌtʃʌ]
4. Articulate these syllable pairs:

   Easy to contrast: [itʃ-ip] [itʃ-ik]
   [tʃi-pi] [tʃi-ki]
   [itʃi-ipi] [itʃi-iki]
   Difficult to contrast: [itʃ-idʒ] [itʃ-iʃ] [itʃ-it] [itʃ-iθ]
   [tʃi-dʒi] [tʃi-ʃi] [tʃi-ti] [tʃi-θi]
   [itʃi-idʒi] [itʃi-iʃi] [itʃi-iti] [itʃi-iθi]

   Repeat by substituting [ɑɪ], [oʊ], and [ʌ] for [i].

Word Practice

5. Read these words aloud:

Initial: chair, chap, check, cheek, chew, child, choose, chump
Medial: bachelor, coaching, etching, itching, matching, reaching, switching, watching
Final: blotch, coach, each, etch, itch, leach, match, notch
Special [tʃ] *combinations:* butcher, marcher, pitcher, suture, watcher, hatched, launched, patched, scratched, starched, filch, gulch, mulch, pilchard, lunch, munch, staunch, winch, wrench, parch, perch, research, search, smirch

6. Read these word pairs aloud:

Easy to contrast:
[tʃ-p] chair-pair, check-peck, child-piled, coaching-coping, matching-mapping, reaching-reaping, suture-super, coach-cope, leach-leap, match-map
[tʃ-k] chair-care, chap-cap, choose-coos, hatched-hacked, marcher-marker, patched-packed, reaching-reeking, coach-coke, each-eke, patch-pack
Difficult to contrast:
[tʃ-dʒ] cheap-jeep, chin-gin, chump-jump, etcher-edger, etching-edging, lecher-ledger, riches-ridges, etch-edge, perch-purge, search-serge
[tʃ-ʃ] chair-share, cheap-sheep, chop-shop, ditches-dishes, hatched-hashed, latched-lashed, matching-mashing, catch-cash, crutch-crush, leach-leash
[tʃ-t] chair-tear, chap-tap, chin-tin, coaching-coating, lecher-letter, marcher-martyr, matching-matting, catch-cat, coach-coat, perch-pert
[tʃ-θ] chick-thick, chief-thief, chin-thin, chum-thumb, chump-thump, filch-filth, latch-lath, patch-path, reach-wreath, teach-teeth

Sentence Practice

7. Read these sentences aloud:

Charlie was a cherubic chimpanzee.
The child watched for each chance to chase the chickens.
The teacher found that mischievous Richard had filched the watch.

Chester was the gum-chewing champion of Charleston.
Richard searched for the satchel.

DEVIATIONS for [dʒ]

1. Substitution of [tʃ] so that *badge* sounds like [bætʃ].
2. Substitution of [ʒ] so that *magic* sounds like ['mæʒik].
3. Substitution of [d] so that *just* sounds like [dʌst].
4. Substitution of [ð] so that *large* sounds like [lɑrð].
5. Addition of [ə] so that *huge* sounds like ['hjudʒə].
6. Omission of [dʒ] so that *engine* sounds like ['ɛnən].
7. Excessive pressure in production. This sound distortion occurs when the tongue position reduces the size of the required opening and there is excessive audible friction in the resulting sound.
8. Lateral production. This sound distortion occurs when the tongue is held in such a way that the breath stream is diverted and escapes over one or both of the sides of the tongue.

EXERCISES for [dʒ]

Sound Practice

1. Articulate a series of staccato [dʒ] sounds.
2. Articulate these sound pairs:

   Easy to contrast: [dʒ-b] [dʒ-g]
   Difficult to contrast: [dʒ-tʃ] [dʒ-ʒ] [dʒ-d] [dʒ-ð]

Syllable Practice

3. Articulate these syllables: [dʒi] [dʒaɪ] [dʒoʊ] [dʒʌm]
   [idʒ] [aɪdʒ] [oʊdʒ] [ʌdʒ]
   [idʒi] [aɪdʒaɪ] [oʊdʒoʊ] [ʌdʒʌ]
4. Articulate these syllable pairs:

   Easy to contrast: [idʒ-ib] [idʒ-ig]
   [dʒi-bi] [dʒi-gi]
   [idʒi-ibi] [idʒi-igi]
   Difficult to contrast: [idʒ-itʃ] [idʒ-iʒ] [idʒ-id] [idʒ-ið]
   [dʒi-tʃi] [dʒi-ʒi] [dʒi-di] [dʒi-ði]
   [idʒi-itʃi] [idʒi-iʒi] [idʒi-idi] [idʒi-iði]

   Repeat by substituting [ɑɪ], [oʊ], and [ʌ] for [i].

Word Practice

5. Read these words aloud:

   Initial: jagged, jar, jaw, jest, judge, jump, jury, just
   Medial: aged, agent, agile, changes, cogent, sieges, stages, wedges
   Final: age, badge, budge, edge, hedge, ledge, lodge, nudge
   Special [dʒ] *combinations:* aged, charged, raged, sieged, surged, avenger, badger, edger, ledger, major, bilge, bulge, divulge, indulge, binge, fringe, lounge, plunge, range, strange, enlarge, gorge, merge

6. Read these word pairs aloud:

   Easy to contrast:
   [dʒ-b] jar-bar, jest-best, judge-budge, edging-ebbing, lodging-lobbing, ridged-ribbed, wedging-webbing, lodge-lob, nudge-nub, ridge-rib
   [dʒ-g] jag-gag, jest-guest, just-gust, badged-bagged, badging-bagging, ridged-rigged, ridging-rigging, badge-bag, budge-bug, ridge-rig
   Difficult to contrast:
   [dʒ-tʃ] gin-chin, jeep-cheap, jump-chump, edger-etcher, edging-etching, ledger-lecher, ridges-riches, edge-etch, purge-perch, surge-search
   [dʒ-ʒ] legion-lesion, legion-lesion, legion-lesion, legion-lesion, legion-lesion, legion-lesion, legion-lesion, legion-lesion, legion-lesion, legion-lesion
   [dʒ-d] jeer-dear, jump-dump, just-dust, aged-aided, hedging-heading, ridging-ridding, wedging-wedding, badge-bad, budge-bud, ledge-led
   [dʒ-ð] gem-them, jay-they, Joe-though, hedger-heather, ledger-leather, sieging-seething, wedger-weather, rage-rathe, siege-seethe, swage-swathe

Sentence Practice

7. Read these sentences aloud:

   Jack joined Jim on the edge of the ledge.
   The jalopy wouldn't budge until Jerry adjusted the engine.
   The judge jumped when Judy joined the jury.
   "This joint is jumping," said John as he joined Jane.
   "I was just joking, Jerry," said Roger.

11. *Improving* PRONUNCIATION

test your pronunciation

Read the following words and sentences aloud while your instructor evaluates your pronunciation.

PRONUNCIATION ERRORS

(EXPLANATION, P. 261; EXERCISES, PP. 262-68.)

1. Get, catch, just, because
   Height is no guarantee of strength.
2. Wash, athlete, film, subtle
   The column of the Fifth Corps escaped twice through subtle maneuvers.
3. Government, library, picture, February
   You probably recognize the fact that twenty architects would be too many.
4. Asterisk, cavalry, irrelevant, imminent
   The action of the larynx is irrelevant to the phenomenon of assimilation.
5. Formidable, hospitable, infamous, lamentable
   A comparable catastrophe had left him irrevocably vehement.

PRONUNCIATION AND CONNECTED SPEECH

(EXPLANATION, P. 268; EXERCISES, P. 270.)

6. Coxswain, column, forecastle, good night, issue, palm, raspberry, theater, whipped, Worcestershire
   One feature of his candidacy is that he remained judiciously calm.

Instructor's Test Sheet for Chapter 11

*Name*____	*Rating*
1. Student avoids the error of substitution.	_____
2. Student avoids the error of addition.	_____
3. Student avoids the error of omission.	_____
4. Student avoids the error of transposition.	_____
5. Student avoids the error of misplaced accent.	_____
6. Student achieves proper assimilation in connected speech.	_____
Total	_____

Rating: It is suggested that the student be scored on a 5 to 1 point scale, 5 being used to indicate an excellent and 1 a poor rating.

Introduction Up to this point you have been drilling on the individual sounds of English. You may wish to improve the clarity of your speech further by returning from time to time to the exercises on those sounds which you found troublesome. However, proficiency in sound articulation does not guarantee accuracy in word production. Many speakers who can produce all of the sounds of English without difficulty still mispronounce words. You may have found by experience or through the test at the beginning of this chapter that you do not pronounce certain words as do respected speakers in your region. If you say [æks] for *ask* or ['fɪləm] for *film*, for instance, you may find that the sound of your speech distracts your listener. If you are overly precise and artificially correct in your pronunciation, you may find that you alienate the audience that you wish to impress.

Although it is not possible to establish hard and fast rules for determining correct pronunciation, it now seems clear that we should follow the speech of educated people in one of the three dialect regions of the United States. There are, moreover, several categories of errors of pronunciation. These errors are discussed in this chapter, and exercises are provided in each of these categories. You will find also that certain sounds tend to be altered as they are blended into connected speech, and these changes are discussed briefly in the last part of the chapter.

Errors of Pronunciation

SUBSTITUTION A speaker with substandard speech may substitute another sound for the required one. However, we cannot tell whether the substitution is permissible by looking at the word. If you hear speakers using both [dʒʌst] and [dʒɪst], can you tell which is to be preferred by looking at the word *just?* Unfortunately you cannot, since *u* is not always pronounced [ʌ] in all words by educated speakers. In the word *business,* it is usually pronounced with the [ɪ] that appears in the second pronunciation of *just* given above. However, if you listen to acceptable speech in most parts of the country, you will hear the first pronunciation of *just;* you will hear the second mostly among uneducated people. Thus it is safe to say that [ɪ] is generally an unsatisfactory alternative to [ʌ] in the word *just.* With this standard in mind, pronounce the following words and transcribe them, either in phonetics or diacritics, just as you say them. Then look them up in the dictionary and transcribe the pronunciations given. In the case of alternate pronunciations note those preferred by respected speakers in your region. Wherever your pronunciation differs from that given in the dictionary, make a special note of the word and practice pronouncing it as do respected speakers in your area. If you discover that you have a tendency to substitute sounds, pay particular attention to this error of pronunciation.

Word List	*Your Pronunciation*	*Dictionary Pronunciation*
1. absurd		
2. agile		
3. atrocity		
4. bade		
5. baste		
6. bathe		
7. beige		
8. blatant		
9. butter		
10. cache		
11. caste		
12. catch		
13. cello		
14. chasm		
15. chiropodist		
16. comely		
17. congratulate		
18. dais		
19. deaf		
20. demise		
21. diphtheria		
22. eggs		
23. err		
24. examine		
25. forbade		
26. genuine		
27. gesture		
28. giblet		
29. guarantee		
30. hearth		
31. hover		

32. loath
33. longevity
34. luxury
35. mien
36. niche
37. oil
38. partner
39. poignant
40. pronunciation
41. protocol
42. puerile
43. querulous
44. rabid
45. saline
46. strength
47. such
48. tacit
49. worsted
50. zealous

After you have written down your pronunciation and that given in the dictionary, check the words in the list which you cannot define with accuracy or use with ease. Then look up the definitions, making sure that you understand the connotations of the word. Under each word you look up, write a sentence using that word. Then review the sentences at regular intervals until the word becomes a part of your active vocabulary. Follow the same procedure at the end of each list that follows.

ADDITION A speaker with substandard speech may add one or more sounds to the required sounds. As in the case of substitutions, it is not always possible to tell whether someone has used a superfluous sound by looking at the word. One might argue, by examining the words only, that it is all right to pronounce both the *p* and the *s* in *psychology* since you pronounce both in *flaps*. Yet this is not so. Your standard, as before, must be the one set by educated people.

Make the same kind of transcriptions as before for the following list of words. If in correcting your pronunciations you find that frequently you add sounds not indicated by the dictionary, pay particular attention to this pronunciation error.

Word List	Your Pronunciation	Dictionary Pronunciation
1. accompanist		
2. across		
3. almond		
4. ambidextrous		
5. aperture		
6. asceticism		
7. athlete		
8. balk		
9. balmy		
10. calm		
11. chassis		
12. christen		
13. climb		
14. column		
15. corps		
16. deprecate		
17. drowned		
18. escape		
19. film		
20. gnaw		
21. grievous		
22. harangue		
23. height		
24. heinous		
25. heir		
26. idea		
27. indict		
28. mischievous		
29. monstrous		
30. once		
31. posthumous		
32. schism		
33. singing		
34. statistics		
35. stupendous		
36. subtle		
37. twice		
38. umbrella		

39. victual		
40. viscera		

OMISSION A speaker with substandard speech may omit required sounds. The word itself, however, is no better guide for determining an improper omission than for determining an improper addition. For example, compare the same two words, *psychology* and *flaps*. If it is correct to omit the *p* in the first word, is it proper to omit it in the second? Once again, you must depend on the example set by respected speakers in your area, not on the word itself.

Compare your own usage with that given in the dictionary for the following list of words, and check your speech for the fault of omission if you diverge from accepted usage on more than a few of these words.

Word List	*Your Pronunciation*	*Dictionary Pronunciation*
1. accuracy		
2. adjective		
3. architect		
4. asparagus		
5. barbiturate		
6. candidate		
7. company		
8. deluge		
9. environment		
10. exactly		
11. facsimile		
12. fact		
13. flaccid		
14. fortuitous		
15. government		
16. grand		
17. kept		
18. land		
19. library		
20. medieval		
21. mountain		
22. particular		
23. picture		
24. poem		

Word List	Your Pronunciation	Dictionary Pronunciation
25. probably		
26. recognize		
27. regular		
28. slept		
29. succinct		
30. twenty		

TRANSPOSITION A speaker with substandard speech may *transpose* sounds. An example heard frequently is [ˈæstɚɪks] for *asterisk.* The spelling of the word is a good, though not perfect, guide to the avoidance of improper transpositions. Compare your own pronunciations with those given in the dictionary. Be particularly careful to avoid transpositions, since they are almost wholly unacceptable in educated speech.

Word List	Your Pronunciation	Dictionary Pronunciation
1. animosity		
2. anonymous		
3. ask		
4. assimilation		
5. astronomer		
6. bituminous		
7. cavalry		
8. cinema		
9. diminution		
10. equanimity		
11. equivalent		
12. frivolity		
13. ignominious		
14. illuminate		
15. irrelevant		
16. larynx		
17. phenomenon		
18. remnant		
19. solemnity		
20. tragedy		

MISPLACED ACCENT A speaker with substandard speech may stress syllables that are unstressed in educated speech. It is not uncommon to find speakers stressing the wrong syllable because a similar word is stressed in that way. For example, if you were trying to pronounce *respite* for the first time, you might decide to accent the second syllable since you accent the second syllable in *despite.* Determining the syllable to be accented in this way often leads to the wrong conclusion; therefore, it is best to consult the dictionary whenever you are in doubt.

In transcribing your pronunciation of the words below in phonetics, remember that the syllable that takes the greatest stress is preceded by a mark placed slightly above it, and the syllable with the secondary stress is preceded by the same mark but put below the base line, as in [kən,grætʃə'leɪʃən]. In the diacritic systems of most dictionaries, primary accent is indicated by a heavy mark following, and slightly above, the syllable which is to receive the stress (kŭn·grăch'ŭ·lā'shŭn). The secondary stress is indicated by a lighter mark placed after and slightly above the lightly stressed syllable.

Word List	*Your Pronunciation*	*Dictionary Pronunciation*
1. acumen		
2. aggrandizement		
3. alias		
4. alienate		
5. amicable		
6. apostolic		
7. atrophy		
8. authoritative		
9. blasphemy		
10. catastrophe		
11. centrifugal		
12. comparable		
13. decorous		
14. degradation		
15. demoniacal		
16. demonstrative		
17. diminutive		
18. epitome		
19. erroneous		
20. exemplary		

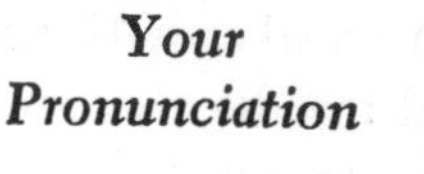

Word List	Your Pronunciation	Dictionary Pronunciation
21. formidable		
22. fortuitous		
23. habitable		
24. horizon		
25. ignominy		
26. illustrative		
27. impious		
28. impotent		
29. incomparable		
30. incongruous		
31. incredulity		
32. indicative		
33. infamous		
34. integral		
35. irreparable		
36. irrevocable		
37. jocose		
38. lamentable		
39. mayoralty		
40. obdurate		
41. omnipotent		
42. posthumous		
43. practicable		
44. preferable		
45. preparatory		
46. prevalence		
47. reputable		
48. respite		
49. superfluous		
50. vehemence		

Pronunciation and Connected Speech

In the study of the articulation of sounds and the pronunciation of words, we sometimes lose sight of the fact that in conversational connected speech we deal with sounds and words not as single units in isolation, but rather as part of a forward-flowing process.

Assimilation (described briefly in Chapter 7, pages 107-08), is of great importance in connected speech, for too little of it produces a stilted and monotonous effect and too much is unacceptable and makes speech unintelligible; whereas just the right amount, that very important and extremely vague standard, produces the most effective speech.

Assimilation of sounds, the running together of adjacent sounds so that they lose some, or all, of their identifiable characteristics, results from the tendency of the speech mechanism to do that which is most efficient.

In one type of assimilation, *progressive assimilation,* the sound which changes is the one which follows the dominant sound. In the word *legs,* the dominant sound is [g], a sound made with the vocal folds vibrating. In other words it is a voiced sound. It is easier for the speech mechanism to follow this with the voiced [z] than the unvoiced [s], so *s* is articulated [z]. The same kind of progressive assimilation is found in the articulation of the final *s* in words like *builds* and *hives.* Similarly, the unvoiced [ʃ] in words like *lashed* and *clashed* causes the *d* to become the unvoiced [t], since, in this situation, the speech mechanism can produce this sound more easily than the voiced [d], and the meaning of the word is not obscured by the change.

In another type of assimilation, *regressive assimilation,* the dominant sound affects the sound or sounds which precede it. The phrase *that book* is usually said with an indefinite second *t* since the articulators move quickly through the [t] position to assume the one for [b], the dominant sound. In *this ship* the *s* may not be articulated as a distinct sound but may be produced as [ʃ] as the two words are blended together.

Often two adjacent sounds so influence each other that another sound appears in their place. This is sometimes called *reciprocal assimilation,* and is exemplified in words like *picture* and *literature* where the *tu* becomes a [tʃ]. See how much simpler it is for the articulators to form ['pɪktʃɚ] than to form ['pɪktjur]. In connected speech, you frequently find this kind of assimilation in phrases like *meet you* where the two words flow together as ['mitʃu].

Though efficient movement of the articulators produces assimilation, speech loses its effectiveness if only the *easiest* way of speaking is considered. It may be easier to say [sjə'toum] than ['sijə æ'toum], but unless you are speaking to a very good friend, your message may never get through or you may have to go to the trouble of repeating the statement to your somewhat irritated companion. Therefore, assimilate sounds, but not beyond the point where the average person can hear what you are saying with ease. In this way you will preserve the natural flow of good speech and yet avoid substandard or confusing assimilation.

Transcribe your pronunciation of the following words. Use them in connected speech paying particular attention to proper assimilation of speech sounds.

Word List	*Your Pronunciation*	*Dictionary Pronunciation*
1. aperture		
2. appreciation		
3. azure		
4. blackguard		
5. boatswain		
6. celestial		
7. education		
8. feature		
9. fission		
10. issue		
11. judicial		
12. judicious		
13. nuptials		
14. official		
15. officious		
16. pasture		
17. propitious		
18. transient		
19. virtuous		
20. waistcoat		

4. *Expanding Your Expression*

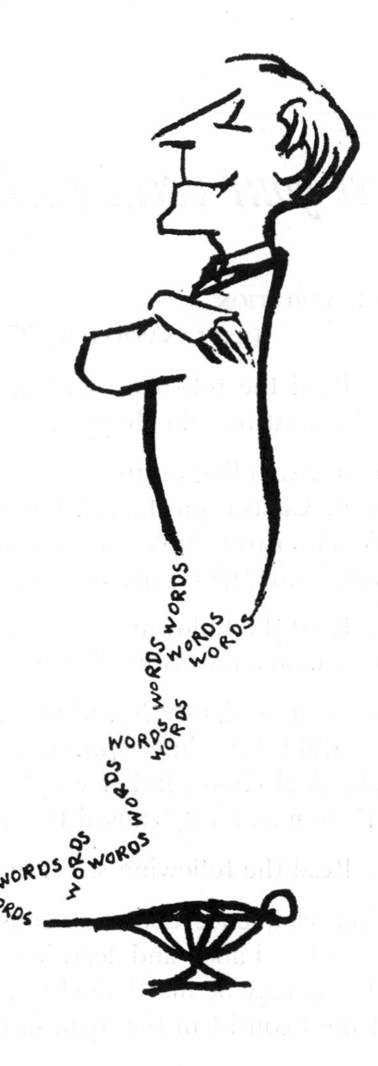

12. *Expanding* VOCAL VARIETY

test your vocal variety

PITCH VARIATION

(EXPLANATION, P. 277; EXERCISES, PP. 278-82.)

1. Read the following sentences aloud as if speaking to a "pushy," ill-mannered bargain shopper.

You're standing on my toe.
Santa Claus is on the third floor.
What do you think good manners means?
The boxing gloves are on aisle four.

2. Read the following sentences aloud, reading the italicized word as if to reinforce the entire meaning of the sentence with the one word.

What a gloriously *beautiful* day!
He will be absolutely *furious* if you tell.
The dead child's father was *heartbroken.*
His own *stupidity* caused the accident.

3. Read the following selection aloud:

True eloquence does not consist in speech. It cannot be brought from far. Labor and learning may toil for it in vain. Words and phrases may be marshalled in every way, but they cannot compass it. It must consist in the man, in the subject, and in the occasion.

—Daniel Webster

LOUDNESS VARIATION

(EXPLANATION, P. 282; EXERCISES, PP. 283-85.)

4. Read the following sentences aloud as if you are speaking to a small group of normal, mature adults.

We will need thirty cents.
The meeting begins at 8 o'clock.
These scissors are very dangerous.
The telephone number is ULysses 3-1212.

Repeat as if to a class of thirty first-graders.
Repeat as if to a deaf person.

TIME VARIATION

(EXPLANATION, P. 285; EXERCISES, PP. 286-90.)

5. Read the following selection aloud:

A man may be a miser of his wealth; he may tie up his talent in a napkin; he may hug himself in his reputation; but he is always generous in his love. Love cannot stay at home; a man cannot keep it to himself. Like light, it is constantly travelling. A man must spend it, must give it away.

—Alexander Macleod

6. Read the following selection aloud:

Never say of anything, "I have lost it"; but, "I have restored it." Is your child dead? It is restored. Is your wife dead? She is restored. Is your estate taken away? Well, and is that not likewise restored? "But he who took it away is a bad man." What is it to you by whose hands he, who gave it, hath demanded it back again? While he gives you to possess it, take care of it; but as of something not your own, as passengers do of an inn.

—Epictetus

7. Read the following selection aloud:

It is all very well to tell me that young man has distinguished himself by a brilliant first speech. He may go on, or he may be satisfied with his first triumph; but show me a young man who has not succeeded at first, and nevertheless has gone on, and I will back that young man to do better than most of those who have succeeded at the first trial.

—C. J. Fox

INTEGRATING THE VOCAL ELEMENTS

(EXPLANATION, P. 290; EXERCISES, PP. 291-96.)

8. Read the following sonnet aloud:

Let me not to the marriage of true minds
Admit impediments. Love is not love
Which alters when it alteration finds,
Or bends with the remover to remove:
O, no! it is an ever-fixèd mark,
That looks on tempests and is never shaken;
It is the star to every wandering bark,
Whose worth's unknown, although his height be taken,
Love's not Time's fool, though rosy lips and cheeks
Within his bending sickle's compass come;
Love alters not with his brief hours and weeks,
And bears it out even to the edge of doom.
If this be error and upon me proved,
I never writ, nor no man ever loved.

—William Shakespeare, Sonnet CXVI

Instructor's Test Sheet for Chapter 12

*Name*____	*Rating*
1. Pitch steps help to sustain interest.	____
2. Pitch inflections help to sustain interest.	____
3. Intonations help to sustain interest.	____
4. Loudness variations help to sustain interest.	____
5. Rate is neither too fast nor too slow.	____
6. Rate variations help to sustain interest.	____
7. Phrasing helps to sustain interest.	____
8. Pitch, loudness, and time variations are integrated properly to sustain interest.	____
Total	____

Rating: It is suggested that the student be scored on a 5 to 1 point scale, 5 being used to indicate an excellent and 1 a poor rating.

Introduction Does the test show that your speech attracts listeners? Do variations in pitch make your voice express the meaning you wish to convey? Does your loudness change as your thought changes? How about your speaking rate? Is it always too fast, or is it too slow? Is it appropriate for every situation?

The effective speaker varies loudness, pitch, and time, adjusts these individual elements, and integrates them for over-all interest. Vocal variety is not an end in itself, but is used to achieve more effective communication of meaning and feeling.

You may have received high scores in the various aspects of speech studied so far, and yet your speech may still be ineffective in attracting and holding your audience. The material in this chapter will help you integrate these vocal elements of pitch, loudness, and time. Such integration will do much to make you a more interesting and effective speaker.

Pitch Variation

Repeat the following quotation by Cowper aloud in a monotone (without varying your pitch level): "Variety is the very spice of life, that gives it all its flavor." Notice how uninteresting—how boring—this is. Repeat the sentence using mechanical (sing-song) pitch variations unrelated to the meaning, as a young child might do. Do you agree that the potential listener will be lulled rather than aroused? Now read the sentence a third time, concentrating on its meaning. Note that a word may be emphasized by setting it apart from words adjacent to it by means of changes in pitch. This is particularly apparent if surrounding words are uttered at relatively unvarying pitch levels. Emphasize the important words; de-emphasize the unimportant. Do your utmost to express Cowper's meaning. If you are doing this correctly, your pitch variations (steps, inflections, and intonation) are giving your speech the variety, which Cowper says is "spice" and "flavor."

The *step* in pitch (in which phonation is interrupted during the change in pitch) may be illustrated by saying "Look here!" Use one pitch level for *look* and a higher or lower pitch level for *here,* with a break in phonation between them. ("Look here!" "Look here!")

Inflection (in which phonation continues throughout the change in pitch) may be illustrated with a single word. For simple upward or downward inflections, begin at one level and vary the pitch upward or downward as you say "Say!" ("Say!" "Say!") For the circumflex inflection start at one pitch level, vary it upward or downward, then reverse again, without interruption. ("Say!")

Intonation refers to the over-all melody of a given sample of speech. Speech steps and inflections may be likened to the individual notes of a song; intonation to many notes, or a complete song. One might carry the analogy further by saying that American speech, with its typical upward steps and downward inflections has one melody, Spanish speech another, Swedish another, and so on.

You may need to train your ear to recognize the intonation pattern of American English, especially if you speak another language. Then you will need to practice typical patterns in order to make them a part of your conversational speech.

Exercises for Pitch Variation

1. Make definite steps in pitch as indicated by the arrows.

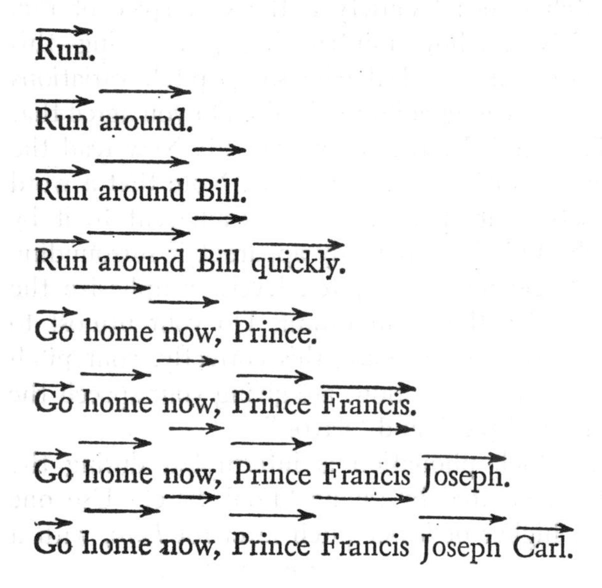

2. Read the following words aloud. Express the meaning intended by using the inflection indicated.

Go (Get out of here!)

Go	(You mean you want me to go?)
Oh	(I'm surprised.)
Oh	(I understand.)
Hate	(I despise him.)
Hate	(How could I feel that way?)
Love	(I love you.)
Love	(She doesn't love anyone but herself.)
Wait	(Don't leave.)
Wait	(I've already been waiting for three hours.)
Great	(That's wonderful.)
Great	(That's just awful.)
Preposterous	(His story is ridiculous.)
Preposterous	(What do you mean, "This isn't true?")
Unfortunately	(Our team lost.)
Unfortunately	(Your team lost.)

Repeat the above words and express as many additional meanings as possible by varying the inflections.

3. Read the following pairs of sentences, first as statements and then as questions. Change the meaning by giving a downward inflection to the last word and then by giving the last word an upward inflection.

Is she beautiful!	I have passed the examination.
Is she beautiful?	I have passed the examination?

This is the prize.
This is the prize?

I've been fired.
I've been fired?

I received a raise.
I received a raise?

He can't stay.
He can't stay?

Al is ineligible.
Al is ineligible?

He plays the trumpet.
He plays the trumpet?

4. Read the following conversations aloud, expressing the meanings indicated in parenthesis by means of inflection. Draw a line above each word to indicate the inflection which is appropriate to express the meaning.

Hello	(How do you do?)
Hello	(How are you?)
Fine	(I'm fine, thank you.)
Fine	(Wonderful!)
Pass	(Did I pass?)
Pass	(I should say not!)
Fail	(Did I fail?)
Fail	(I'm afraid you did.)
Green	(Is it green?)
Blue	(No, it's blue.)
Blue	(You mean it's blue?)
Blue	(Yes, it's blue.)
Surprise	(I'll bet you're surprised to see me.)
Greetings	(Welcome.)
Greetings	(Hello everyone.)
Surprise	(This is a surprise.)
Snow	(Look, it snowed last night.)
Snow	(Are you kidding?)
Snow	(No, come see for yourself.)
Snow	(Isn't it beautiful?)
Well	(Is he well?)
Well	(I'm not sure.)
Well	(I'm surprised.)
Well	(After all, what can you expect?)

Lazy	(You're lazy.)
Lazy	(I'm not lazy.)
Lazy	(Yes, you are lazy.)
Lazy	(So, I'm lazy.)
Seventeen	(Is seventeen the answer to that problem?)
Seventeen	(Did you say seventeen?)
Seventeen	(Yes, that's what I said.)
Seventeen	(Yes, that's the answer.)

5. Read the following sentences aloud. Produce steps and inflections as indicated.

I will.

I will not.

I will not say.

I will not say *git*.

I will not say *git* or *jist*.

I will not say *git* or *jist* today.

I will not say *git* or *jist* today or tomorrow.

I will not say *git* or *jist* today or tomorrow or ever.

Read the following sentences aloud, using appropriate steps and inflections.

Who?
Who came?
Who came here?
Who came here today, Jim?
Who came here today, Jim Arthur?
Who came here today, Jim Arthur? Mary?
Who came here today, Jim Arthur? Mary Smith?

6. Read the following selections aloud. Pay particular attention to using steps and inflections which are appropriate to the intonation pattern of American speech.

We shall go on to the end; we shall fight in France; we shall fight on the seas and oceans; we shall fight with growing confidence and growing strength in the air; we shall defend our Island, whatever the cost may be; we shall fight on the beaches; we shall fight on the landing grounds; we shall fight in the fields and in the streets; we shall fight in the hills. We shall never surrender, and even if, which I do not for a moment believe, this Island or a large part of it were subjugated and starving, then our Empire beyond the seas, armed and guarded by the British Fleet, would carry on the struggle, until, in God's good time, the New World, with all its power and might, steps forth to the rescue and the liberation of the old.[1]

—Winston Churchill

Abou Ben Adhem (may his tribe increase!)
Awoke one night from a deep dream of peace,
And saw within the moonlight in his room,
Making it rich, and like a lily in bloom,
An angel, writing in a book of gold:
Exceeding peace had made Ben Adhem bold,
And to the presence in the room he said,
"What writest thou?"—The vision raised its head,
And with a look made of all sweet accord,
Answer'd, "The names of those who love the Lord."
"And is mine one?" said Abou. "Nay, not so,"
Replied the angel. Abou spoke more low,
But cheerily still; and said, "I pray thee, then,
Write me as one that loves his fellow men."
The angel wrote and vanish'd. The next night
It came again, with a great wakening light,
And show'd the names whom love of God had bless'd,
And, lo! Ben Adhem's name led all the rest.

—Leigh Hunt, "Abou Ben Adhem"

Loudness Variation

Read the following quotation by Pope aloud, giving each word equal loudness: "Order in variety we see; though all things differ, all agree."

[1] Winston S. Churchill, *Blood, Sweat, and Tears* (New York, G. P. Putnam's Sons, 1941), p. 297. Reprinted by permission of the publisher.

Notice how much of the meaning is lost. Now read the sentence aloud again, making abrupt and excessive changes in loudness. Speaking in this fashion destroys the meaning by calling attention to the technique of variety. Read the sentence a third time, increasing the loudness of the important words and decreasing the loudness of unimportant connecting words. Varying loudness in this manner enhances communication. The skillful speaker, just as the good musical conductor, sustains interest through such variations. If you are in doubt about how to achieve these differing degrees of loudness, review Chapter 6, "Increasing Vocal Power," before doing the following exercises.

Exercises for Loudness Variation

1. Read each of the following sentences aloud three times. First, read as though you were engaging in a normal conversation; second, as though you were responding to your listener's inquiry, "What?" and third, as though you were responding to his second inquiry, "What was that?"

It looks as though the Yankees will win the pennant this year.

Johnson's batting average, for the season, is .375.

The score at half-time is 13 to 6.

The injured right halfback, McMurtry, was carried off the field with a broken arm.

State scored in the last minute, on a 63 yard touchdown pass from Marshall to Jones.

Barnes won the second set 7–5 and now leads two sets to one.

Central won 78 to 77 in the third overtime period.

The third race was won by Topsy Turvy who paid $18.30 to win.

2. Make ten-word telegrams of each of the following sentences by underlining the ten words which are most essential to the meaning. First, read just the ten words aloud, as if reading a telegram. Then, read the entire sentence aloud, making the ten words stand out by increasing the loudness.

Since both engines of the plane failed, we made a forced landing with only one passenger slightly injured and all other damage negligible.

Mother arrived last night feeling fine, even though she forgot her brown suitcase which she wants you to send to her at Uncle John's.

The line between mental health and mental illness is vague and shadowy and everyone has certain traits or characteristics which might be called abnormal.

Tell Mary and her family to bring the salad and dessert, and tell Jane to bring sandwiches and pickles, and you can all meet us at seven.

If there's one thing I can't stand, it's the kind of person who says one thing and means something entirely different.

I've told you a hundred times that civilized human beings do not act like caged animals just because they can't have everything they want.

Some people believe that it is perfectly acceptable to steal a dollar but that it is a horrible crime to steal ten thousand dollars.

Madalyn has been terribly unhappy since she left home and would like to return if you can find it in your heart to forgive her.

3. Read the following sentences aloud. Give the unimportant connecting words relatively little prominence by decreasing the loudness.

There are three sides to a triangle.
A rectangle has four sides.
Five sides enclose a pentagon.
A polygon with six sides is called a hexagon.
Seven-sided polygons are known as heptagons.
An eight-sided figure is called an octagon.
Polygons with nine sides are nonagons.
Decagons have ten sides.

4. Read the following selection aloud. Avoid loudness patterns as you read.

'Twas on the shores that round our coast
From Deal to Ramsgate span,
That I found alone on a piece of stone
An elderly naval man.

His hair was weedy, his beard was long,
And weedy and long was he;
And I heard this wight on the shore recite,
In a singular minor key:

"Oh, I am a cook, and a captain bold,
And the mate of the *Nancy* brig.

And a bo'sun tight, and a midshipmite,
And the crew of the captain's gig." [2]
—W. S. Gilbert, "The Yarn of the Nancy Bell"

Time Variation

Read the following quotation by Richter aloud, giving each word equal duration and setting each word apart with pauses of equal length. "Variety of mere nothing gives more pleasure than uniformity of something." Now read the same sentence aloud with random and exaggerated changes in tempo, making some words excessively staccato and prolonging the durations of other words unduly. Finally, read the sentence using variations in time. Try to enhance interest by varying pause lengths. Phrase according to the meaning you wish to express, pausing sufficiently at appropriate intervals to make your meaning clear. Durations of phonations and durations of pauses between phonations contribute to expression of meaning. Important words are frequently longer in duration than are adjacent unimportant words. Important words are also frequently set apart from unimportant words by means of pauses of longer than normal duration. Increasing your rate during unimportant phrases and decreasing your rate during important ones will also increase the interest of your speech.

Rate (the speed of speech) usually is referred to in terms of words per minute. You might ask, "How rapidly should I speak?" There is no absolute answer. It depends upon your personality, your topic, and the particular situation. If you are dedicating a monument, 110 words per minute may be fast enough. In a conversation 150 words per minute may be acceptable. If you are a newscaster you may talk 175 words per minute. 210 words per minute may not be too fast if you are reporting a football game. In the final analysis, your speech is too fast or too slow only as your listeners judge it to be.

If your test indicated that your rate was improper in a given situation, there are two ways in which this rate may be altered. You may change the durations of the sounds produced or you may change the durations of pauses between sounds.

[2] "The Yarn of the Nancy Bell" by W. S. Gilbert. Reprinted from *The Bab Ballads*, p. 101, by permission of St. Martin's Press and Macmillan and Company, London.

All sounds do not take the same length of time to articulate. Say *arena* and then *pippin.* Each word contains five sounds, and yet the first takes longer to say than the second. Vowels and diphthongs are more susceptible to changes in duration than are consonants—particularly plosive consonants. Therefore, to change rate, concentrate particularly on altering the durations of vowels and diphthongs.

Do not attempt to adjust your rate merely by varying the duration of your phonations. Examine, also, your pause lengths. Speech which is too rapid may include few pauses, those being of short duration. Speech which is too slow frequently has many long pauses, punctuated all too often with distracting vocalized *uh*'s and *er*'s.

Phrasing was discussed in Chapter 3, "Controlling Breathing," because of its relationship to inhalation. We need to note here only that there may be many correct ways to phrase any given sentence, and that varying the lengths of your phrases is essential if you would hold the attention of your listeners.

Exercises for Time Variation

1. If your rate of speech has been judged as too fast or too slow, read the following passage aloud and take note of the number of seconds required to complete it. On the accompanying scale, compare the reading time in seconds with the number of words per minute, and you will have a record of your reading rate. If your rate of speech continues to be too fast or too slow, return to this exercise regularly until you have acquired a rate of speech which is appropriate for you.

Although it can be said, in general, that a speaking	10
rate of about one hundred and fifty words per minute	20
will be judged as normal for many people in many	30
speaking situations, it can not be stated with finality that	40
this is the correct speaking rate for all people in	50
all situations. A slow-moving, deliberative type of person may	60
have normal speech which is slower than this. A rapid-	70
moving, quick type of person may have normal speech which	80
is faster than this. Similarly, a slower rate than one	90
hundred and fifty words per minute may be normal in	100
the pulpit; a faster rate than one hundred and fifty	110
words per minute may be appropriate at a football game.	120
If you need to correct your speaking rate, always be	130

sure you retain the proper relationship between the durations of 140
your phonations and the lengths of the pauses between them. 150

(Compare your reading time in seconds with the number listed above it to determine your reading rate in words per minute.)

Rate			*Too slow*						*Too fast*			
WORDS PER MINUTE	100	106	113	120	129	138	150	163	180	200	225	259
READING TIME IN SECONDS	90	85	80	75	70	65	60	55	50	45	40	35

2. Read the following words and phrases aloud at a rate appropriate to the meaning expressed by each.

Begin slowly—then talk faster—a little faster still—now more slowly—now very slowly—speak at your normal rate—now very fast—now normal—now very slowly—now slower still.

3. Read the following material at a slow, medium, or rapid rate, as indicated.

(*Medium*) Yesterday, as I was walking home from the corner drugstore, I noticed two youngsters playing ball in the middle of the street. (*Fast*) Suddenly, the sound of a siren pierced the air and a fire engine came racing toward them. They scrambled out of the way just as it roared by. (*Slow*) Meanwhile, their mother, unaware of the danger, was in the house preparing dinner.

4. Read the following sentences aloud. Vary the durations of your phonations in a manner appropriate to the meaning expressed.

She is beautiful, charming, graceful, and refined.
He is handsome, hospitable, generous, and brilliant.
Run for your life!
The monster has two heads, four legs, eight arms, and breathes fire.
The diamond was dazzling as it lay there sparkling in all of its brilliance.
Look out!
Lazily, the boat moved down the stream.

5. Read each of the following Chinese proverbs aloud, making the first half prolonged and the second half staccato.

Among mortals—who is faultless?
Good words are like—a string of pearls.

Birth is not a beginning—death is not an end.
Pale ink is better—than the most retentive memory.
One dog barks at something—and a hundred bark at the sound.
Knowledge is boundless—but the capacity of one man is limited.
Better be kind at home—than burn incense in a far place.
Even the Emperor—has straw-sandaled relatives.

Read each of the following Chinese proverbs aloud, making the first half staccato and the second half prolonged.

Hunger is cured by food—ignorance by study.
Yellow gold has its price—learning is priceless.
Rats know the way—of rats.
He who soars not—suffers not by a fall.
There is a time to fish—and a time to dry nets.
Rotten wood—cannot be carved.
Suppress slanders—and protect the innocent.
In clothes we value novelty—in men old age.

6. Read the following short statements from history aloud. First, read them with staccato phonations and with long pauses where the slant marks appear; then with staccato phonations and short pauses; then with prolonged phonations and short pauses; then with prolonged phonations and long pauses. Where the duration of phonation and pause length are mismatched, exaggerate the difference. When they are balanced, concentrate on blending sound duration and pause length appropriately.

Don't fire / until you see / the whites of their eyes.
I only regret / that I have but one life / to lose for my country.
Don't / give up the ship!
Put none but Americans / on guard tonight.
Millions for defense, / but not one cent / for tribute.
I propose / to fight it out on this line / if it takes / all summer.
Fifty-four forty / or fight.
You may fire / when ready, / Gridley.

7. Read the following sentences aloud. Phrase each sentence as indicated and make a clear distinction between the two meanings expressed.

You might marry Miss Susabelle Brown.
You might marry, / Miss Susabelle Brown.

The bus stopped with a jerk and you got off.
The bus stopped with a jerk, / and you got off.

John struck / his wife Mary consoled him.
John struck his wife / Mary consoled him.

What's the latest dope?
What's the latest / dope?

I don't know Karen.
I don't know / Karen.

Joan read the book, / sighed / and went to sleep.
Joan read / the book sighed / and went to sleep.

As he was phoning / Rosalie, his wife walked in.
As he was phoning Rosalie / his wife walked in.

While Frieda fed the cat / to her son she said, "Come here."
While Frieda fed the cat to her son / she said, "Come here."

8. Read the following selections aloud. Read each phrase as a single thought, concentrating on revealing the meaning of the ideas expressed, rather than upon the words themselves. You will notice that the materials are placed in thought groups rather than in single lines. Some students find this arrangement helpful in organizing materials for meaningful phrasing.

The quality	it	as the gentle	upon the
of mercy is	droppeth	rain	place
not strain'd;		from heaven	beneath.

It is	it blesseth	and him	'Tis mightiest
twice	him	that	in the
blest—	that gives	takes.	mightiest.

It becomes the thronèd	His	shows the
monarch better than	scepter	force of
his crown.		temporal power,

The attribute	Wherein	the dread
to awe and	doth	and fear
majesty,	sit	of kings.

Phrase the remainder of this speech as illustrated above.

But mercy is above this sceptered sway;
It is enthronèd in the hearts of kings,
It is an attribute to God himself;
And earthly power doth then show likest God's
When mercy seasons justice. Therefore, Jew,
Though justice be thy plea, consider this—
That, in the course of justice, none of us
Should see salvation. We do pray for mercy,
And that same prayer doth teach us all to render
The deeds of mercy. I have spoke thus much
To mitigate the justice of thy plea;
Which if thou follow, this strict court of Venice
Must needs give sentence 'gainst the merchant there.

—William Shakespeare, *The Merchant of Venice*

9. Read the following selection aloud. Concentrate on setting each phrase apart clearly to reveal the intended meaning.

Will Will Marry Mary?

Will Mary Fall fall for Will Winter in the winter or will Will Winter win her, Mary Fall, in the fall? Will Will marry Mary or will Mary marry Will? If Mary will marry Will, will not Will will to marry Mary? Or will winter fall before Will Winter will fall for Mary Fall? Now if Mary is merry enough to marry Will, will Will will to marry merry Mary? Merry Mary Fall will fall for Will in the fall. Which means Will will fall for merry Mary Fall in the fall. If they both fall who will be merry? Will Will be merry or will Mary be merry and who will be married? Will Will will to be married or will Will's Mary will to be married? After Will marries merry Mary will Mary Fall's will will all to Will if it is his will and will Will's will will all to Mary Fall or will Will will to will all to Betty who shouldn't be in this story at all?

Integrating the Vocal Elements

Not chaos-like together crush'd and bruis'd,
But, as the word, harmoniously confus'd:
Where order in variety we see,
And where, though all things differ, all agree.

—Alexander Pope, "Windsor Forest"

Speech is an integrated process. This chapter has dealt with the individual elements of vocal variety: pitch, loudness, and time. Each of these factors may be used as a means of emphasizing a single word. A particularly skillful speaker may combine all three, making a given word greater in loudness, higher in pitch, and longer in duration than the less important words adjacent to it. In this way he gives the word a more complex or particular meaning and adds to the interest for his listener. In your speaking, alter the levels of pitch, use differing degrees of loudness, and employ variations in time in keeping with the meaning and feeling which you want to express. Blend these vocal elements so that they reinforce meaning and sustain interest. These variations should be natural—not studied or affected. As Pope suggests, your goal is "order in variety."

Exercises for Integrating the Vocal Elements

1. Count from 1 to 10 expressing each of the following emotions in turn.

Fear Anger Disgust Grief Joy Surprise Yearning

2. Repeat the following selection aloud expressing, in turn, the emotions of fear, anger, joy, and surprise.

Row, row, row your boat
Gently down the stream.
Merrily, merrily, merrily, merrily.
Life is but a dream.

Repeat the above selection expressing fear on the first line, anger on the second line, joy on the third line, and surprise on the fourth line.

3. Read the following sentence aloud varying the vocal elements to reveal the emotional meanings intended.

I wouldn't say that. (That isn't exactly what I mean.)
I wouldn't say that. (That is too horrible to say.)
I wouldn't say that. (I would be too frightened.)
I wouldn't say that. (I'm too happy to say a thing like that.)
I wouldn't say that. (It would be too disgusting.)
I wouldn't say that. (I'm surprised that you think I would.)
I wouldn't say that. (I'd like to say it, though.)
I wouldn't say that. (You'd better not say that.)

4. Repeat the following conversational compliments. Be enthusiastic and sincere. Avoid affectation.

It's wonderful to see you again after all these years.
That's the brightest looking baby I've ever seen.
That hat is most becoming.
You have a commanding presence before an audience.
I don't know when I have enjoyed myself so much.
Please give me the recipe, this dessert is delicious.
You must use Glosso, you have the whitest wash in the neighborhood.
You have marvelous taste. I want to tell you how much I admire your new suit.

5. Read the following verses from the *Rubáiyát* aloud. Reveal the intended meaning through the integration of the vocal elements.

12

A Book of Verses underneath the Bough,
A Jug of Wine, a Loaf of Bread—and Thou
  Beside me singing in the Wilderness—
Oh, Wilderness were Paradise enow!

24

Ah, make the most of what we yet may spend,
Before we too into the Dust descend;
  Dust into Dust, and under Dust, to lie,
Sans Wine, sans Song, sans Singer, and—sans End!

32

There was the Door to which I found no Key;
There was the Veil through which I could not see:
  Some little talk awhile of ME and THEE
There was—and then no more of THEE and ME.

71

The Moving Finger writes; and, having writ,
Moves on: nor all your Piety nor Wit,
  Shall lure it back to cancel half a Line,
Nor all your Tears wash out a Word of it.

—*Rubáiyát of Omar Kháyyám*, tr. by Edward Fitzgerald

6. Read the following selections aloud. Pay particular attention to integrating the vocal elements.

And all men kill the thing they love,
  By all let this be heard,
Some do it with a bitter look,
  Some with a flattering word,
The coward does it with a kiss,
  The brave man with a sword!

—Oscar Wilde, "Ballad of Reading Gaol"

When in disgrace with Fortune and men's eyes,
I all alone beweep my outcast state,
And trouble deaf heaven with my bootless cries,
And look upon myself and curse my fate,
Wishing me like to one more rich in hope,
Featur'd like him, like him with friends possess'd,
Desiring this man's art, and that man's scope,
With what I most enjoy contented least;
Yet in these thoughts myself almost despising,
Haply I think on thee, and then my state,
Like to the lark at break of day arising
From sullen earth, sings hymns at heaven's gate;
  For thy sweet love rememb'red such wealth brings
  That then I scorn to change my state with kings.

—William Shakespeare, Sonnet XXIX

Dear Madam:

I have been shown in the files of the War Department a statement of the Adjutant-General of Massachusetts that you are the mother of five sons who have died gloriously on the field of battle. I feel how weak and fruitless must be any words of mine which should attempt to beguile you from the grief of a loss so overwhelming. But I cannot refrain from tendering to you the consolation that may be found in the thanks of the Republic they died to save. I pray that our heavenly Father may assuage the anguish of your bereavement, and leave you only the cherished memory of the loved and lost, and the solemn pride that must be yours to have laid so costly a sacrifice upon the altar of freedom.[3]

—Abraham Lincoln

[3] Letter to Mrs. Bixby whose five sons had been reported killed in battle, November 21, 1864.

JEALOUSY's an awful thing and foreign to my nature;
I'd punish it by law if I was in the Legislature.
One can't have all of anyone, and wanting it is mean,
But still, there is a limit, and I speak of Miss Duveen.

I'm not a jealous woman,
But I can't *see what he sees in her,*
I can't see what *he sees in her,*
I can't see what he sees *in her!*

If she was something striking
I could understand the liking,
And I wouldn't have a word to say to that;
But I can't see why he's fond
Of that objectionable blonde—
That fluffy little, stuffy little, flashy little, trashy little,
creepy-crawly, music-hally, horrid little CAT!

I wouldn't say a word against the girl—be sure of that;
It's not the creature's fault she has the manners of a rat.
Her dresses may be dowdy, but her hair is always new,
And if she squints a little bit—well, many people do.

I'm not a jealous woman,
But I can't *see what he sees in her,*
I can't see what *he sees in her,*
I can't see what he sees *in her!*

He's absolutely free—
There's no bitterness in me,
Though an ordinary woman would explode;
I'd only like to know
What he sees in such a crow,
As that insinuating, calculating, irritating, titivating,
sleepy little, creepy little, sticky little TOAD.[4]
—A. P. Herbert, "I Can't Think What He Sees in Her"

THE VISCOUNT. (He goes up to Cyrano, who is watching him, and with a conceited air.) Sir, your nose is . . . hm . . . it is . . . very big!

CYRANO (gravely). Very!

[4] "I Can't Think What He Sees in Her," from *Plain Jane*, copyright 1930, 1931 by Sir Alan Herbert. Reprinted by permission of Sir Alan, the Proprietors of *Punch*, Benn and Doubleday and Co., Inc.

THE VISCOUNT (laughing). Ha!
CYRANO (imperturbably). Is that all?
THE VISCOUNT. What do you mean?
CYRANO.

Ah no! young blade! That was a trifle short!
You might have said at least a hundred things
By varying the tone . . . like this, suppose. . . .
Aggressive: "Sir, if I had such a nose
I'd amputate it!" Friendly: "When you sup
It must annoy you, dipping in your cup;
You need a drinking-bowl of special shape!"
Descriptive: " 'Tis a rock! . . . a peak! . . . a cape!
—A cape, forsooth! 'Tis a peninsular!"
Curious: "How serves that oblong capsular?
For scissors-sheath? or pot to hold your ink?"
Gracious: "You love the little birds, I think?
I see you've managed with a fond research
To find their tiny claws a roomy perch!"
Truculent: "When you smoke your pipe . . . suppose
That tobacco-smoke spouts from your nose—
Do not the neighbors, as the fumes rise higher,
Cry terror-struck: 'The chimney is afire'?"
Considerate: "Take care . . . your head bowed low
By such a weight . . . lest head o'er heels you go!"
Tender: "Pray get a small umbrella made,
Lest its bright color in the sun should fade!"
Pedantic: "That beast Aristophanes
Names Hippocamelelephantoles
Must have possessed just such a solid lump
Of flesh and bone, beneath his forehead's bump!"
Cavalier: "The last fashion, friend, that hook?
To hang your hat on? 'Tis a useful crook!"
Emphatic: "No wind, O majestic nose,
Can give *thee* cold!—save when the mistral blows!"
Dramatic: "When it bleeds, what a Red Sea!"
Admiring: "Sign for a perfumery!"
Lyric: "Is this a conch? . . . a Triton you?"
Simple: "When is this monument on view?"
Rustic: "That thing a nose? Marry-come-up!
'Tis a dwarf pumpkin, or a prize turnip!"

Military: "Point against cavalry!"
Practical: "Put it in a lottery!"
Or . . . parodying Pyramus' sighs . . .
"Behold the nose that mars the harmony
Of its master's phiz! blushing its treachery!"
—Such, my dear sir, is what you might have said,
Had you of wit or letters the least jot:
But, O most lamentable man!—of wit
You never had an atom, and of letters
You have three letters only!—they spell Ass!
And—had you had the necessary wit,
To serve me all the pleasantries I quote
Before this noble audience . . . e'en so,
You would not have been let to utter one—
Nay, nor the half or quarter of such jest!
I take them from myself all in good part,
But not from any other man that breathes!" [5]

—Edmond Rostand, "Cyrano De Bergerac"

[5] Edmond Rostand, "Cyrano De Bergerac," trans. by Gladys Thomas and Mary F. Guillemard (London, William Heinemann, Ltd., 1898).

13. *Increasing* CREATIVE EXPRESSION

test your creative expression

DEVELOPING A PLEASANT SPEAKING PERSONALITY

(EXPLANATION, P. 301; EXERCISES, PP. 303-04.)

Read the following selections aloud.

1. Sincerity is to speak as we think, to do as we pretend and profess, to perform what we promise, and really to be what we seem and appear to be.

—John Tillotson

2. Good nature is more agreeable in conversation than wit, and gives a certain air to the countenance which is more amiable than beauty. —It shows virtue in the fairest light; takes off, in some measure, from the deformity of vice; and makes even folly and impertinence supportable.

—Joseph Addison

3. Nothing is so contagious as enthusiasm; it moves stones, it charms brutes. . . . Enthusiasm is the genius of sincerity and truth accomplishes no victories without it.

—Edward Bulwer-Lytton

4. The block of granite which is an obstacle in the pathway of the weak, becomes a stepping-stone in the pathway of the strong.

—Thomas Carlyle

DEVELOPING A CREATIVE APPROACH TO LIVING

(EXPLANATION, P. 304; EXERCISES, PP. 307-10.)

Being an interesting speaker involves many variables which do not lend themselves to measurement. However, you can arrive at some conclusions through self-analysis. Evaluate your interest as a speaker by answering the following questions as objectively as possible.

1. Are you sharply aware of the things you see, hear, smell, taste, and touch?
2. Are you keenly sensitive to ideas, feelings, and beauty?
3. Is your imagination stimulated vividly by visual and verbal symbols?

Instructor's Test Sheet for Chapter 13

*Name*____	*Rating*
1. Voice reveals sincerity of speaker.	____
2. Voice reveals friendliness of speaker.	____
3. Voice reveals vitality of speaker.	____
4. Voice reveals adaptability of speech personality.	____
5. Student reports he is sharply aware of the things he sees, hears, smells, tastes, and touches.	____
6. Student reports he is keenly sensitive to ideas, feelings, and beauty.	____
7. Student reports his imagination is stimulated vividly by visual and verbal symbols.	____
Total	____

Rating: It is suggested that the student be scored on a 5 to 1 point scale, 5 being used to indicate an excellent and 1 a poor rating.

Introduction This book introduced you to speech improvement by giving you an overview of the entire speech process. Speech was then broken into its individual elements. Your proficiency was evaluated, and you improved your speech by working on these elements.

This final chapter is again concerned with an overview of the speech process. The test you have just taken may indicate that your voice reveals vitality, sincerity, friendliness, and adaptability. You may now be keenly aware, sensitive, and imaginative. If this is so, and if you have overcome all other speech difficulties, undoubtedly you have experienced the great satisfaction of communicating successfully with those around you.

On the other hand, if your speech is not as interesting as you wish it might be, despite a proficiency in the various elements, you may need to expand your intellectual and emotional horizons. Becoming a more interesting speaker goes hand-in-hand with becoming a more interesting person. To the degree that you participate in and react to your environment you will increase the interest-potential of your speech.

Developing a Pleasant Speaking Personality

Your speech reflects your personality. The speaker who most easily wins over his audience, whether in informal or formal speech, is almost invariably sincere and friendly. His voice probably has a healthful vigor, and is in every way suited to his audience.

Occasionally a misguided person will get the impression that clever manipulation of the voice and careful control of other elements of speech are ends in themselves. At times such a person may even succeed in sounding sincere, when in reality he is simulating his sincerity or conviction. A certain stereotype of high pressure salesman, confidence man, or silver-tongued politician would fit into this category. Undoubtedly, you have detected this insincerity in the voices of some speakers and have been repelled. The speaker assumes a role, but in unguarded moments his speech may reveal him to be what he really is. In the same way the voice reveals the sincere speaker to be what he is. The better you train your voice, the more emphatically this trait of your personality will be revealed.

One way of showing sincerity in your speech is by using regional speech only where it is natural for you to do so. For instance, if you live in Chicago, vacation in Florida for a few weeks and return to Illinois with a Southern drawl, you are being affected rather than sincere in your speech. But beyond this, a genuine belief in what you are saying will give your speech conviction. If you care deeply about sharing your thoughts and emotions, it is likely that your speech will arouse and hold your listener's interest.

Friendliness also arouses your listener's interest in you and what you are saying. Prove this to yourself by using two different manners of speaking in two somewhat similar situations. First, let your voice reflect an aloof lack of interest in the person or persons to whom you speak. Second, speak to a group of people as though they were your intimate friends. Let your voice reflect a genuine regard for them and the things they are talking about. The results will show that friendliness is an important element in successful communication.

Vitality also makes your speech more interesting. If you are chronically ill or always tired, this lifelessness will be reflected in your voice. If you find nothing exciting, people will judge your voice to be dull. On the other hand, if you are physically fit, alert, and enthusiastic, your voice will reveal these feelings and attitudes and you will be considered an interesting person.

In addition to having the characteristics of sincerity, friendliness, and vitality, interesting speech is adaptable. Ordinarily you are repelled by voices which are not appropriate to the material, age, and sex of the speaker, or to the situation in which he is speaking. You are deeply attracted, on the other hand, by the speaker whose voice responds with equal sensitivity to the magnificence of the cathedral and the rustic charm of the country school house.

You may find it difficult to be expressive in certain situations or before certain audiences, not because you lack physical or mechanical ability, but because you are apprehensive or lack confidence in your speaking.

As a result of your study about speech and speech improvement, you have undoubtedly become more confident. If, however, you are still unsure of yourself, remember that it is natural and actually desirable to be keyed up somewhat in order that you may have reserve energy when you speak. You do not consider it unusual if, during a time of excitement, your heart beats faster, your breathing becomes interrupted, or your throat gets dry. Your speech reflects this excitement. At an accident your voice undoubtedly reveals fright. Your voice reacts the way it does because it is affected by physical changes which emotions bring about in the body. These physical changes are set in motion by fear-producing situations whether the fear is physical, as in an accident, or emotional, as when you appear before an audience.

The vast majority of professional speakers, actors, and public figures would recite the same list of physical symptoms. They simply turn these feelings about speech to their advantage because they have found, as you may have, that these physical reactions, if properly controlled and channeled, help them to communicate more effectively.

If you are not positive that your voice indicates sincerity, friendliness, and vitality and that it is adaptable to many differing needs and situations, you may need to evaluate your personal attitudes and philosophy. Is it your voice control that is at fault, or are you really insincere, unfeeling of others, too timid, too aggressive? Perhaps you may need professional assistance with a personality rather than a voice problem. But perhaps you merely need practice in making your voice reflect you as you are. The following exercises will help you in this latter practice.

Exercises for Developing a Pleasant Speaking Personality

1. Count from one to ten imitating the most pedantic, affected, conceited, superficial person you can imagine. Note, so that you can avoid, the quality of the tone which results from lack of sincerity, even though it is only a simulated lack. Now, count from one to ten as if you were telling someone something you believe sincerely, and that you want him to believe thoroughly. Note the nature of the quality produced and practice it.

2. Count from one to ten imitating the most antagonistic, hostile, bitter, malicious person you can imagine. Note and avoid the quality of the tone which results from lack of friendliness. Now, count from one to ten as if you were telling your best friend how much his (or her) friendship means to you. Note the nature of the quality produced, so that you can practice and develop it.

3. Count from one to ten imitating the most listless, lifeless, inactive, inert person you can imagine. Note and avoid the quality of this speech. Now, count from one to ten as if you were in perfect physical health, happy, and enthusiastic. Note the nature of the quality produced, and practice it.

4. Count from one to ten, imitating the most insensitive, rigid, intolerant, unaccommodating person you can imagine. Note and avoid the quality of the tone which results from lack of adaptability. Now, count from one to ten as if you were sensitively aware of a stranger's

problem and were obliging him by giving him directions. Note the nature of the quality produced and practice using it.

Developing a Creative Approach to Living

One of the best ways to become an interesting person is to be aware of the things which go on around you. Don't go through life seeing without being aware of what you see. You may have taken part in an experiment in your psychology class in which several young men rush into the room and simulate a hold-up. One points an object at another and says, "Bang, bang, bang!" The victim falls, "wounded." How many entered the room? How many "shots" were fired? What kind of "gun" was used? Although you cannot always be sure of what you have seen, your range of expression will be improved as you train yourself to be more aware of the visual stimuli around you.

Being more aware of what you see is not enough. You must also be particularly conscious of sound. If you live in a large city you may have become oblivious of the usual sounds around you and excluded crowd and traffic noises from your conscious perception. This exclusion may be essential if you wish to concentrate or rest. But try listening to all the sounds for short periods. See how many you can identify and describe. If you live in the country, try listening to sounds at different times of the day and describing them.

An awareness of sound is important in identifying errors of speech. The exercises in this book have alerted you to hearing yourself as well as others. Would you hear the sound of a coin dropped on the sidewalk—even in the midst of traffic din? Try an experiment. You will probably find that a surprising number of pedestrians respond to such a noise, because the coin provides a reason for listening. This same reason for listening apparently does not hold true for many persons who hear and produce speech sounds. If you were to tell a friend about a lecture you heard on the subject of propaganda devices, you might say, "You can prove anything with *stastistics*." A critical listener might observe, "You mean with *statistics*." If you are a careless listener, you might reply, "That's what I said—with *stastistics*." Even more important than listening for the purpose of identifying speech sounds is listening to absorb the meaning of things which go on around us. Listening comprehension is taught in many college classrooms because experimenters have found "that after a lapse of two months or more, learning through listening seldom operates at more than a 25 per cent level of efficiency."[1] Out of the time we spend in verbal communication (reading, writing, listening, and speaking), 45 per cent of the time is spent in listening.[2] Don't let the saying "None is so deaf as he who will not hear" be applied to you.

To sight and sound must be added an awareness of the sense of touch. If you are to express in words the "softness" of a baby's skin, the texture of wool, the coolness of water, you must first be keenly aware of the experience itself. Only then can you communicate this impression to your listener.

No doubt you have found that food is more delicious when served in a terraced banquet room or a luxury hotel than when served over a counter. Successful restaurateurs believe that beautiful surroundings—pleasing to both sight and sound—increase the delectability of a meal. Even in the absence of soft lights and beautiful music, appreciation of taste also contributes to the total awareness pattern.

Tiny gift shops, quaint coffee houses, and exquisite garden spots frequently bid for public acceptance on the basis of sensory appeal. The delicate aroma of roasting coffee beans may be a subtle lure to the coffee house, while the fragrance of honeysuckle may be as impelling an attraction to the garden as the vivid hues of thousands of bursting blossoms. As you look back on Thanksgiving at Grandmother's, was it the fact that it was a family reunion that made it so nostalgic or was it the tasty dinner? Was it perhaps the smells from the kitchen—the whiff of turkey being taken out of the oven—the odor of freshly baked mince pie?

Being aware of the stimuli which surround you is the first, but not the only, requirement if you are to be an interesting person. You must also be sensitive to ideas, to the feelings, and to the varying degrees of beauty which are transmitted to you through your senses.

The more understanding you bring to an intellectual concept, the more you can reveal to your listeners. You may be sure that you remember the simple story of Alice in Wonderland. But are you sensitive to the subtle shades of meaning which this tale includes? Could you really tell the story of Alice without referring once again to the narrative and reacting to its elements? Reread the poem "Fool's Prayer" by Edward Rowland Sill. Then try to summarize its message in one succinct sen-

[1] Ralph G. Nichols and Thomas R. Lewis, *Listening and Speaking* (Dubuque, Iowa, William C. Brown Co., 1954), p. 4.

[2] Paul T. Rankin, "The Importance of Listening Ability," *English Journal*, College Edition, Vol. 17 (October 1928), pp. 623-30.

tence. Until you have developed a sensitivity to its meaning, you cannot expect to relate that meaning to another.

Unless you are sensitive to the imagery and the figures of speech in man's writing, you cannot expect to appreciate fully what he has written. Norman Corwin has written much for the medium of radio. You may have heard his radio plays. What does Corwin mean, however, when he says, "His states were 48, and his respiration normal," [3] or "He died of the multiple abrasions of the skin of a Chinese"? [4] You must know if you are to understand his ideas.

Being sensitive to meaning is not always easy, but being sensitive to feeling is even more demanding, for here you must often look beyond the surface meaning. It is possible to say, "I despise her," but to mean "I adore her." It is equally possible to say, "I can't stand being away from her," and to mean, "I hope I never see her again."

Psychiatrists and professional counselors spend much of their time trying to understand what people really mean. They must be able to put themselves into the position of the patient. When a client says, "I want nothing more than to devote my life to my parents," perhaps he means "I am trapped into this pattern." If you would be a truly effective oral communicator, you too must cultivate the ability to react sensitively to the emotional content of the stimuli around you.

You must cultivate, also, a sensitivity to beauty if, in your speaking, you wish to reveal a sense of beauty to others. Beauty is an elusive, intangible concept. It is something that is felt or experienced, but is not easily described. But by developing your sensitivity so that you capture a feeling of beauty in what you see, hear, feel, smell, and taste, you will better be able to express it.

To be an effective speaker you must not only be aware of and sensitive to your surroundings, you must be imaginative.

Imagination enables a man to fashion a piece of soft wire, one thirty-second of an inch in diameter and four and a quarter inches long into a device of incomparable value to the household and office—a paper clip. Imagination will make the oratory of Churchill live long after the death of men who lived during World War II. Churchill used the language which is our common heritage; he spoke of events well known to all; he was aware of the situation around him; he was sensitive to the implications of events. He used his imagination to draw together that which

[3] Norman Corwin, "Untitled," *Untitled and Other Radio Dramas* (New York, Henry Holt and Co., 1945), p. 51.
[4] *Ibid.*, p. 50.

was significant and to discard that which should be overlooked. His imagination led him to compose word-pictures which reflected the needs and feelings of the common man. He was able to move his audience as few other leaders have done.

There are few Churchills. Yet all of us are surrounded by the continual bombardment of sensory stimuli, ideas, and feelings. Developing your imagination will increase your capacity to be interesting—to yourself and, through your speech, to others, even though you do not discover radium, write a new *Gulliver's Travels,* or deliver another Gettysburg Address.

Exercises for Developing a Creative Approach to Living

1. Try to increase your awareness of what you see.
   a. Without looking, tell how many windows there are in this room, in this building, and in your home.
   b. Without looking, tell what color are the eyes of your teacher, the person on your right, and the person on your left.
   c. The next time you go shopping take one minute to look at a window display. Describe the merchandise on view and the prices asked for each item.
   d. Which of the following spellings is correct: accommodate, acomodate, accomodate, acommodate?
2. Try to increase your awareness of what you hear.
   a. Describe the sound which accompanies a blowout.
   b. Describe the sound of Big Ben.
   c. Compare the tempos of a fox trot, a march, and a waltz.
   d. Compare the pitch ranges of a French horn, a trumpet, and a Sousaphone.
3. Try to increase your awareness of what you smell.
   a. Describe the odor of a steak cooking at a barbecue.
   b. Describe the odor of honeysuckle.
   c. Compare the odors of sulfur dioxide, nitrous oxide, and sodium chloride.
   d. Compare the odors of a waterfront with those of a forest.
4. Try to increase your awareness of what you taste.
   a. Compare the tastes of a dill pickle, a French pastry, and a grapefruit rind.
   b. Describe the taste of an avocado.

   c. Describe the difference between the tastes of coffee and tea.
   d. Describe the taste of cotton candy.
5. Try to increase your awareness of what you touch.
   a. Take some loose change out of your pocket and count it without looking at it.
   b. Compare the textures of wool, cotton, and nylon.
   c. Compare the textures of a glass brick, a cement brick, and a clay brick.
   d. Compare the textures of hair of a Pekinese, a Spitz, and an Airedale.
6. Try to be more sensitive to ideas.
   a. What is the answer to the following riddle: As I was going to St. Ives, I met a man with seven wives; each wife had seven sacks; each sack had seven cats; each cat had seven kits; kits, cats, sacks, and wives, how many went to St. Ives?
   b. What did Hamlet mean when he said, "when we have shuffled off this mortal coil"?
   c. Give the meaning of the following headline: "Show Biz Fizz; New Pic Lays Egg."
7. Try to be more sensitive to feeling.
   a. What one word best describes Petruchio's feeling in the following scene?
   b. What one word best describes Katharina's feeling?

PET. Good morrow, Kate; for that's your name, I hear.
KATH. Well have you heard, but something hard of hearing.
They call me Katharine that do talk of me.
PET. You lie, in faith! for you are call'd plain Kate,
And bonny Kate, and sometimes Kate the Curst;
But, Kate, the prettiest Kate in Christendom,
Kate of Kate-Hall, my super-dainty Kate,
For dainties are all Kates—and therefore, Kate,
Take this of me, Kate of my consolation:
Hearing thy mildness praised in every town,
Thy virtues spoke of, and thy beauty sounded,
Yet not so deeply as to thee belongs,
Myself am mov'd to woo thee for my wife.
KATH. Mov'd! In good time. Let him that moved you hither
Remove you hence. I knew you at the first
You were a movable.

—William Shakespeare, *The Taming of the Shrew*

c. What emotion is predominant in the following sentence?

You would think that a college student would be old enough to decide on an objective in life and to take the steps which are necessary to reach his goal.

d. What is the predominant emotion in Milton's "On His Blindness"?

When I consider how my light is spent
Ere half my days in this dark world and wide,
And that one talent which is death to hide
Lodged with me useless, though my soul more bent
To serve therewith my Maker, and present
My true account, lest He returning chide,
"Doth God exact day-labor, light denied?"
I fondly ask. But Patience, to prevent
That Murmur, soon replied, "God doth not need
Either man's work or his own gifts. Who best
Bear his mild yoke, they serve him best. His state
Is kingly: thousands at his bidding speed,
And post o'er land and ocean without rest;
They also serve who only stand and wait."

—John Milton

8. Try to be more sensitive to beauty.
   a. Describe the most beautiful sunset you have ever seen.
   b. Describe the most beautiful orchestral selection you have heard.
   c. Describe the most beautiful poem you have ever read.
   d. Which of the following three first stanzas of poems by Edgar Allan Poe do you consider to be the most beautiful?

Helen, thy beauty is to me
  Like those Nicean barks of yore,
That gently, o'er a perfumed sea,
  The weary, wayworn wanderer bore
To his own native shore.

—"To Helen"

The skies they were ashen and sober;
  The leaves they were crispèd and sere—
  The leaves they were withering and sere:
It was night, in the lonesome October
  Of my most immemorial year;

It was hard by the dim lake of Auber,
In the misty mid region of Weir—
It was down by the dank tarn of Auber,
In the ghoul-haunted woodland of Weir.

—"Ulalume"

It was many and many a year ago,
In a kingdom by the sea
That a maiden there lived whom you may know
By the name of Annabel Lee;
And this maiden she lived with no other thought
Than to love and be loved by me.

– "Annabel Lee"

Appendix

The following selections may be used when longer reading passages are required. In reading these selections, incorporate all of the techniques you have been developing. Concentrate on expressing the author's intended meaning through your use of controlled, well-initiated and well-resonated vocal tone, precise articulation, accurate pronunciation, vocal variety, and creative expression.

The Babies (*an excerpt*)

I like the idea that a baby doesn't amount to anything! Why, one baby is just a house and a front yard full by itself; one baby can furnish more business than you and your whole interior department can attend to; he is enterprising, irrepressible, brimful of lawless activities; do what you please, you can't make him stay on the reservation. Sufficient unto the day is one baby. As long as you are in your right mind don't you ever pray for twins. Twins amount to a permanent riot; and there ain't any real difference between triplets and insurrection.

Among the three or four million cradles now rocking in the land, are some which this nation would preserve for ages as sacred things if we could know which ones they are. For in one of these cradles the unconscious Farragut of the future is at this moment teething. Think of it! and putting a word of dead earnest, unarticulated, but justifiable, profanity over it, too; in another, the future renowned astronomer is blinking at the shining Milky Way with but a languid interest, poor little chap, and wondering what has become of that other one they call the wet-nurse; in another, the future great historian is lying, and doubtless he will continue to lie until his earthly mission is ended; in another, the future President is busying himself with no profounder problem of State than what the mischief has become of his hair so early; and in a mighty array of other cradles there are now some sixty thousand future office-seekers getting ready to furnish him occasion to grapple with that same old problem a second time! And in still one more cradle, somewhere under the flag, the future illustrious commander-in-chief of the American armies is so little burdened with his approaching grandeurs and responsibilities as to be giving his whole strategic mind, at this moment, to trying to find out some way to get his own big toe into his mouth, an achievement which (meaning no disrespect) the illustrious guest of this evening also turned his attention to some fifty-six years ago! And if the child is but the prophecy of the man there are mighty few will doubt that he succeeded.

—Mark Twain

Speech of Acceptance upon the Award of the Nobel Prize for Literature

Our tragedy today is a general and universal physical fear so long sustained by now that we can even bear it. There are no longer problems of the spirit. There is only the question: When will I be blown up? Because of this, the young man or woman writing today has forgotten the problems of the human heart in conflict with itself which alone can make good writing because only that is worth writing about, worth the agony and the sweat.

He must learn them again. He must teach himself that the basest of all things is to be afraid; and, teaching himself that, forget it forever, leaving no room in his workshop for anything but the old verities and truths of the heart, the old universal truths lacking which any story is ephemeral and doomed—love and honor and pity and pride and compassion and sacrifice. Until he does so, he labors under a curse. He writes not of love but of lust, of defeats in which nobody loses anything of value, of victories without hope and, worst of all, without pity or compassion. His griefs grieve on no universal bones, leaving no scars. He writes not of the heart but of the glands.

Until he relearns these things, he will write as though he stood among and watched the end of man. I decline to accept the end of man. It is easy enough to say that man is immortal simply because he will endure: that when the last ding-dong of doom has clanged and faded from the last worthless rock hanging tideless in the last red and dying evening, that even then there will still be one more sound: that of his puny inexhaustible voice, still talking. I refuse to accept this. I believe that man will not merely endure: he will prevail. He is immortal, not because he alone among creatures has an inexhaustible voice, but because he has a soul, a spirit capable of compassion and sacrifice and endurance. The poet's, the writer's, duty is to write about these things. It is his privilege to help man endure by lifting his heart, by reminding him of the courage and honor and hope and pride and compassion and pity and sacrifice which have been the glory of his past. The poet's voice need not merely be the record of the man, it can be one of the props, the pillars to help him endure and prevail.[1]

—William Faulkner

Farewell Address at Springfield

My Friends:—No one not in my position can appreciate the sadness I feel at this parting. To this people I owe all that I am. Here I have lived more than a quarter of a century; here my children were born, and here one of them lies buried. I know not how soon I shall see you again. A duty devolves upon me which is, perhaps, greater than that which has devolved upon any other man since the days of Washington. He never could have succeeded except for the aid of Divine Providence, upon which he at all times relied. I feel that I cannot succeed without the same Divine Aid which sustained him; and in the same Almighty Being I place my reliance for support; and I hope you, my friends, will all pray that I may receive that Divine Assistance, without which I cannot succeed, but with which success is certain. Again I bid you all an affectionate farewell.

—Abraham Lincoln

Eulogy to Robert E. Lee

He was a foe without hate; a friend without treachery; a soldier without cruelty; a victor without oppression, and a victim without murmuring. He was a public officer without vices; a private citizen without wrong; a neighbor without reproach; a Christian without hypocrisy, and a man without guile. He was Caesar without his ambition; Frederick without his tyranny; Napoleon without his selfishness, and Washington without his reward. He was as obedient to authority as a servant, and royal in authority as a true king. He was gentle as a woman in life, and modest and pure as a virgin in thought; watchful as a Roman vestal in duty; submissive to law as Socrates, and grand in battle as Achilles!

—Benjamin H. Hill

[1] William Faulkner, *The Faulkner Reader* (New York, Random House, 1954), p. 3.

The Fool's Prayer

The royal feast was done; the King
  Sought some new sport to banish care,
And to his jester cried: "Sir Fool,
  Kneel now, and make for us a prayer!"

The jester doffed his cap and bells,
  And stood the mocking court before:
They could not see the bitter smile
  Behind the painted grin he wore.

He bowed his head, and bent his knee
  Upon the monarch's silken stool;
His pleading voice arose: "O Lord,
  Be merciful to me, a fool!

"No pity, Lord, could change the heart
  From red with wrong to white as wool;
The rod must heal the sin: but, Lord,
  Be merciful to me, a fool!

" 'Tis not by guilt the onward sweep
  Of truth and right, O Lord, we stay;
'Tis by our follies that so long
  We hold the earth from heaven away.

"These clumsy feet, still in the mire,
  Go crushing blossoms without end;
These hard, well-meaning hands we thrust
  Among the heart-strings of a friend.

"The ill-timed truth we might have kept
  Who knows how sharp it pierced and stung?
The word we had not sense to say—
  Who knows how grandly it had rung?

"Our faults no tenderness should ask,
  The chastening stripes must cleanse them all;
But for our blunders—oh, in shame
  Before the eyes of heaven we fall.

"Earth bears no balsam for mistakes;
  Men crown the knave; and scourge the tool
That did his will; but Thou, O Lord,
  Be merciful to me, a fool!"

The room was hushed; in silence rose
  The King, and sought his gardens cool,
And walked apart, and murmured low,
  "Be merciful to me, a fool!"

—Edward Rowland Sill

Psalm XXIV

The earth is the Lord's, and the fulness thereof;
The world, and they that dwell therein.
  For he hath founded it upon the seas,
And established it upon the floods.
  Who shall ascend into the hill of the Lord?
Or who shall stand in his holy place?
  He that hath clean hands, and a pure heart;
Who hath not lifted up his soul unto vanity, nor sworn deceitfully.
  He shall receive the blessing from the Lord,
And righteousness from the God of his salvation.
  This is the generation of them that seek him,
That seek thy face, O Jacob. Selah.
  Lift up your heads, O ye gates; and be ye lift up,
Ye everlasting doors; and the King of glory shall come in.
  Who is this King of glory?
The Lord strong and mighty, the Lord mighty in battle.
  Lift up your heads, O ye gates; even lift them up,
Ye everlasting doors; and the King of glory shall come in.
  Who is this King of glory?
The Lord of hosts, he is the King of glory. Selah.

Ozymandias

I met a traveller from an antique land
Who said: Two vast and trunkless legs of stone
Stand in the desert . . . Near them, on the sand,
Half sunk, a shattered visage lies, whose frown,
And wrinkled lip, and sneer of cold command,
Tell that its sculptor well those passions read
Which yet survive, stamped on these lifeless things,
The hand that mocked them, and the heart that fed:
And on the pedestal these words appear:
"My name is Ozymandias, king of kings:
Look on my works, ye Mighty, and despair!"

Nothing beside remains. Round the decay
Of that colossal wreck, boundless and bare
The lone and level sands stretch far away.

—Percy Bysshe Shelley

Upon Westminster Bridge

Earth has not anything to show more fair:
Dull would he be of soul who could pass by
A sight so touching in its majesty:
This City now doth, like a garment, wear
The beauty of the morning; silent, bare,
Ships, towers, domes, theaters and temples lie
Open unto the fields, and to the sky;
All bright and glittering in the smokeless air.
Never did sun more beautifully steep
In his first splendor, valley, rock, or hill;
Ne'er saw I, never felt, a calm so deep!
The river glideth at his own sweet will:
Dear God! the very houses seem asleep;
And all that mighty heart is lying still!

—William Wordsworth

Sonnet XVIII

Shall I compare thee to a summer's day?
Thou art more lovely and more temperate:
Rough winds do shake the darling buds of May,
And summer's lease hath all too short a date:
Sometimes too hot the eye of heaven shines,
And often is his gold complexion dimmed;
And every fair from fair sometime declines,
By chance or nature's changing course untrimmed:
But thy eternal summer shall not fade
Nor lose possession of that fair thou owest;
Nor shall Death brag thou wanderest in his shade,
When in eternal lines to time thou growest:
So long as men can breathe, or eyes can see,
So long lives this, and this gives life to thee.

—William Shakespeare

Dover Beach

The sea is calm tonight.
The tide is full, the moon lies fair
Upon the straits;—on the French coast the light
Gleams and is gone; the cliffs of England stand,
Glimmering and vast, out in the tranquil bay.
Come to the window, sweet is the night air!
Only, from the long line of spray
Where the sea meets the moon-blanched land,
Listen! you hear the grating roar
Of pebbles which the waves draw back, and fling,
At their return, up the high strand,
Begin, and cease, and then again begin,
With tremulous cadence slow, and bring
The eternal note of sadness in.

Sophocles long ago
Heard it on the Ægæan, and it brought
Into his mind the turbid ebb and flow
Of human misery; we
Find also in the sound a thought,
Hearing it by this distant northern sea.
The Sea of Faith
Was once, too, at the full, and round earth's shore
Lay like the folds of a bright girdle furled.
But now I only hear
Its melancholy, long, withdrawing roar,
Retreating, to the breath
Of the night wind, down the vast edges drear
And naked shingles of the world.
Ah, love, let us be true
To one another! for the world, which seems
To lie before us like a land of dreams,
So various, so beautiful, so new,
Hath really neither joy, nor love, nor light,
Nor certitude, nor peace, nor help for pain;
And we are here as on a darkling plain
Swept with confused alarms of struggle and flight
Where ignorant armies clash by night.

—Matthew Arnold

Prospice

Fear death?—to feel the fog in my throat,
  The mist in my face,
When the snows begin, and the blasts denote
  I am nearing the place,
The power of the night, the press of the storm,
  The post of the foe;
Where he stands, the Arch Fear in a visible form,
  Yet the strong man must go;
For the journey is done and the summit attained,
  And the barriers fall,
Though a battle's to fight ere the guerdon be gained,
  The reward of it all.
I was ever a fighter, so—one fight more,
  The best and the last!
I would hate that death bandaged my eyes, and forebore,
  And bade me creep past.
No! let me taste the whole of it, fare like my peers
  The heroes of old,
Bear the brunt, in a minute pay glad life's arrears
  Of pain, darkness and cold.
For sudden the worst turns the best to the brave,
  The black minute's at end,
And the elements' rage, the fiend-voices that rave,
  Shall dwindle, shall blend,
Shall change, shall become first a peace out of pain,
  Then a light, then thy breast,
O thou soul of my soul! I shall clasp thee again,
  And with God be the rest!

—Robert Browning

Index

C

D

W

Y

H
I 8
J 9
K 0
L 1